S. L. CLEMENS

THE MAN THAT

CORRUPTED HADLEYBURG

AND

OTHER STORIES AND ESSAYS

By MARK TWAIN

ILLUSTRATED

HARPER & BROTHERS PUBLISHERS

NEW YORK AND LONDON

1900

CONTENTS

ILLUSTRATIONS

THE MAN THAT CORRUPTED

HADLEYBURG

THE MAN THAT CORRUPTED HAD-LEYBURG

I

IT was many years ago. Hadleyburg was the most honest and upright town in all the region round about. It had kept that reputation unsmirched during three generations, and was prouder of it than of any other of its possessions. It was so proud of it, and so anxious to insure its perpetuation, that it began to teach the principles of honest dealing to its babies in the cradle, and made the like teachings the staple of their culture thenceforward through all the years devoted to their education. Also, throughout the formative years temptations were kept out of the way of the young people, so that their honesty could have every chance to harden and solidify, and become a part of their very bone. The neighboring towns were jealous of this honorable supremacy, and affected to sneer at Hadleyburg's pride in it and call it vanity; but all the same they were obliged to acknowledge that Hadleyburg was in reality an incorruptible town; and if pressed they would also acknowledge that the mere fact that a young man hailed from Hadleyburg was all the recommendation he needed when he went forth from his natal town to seek for responsible employment.

But at last, in the drift of time, Hadleyburg had the ill luck to offend a passing stranger—possibly without knowing it, certainly without caring, for Hadleyburg was sufficient unto itself, and cared not a rap for strangers or their opinions. Still, it would have been well to make an exception in this one's case, for he was a bitter man and revengeful. All through his wanderings during a whole year he kept his injury in mind, and gave all his leisure moments to trying to invent a compensating satisfaction for it. He contrived many plans, and all of them were good, but none of them was quite sweeping enough; the poorest of them would hurt a great many individuals, but what he wanted was a plan which would comprehend the entire town, and not let so much as one person escape unhurt. At last he had a fortunate idea, and when it fell into his brain it lit up his whole head with an evil joy. He began to form a plan at once,

[Page 2

"IT LIT UP HIS WHOLE HEAD WITH AN EVIL JOY"

saying to himself, "That is the thing to do—I will corrupt the town."

Six months later he went to Hadleyburg, and arrived in a buggy at the house of the old cashier of the bank about ten at night.   He got a sack out of the buggy, shouldered it, and staggered with it through the cottage yard, and knocked at the door. A woman's voice said " Come in," and he entered, and set his sack behind the stove in the parlor, saying politely to the old lady who sat reading the *Missionary Herald* by the lamp:

" Pray keep your seat, madam, I will not disturb you.   There—now it is pretty well concealed ; one would hardly know it was there.   Can I see your husband a moment, madam ?"

No, he was gone to Brixton, and might not return before morning.

" Very well, madam, it is no matter.   I merely wanted to leave that sack in his care, to be delivered to the rightful owner when he shall be found. I am a stranger; he does not know me; I am merely passing through the town to-night to discharge a matter which has been long in my mind.   My errand is now completed, and I go pleased and a little proud, and you will never see me again. There is a paper attached to the sack which will explain everything.   Good-night, madam."

The old lady was afraid of the mysterious big stranger, and was glad to see him go. But her curiosity was roused, and she went straight to the sack and brought away the paper. It began as follows:

"To be Published; or, the right man sought out by private inquiry—either will answer. This sack contains gold coin weighing a hundred and sixty pounds four ounces—"

"Mercy on us, and the door not locked!"

Mrs. Richards flew to it all in a tremble and locked it, then pulled down the window-shades and stood frightened, worried, and wondering if there was anything else she could do toward making herself and the money more safe. She listened awhile for burglars, then surrendered to curiosity and went back to the lamp and finished reading the paper:

"I am a foreigner, and am presently going back to my own country, to remain there permanently. I am grateful to America for what I have received at her hands during my long stay under her flag; and to one of her citizens—a citizen of Hadleyburg—I am especially grateful for a great kindness done me a year or two ago. Two great kindnesses, in fact. I will explain. I was a gambler. I say I was. I was a ruined gambler. I arrived in this village at night, hungry and without a penny. I asked for help—in the dark; I was ashamed to beg in the light. I begged of the right man. He gave me twenty dollars—that is to say, he gave me life, as I considered it. He also gave me fortune; for out of that money I have made myself rich at the gaming-

table. And finally, a remark which he made to me has re-mained with me to this day, and has at last conquered me; and in conquering has saved the remnant of my morals: I shall gamble no more. Now I have no idea who that man was, but I want him found, and I want him to have this money, to give away, throw away, or keep, as he pleases. It is merely my way of testifying my gratitude to him. If I could stay, I would find him myself; but no matter, he will be found. This is an honest town, an incorruptible town, and I know I can trust it without fear. This man can be identified by the remark which he made to me; I feel persuaded that he will remember it.

"And now my plan is this: If you prefer to conduct the in-quiry privately, do so. Tell the contents of this present writ-ing to any one who is likely to be the right man. If he shall answer, 'I am the man; the remark I made was so-and-so,' apply the test—to wit: open the sack, and in it you will find a sealed envelope containing that remark. If the remark mentioned by the candidate tallies with it, give him the money, and ask no further questions, for he is certainly the right man.

"But if you shall prefer a public inquiry, then publish this present writing in the local paper — with these instructions added, to wit: Thirty days from now, let the candidate ap-pear at the town-hall at eight in the evening (Friday), and hand his remark, in a sealed envelope, to the Rev. Mr. Burgess (if he will be kind enough to act); and let Mr. Burgess there and then destroy the seals of the sack, open it, and see if the remark is correct; if correct, let the money be delivered, with my sincere gratitude, to my benefactor thus identified."

Mrs. Richards sat down, gently quivering with excitement, and was soon lost in thinkings — after this pattern: "What a strange thing it is! . . .

And what a fortune for that kind man who set his bread afloat upon the waters! . . . If it had only been my husband that did it!—for we are so poor, so old and poor! . . ." Then, with a sigh—" But it was not my Edward; no, it was not he that gave a stranger twenty dollars. It is a pity too; I see it now. . . ." Then, with a shudder — " But it is *gambler's* money! the wages of sin; we couldn't take it; we couldn't touch it. I don't like to be near it; it seems a defilement." She moved to a farther chair. . . . " I wish Edward would come, and take it to the bank; a burglar might come at any moment; it is dreadful to be here all alone with it."

At eleven Mr. Richards arrived, and while his wife was saying, " I am *so* glad you've come!" he was saying, " I'm so tired — tired clear out; it is dreadful to be poor, and have to make these dismal journeys at my time of life. Always at the grind, grind, grind, on a salary—another man's slave, and he sitting at home in his slippers, rich and comfortable."

" I am so sorry for you, Edward, you know that; but be comforted; we have our livelihood; we have our good name—"

" Yes, Mary, and that is everything. Don't mind my talk—it's just a moment's irritation and doesn't

"BUT IT WAS NOT MY EDWARD"

mean anything. Kiss me—there, it's all gone now, and I am not complaining any more. What have you been getting? What's in the sack?"

Then his wife told him the great secret. It dazed him for a moment; then he said:

"It weighs a hundred and sixty pounds? Why, Mary, it's for-ty thou-sand dollars — think of it — a whole fortune! Not ten men in this village are worth that much. Give me the paper."

He skimmed through it and said:

"Isn't it an adventure! Why, it's a romance; it's like the impossible things one reads about in books, and never sees in life." He was well stirred up now; cheerful, even gleeful. He tapped his old wife on the cheek, and said, humorously, "Why, we're rich, Mary, rich; all we've got to do is to bury the money and burn the papers. If the gambler ever comes to inquire, we'll merely look coldly upon him and say: 'What is this nonsense you are talking? We have never heard of you and your sack of gold before;' and then he would look foolish, and—"

"And in the mean time, while you are running on with your jokes, the money is still here, and it is fast getting along toward burglar-time."

"True. Very well, what shall we do—make the inquiry private? No, not that; it would spoil the romance. The public method is better. Think what a noise it will make! And it will make all the other towns jealous; for no stranger would trust such a thing to any town but Hadleyburg, and they know it. It's a great card for us. I must get to the printing-office now, or I shall be too late."

" But stop—stop—don't leave me here alone with it, Edward!"

But he was gone. For only a little while, how-ever. Not far from his own house he met the edi-tor-proprietor of the paper, and gave him the docu-ment, and said, " Here is a good thing for you, Cox —put it in."

" It may be too late, Mr. Richards, but I'll see."

At home again he and his wife sat down to talk the charming mystery over; they were in no con-dition for sleep. The first question was, Who could the citizen have been who gave the stranger the twenty dollars? It seemed a simple one; both answered it in the same breath—

" Barclay Goodson."

" Yes," said Richards, " he could have done it, and it would have been like him, but there's not another in the town."

" Everybody will grant that, Edward — grant it privately, anyway. For six months, now, the village has been its own proper self once more — honest, narrow, self-righteous, and stingy."

"It is what he always called it, to the day of his death—said it right out publicly, too."

"Yes, and he was hated for it."

"Oh, of course; but he didn't care. I reckon he was the best-hated man among us, except the Reverend Burgess."

"Well, Burgess deserves it—he will never get another congregation here. Mean as the town is, it knows how to estimate *him*. Edward, doesn't it seem odd that the stranger should appoint Burgess to deliver the money?"

"Well, yes—it does. That is—that is—"

"Why so much that-*is*-ing? Would *you* select him?"

"Mary, maybe the stranger knows him better than this village does."

"Much *that* would help Burgess!"

The husband seemed perplexed for an answer; the wife kept a steady eye upon him, and waited. Finally Richards said, with the hesitancy of one who is making a statement which is likely to encounter doubt,

"Mary, Burgess is not a bad man."

His wife was certainly surprised.

"Nonsense!" she exclaimed.

"He is not a bad man. I know. The whole of his unpopularity had its foundation in that one thing—the thing that made so much noise."

"That 'one thing,' indeed! As if that 'one thing' wasn't enough, all by itself."

"Plenty. Plenty. Only he wasn't guilty of it."

"How you talk! Not guilty of it! Everybody knows he *was* guilty."

"Mary, I give you my word—he was innocent."

"I can't believe it, and I don't. How do you know?"

"It is a confession. I am ashamed, but I will make it. I was the only man who knew he was innocent. I could have saved him, and—and—well, you know how the town was wrought up—I hadn't the pluck to do it. It would have turned everybody against me. I felt mean, ever so mean; but I didn't dare; I hadn't the manliness to face that."

Mary looked troubled, and for a while was silent. Then she said, stammeringly:

"I—I don't think it would have done for you to —to— One mustn't—er—public opinion—one has to be so careful—so—" It was a difficult road, and she got mired; but after a little she got started again. "It was a great pity, but— Why, we couldn't afford it, Edward—we couldn't indeed. Oh, I wouldn't have had you do it for anything!"

"It would have lost us the good-will of so many people, Mary; and then—and then—"

"What troubles me now is, what *he* thinks of us, Edward."

"He? *He* doesn't suspect that I could have saved him."

"Oh," exclaimed the wife, in a tone of relief, "I am glad of that. As long as he doesn't know that you could have saved him, he—he—well, that makes it a great deal better. Why, I might have known he didn't know, because he is always trying to be friendly with us, as little encouragement as we give him. More than once people have twitted me with it. There's the Wilsons, and the Wilcoxes, and the Harknesses, they take a mean pleasure in saying, ' *Your friend* Burgess,' because they know it pesters me. I wish he wouldn't persist in liking us so ; I can't think why he keeps it up."

"I can explain it. It's another confession. When the thing was new and hot, and the town made a plan to ride him on a rail, my conscience hurt me so that I couldn't stand it, and I went privately and gave him notice, and he got out of the town and staid out till it was safe to come back."

"Edward! If the town had found it out—"

"*Don't !* It scares me yet, to think of it. I repented of it the minute it was done ; and I was even afraid to tell you, lest your face might betray it to somebody. I didn't sleep any that night, for worrying. But after a few days I saw that no one was going to suspect me, and after that I got to feeling glad I did it. And I feel glad yet, Mary— glad through and through."

"So do I, now, for it would have been a dreadful way to treat him. Yes, I'm glad; for really you did owe him that, you know. But, Edward, suppose it should come out yet, some day!"

"It won't."

"Why?"

"Because everybody thinks it was Goodson."

"Of course they would!"

"Certainly. And of course *he* didn't care. They persuaded poor old Sawlsberry to go and charge it on him, and he went blustering over there and did it. Goodson looked him over, like as if he was hunting for a place on him that he could despise the most, then he says, ' So you are the Committee of Inquiry, are you?' Sawlsberry said that was about what he was. ' Hm. Do they require particulars, or do you reckon a kind of a *general* answer will do?' 'If they require particulars, I will come back, Mr. Goodson; I will take the general answer first.' 'Very well, then, tell them to go to hell—I reckon that's general enough. And I'll give you some advice, Sawlsberry; when you come back

"GOODSON LOOKED HIM OVER"

for the particulars, fetch a basket to carry the relics of yourself home in.' "

" Just like Goodson ; it's got all the marks. He had only one vanity; he thought he could give advice better than any other person."

"It settled the business, and saved us, Mary. The subject was dropped."

" Bless you, I'm not doubting *that*."

Then they took up the gold-sack mystery again, with strong interest. Soon the conversation began to suffer breaks—interruptions caused by absorbed thinkings. The breaks grew more and more frequent. At last Richards lost himself wholly in thought. He sat long, gazing vacantly at the floor, and by-and-by he began to punctuate his thoughts with little nervous movements of his hands that seemed to indicate vexation. Meantime his wife too had relapsed into a thoughtful silence, and her movements were beginning to show a troubled discomfort. Finally Richards got up and strode aimlessly about the room, ploughing his hands through his hair, much as a somnambulist might do who was having a bad dream. Then he seemed to arrive at a definite purpose ; and without a word he put on his hat and passed quickly out of the house. His wife sat brooding, with a drawn face, and did not seem to be aware that she was alone. Now and then she murmured, " Lead us not into t. . . . but—but—we are so poor, so poor !. . . . Lead us not into. . . . Ah, who would be hurt by it ?—and no one would ever know. . . . Lead us. . . ." The voice died out in mumblings. After a little she glanced up and muttered in a half-frightened, half-glad way—

" He is gone ! But, oh dear, he may be too late —too late. . . . Maybe not—maybe there is still time." She rose and stood thinking, nervously clasping and unclasping her hands. A slight shudder shook her frame, and she said, out of a dry throat, " God forgive me—it's awful to think such things—but. . . . Lord, how we are made—how strangely we are made !"

She turned the light low, and slipped stealthily over and kneeled down by the sack and felt of its ridgy sides with her hands, and fondled them lovingly ; and there was a gloating light in her poor old eyes. She fell into fits of absence ; and came half out of them at times to mutter, " If we had only waited !—oh, if we had only waited a little, and not been in such a hurry !"

Meantime Cox had gone home from his office and told his wife all about the strange thing that had happened, and they had talked it over eagerly, and guessed that the late Goodson was the only

man in the town who could have helped a suffering stranger with so noble a sum as twenty dollars. Then there was a pause, and the two became
thoughtful and silent. And by-and-by nervous and
fidgety. At last the wife said, as if to herself,

"Nobody knows this secret but the Richardses
. . . and us . . . nobody."

The husband came out of his thinkings with a
slight start, and gazed wistfully at his wife, whose
face was become very pale; then he hesitatingly
rose, and glanced furtively at his hat, then at his
wife—a sort of mute inquiry. Mrs. Cox swallowed
once or twice, with her hand at her throat, then in
place of speech she nodded her head. In a moment
she was alone, and mumbling to herself.

And now Richards and Cox were hurrying through
the deserted streets, from opposite directions. They
met, panting, at the foot of the printing-office stairs;
by the night-light there they read each other's face.
Cox whispered,

"Nobody knows about this but us?"

The whispered answer was,

"Not a soul—on honor, not a soul!"

"If it isn't too late to—"

The men were starting up-stairs; at this moment
they were overtaken by a boy, and Cox asked,

"Is that you, Johnny?"

"Yes, sir."

"You needn't ship the early mail—nor *any* mail; wait till I tell you."

"It's already gone, sir."

"*Gone?*" It had the sound of an unspeakable disappointment in it.

"Yes, sir. Time-table for Brixton and all the towns beyond changed to-day, sir—had to get the papers in twenty minutes earlier than common. I had to rush; if I had been two minutes later—"

The men turned and walked slowly away, not waiting to hear the rest. Neither of them spoke during ten minutes; then Cox said, in a vexed tone,

"What possessed you to be in such a hurry, *I* can't make out."

The answer was humble enough:

"I see it now, but somehow I never thought, you know, until it was too late. But the next time—"

"Next time be hanged! It won't come in a thousand years."

Then the friends separated without a good-night, and dragged themselves home with the gait of mortally stricken men. At their homes their wives sprang up with an eager "Well?"—then saw the answer with their eyes and sank down sorrowing, without waiting for it to come in words. In both houses a discussion followed of a heated sort—a new thing; there had been discussions before, but not heated ones, not ungentle ones. The discussions to-night were a sort of seeming plagiarisms of each other. Mrs. Richards said,

"If you had only waited, Edward—if you had only stopped to think; but no, you must run straight to the printing-office and spread it all over the world."

"It *said* publish it."

"That is nothing; it also said do it privately, if you liked. There, now—is that true, or not?"

"Why, yes—yes, it is true; but when I thought what a stir it would make, and what a compliment it was to Hadleyburg that a stranger should trust it so—"

"Oh, certainly, I know all that; but if you had only stopped to think, you would have seen that you *couldn't* find the right man, because he is in his grave, and hasn't left chick nor child nor relation behind him; and as long as the money went to somebody that awfully needed it, and nobody would be hurt by it, and—and—"

She broke down, crying. Her husband tried to think of some comforting thing to say, and presently came out with this:

"But after all, Mary, it must be for the best—it

2

must be; we know that. And we must remember that it was so ordered—"

"Ordered! Oh, everything's *ordered*, when a person has to find some way out when he has been stupid. Just the same, it was *ordered* that the money should come to us in this special way, and it was you that must take it on yourself to go meddling with the designs of Providence—and who gave you the right? It was wicked, that is what it was—just blasphemous presumption, and no more becoming to a meek and humble professor of—"

"But, Mary, you know how we have been trained all our lives long, like the whole village, till it is absolutely second nature to us to stop not a single moment to think when there's an honest thing to be done—"

"Oh, I know it, I know it—it's been one everlasting training and training and training in honesty—honesty shielded, from the very cradle, against every possible temptation, and so it's *artificial* honesty, and weak as water when temptation comes, as we have seen this night. God knows I never had shade nor shadow of a doubt of my petrified and indestructible honesty until now—and now, under the very first big and real temptation, I—Edward, it is my belief that this town's honesty is as rotten as mine is; as rotten as yours is. It is a mean town, a hard, stingy town, and hasn't a virtue in the world but this honesty it is so celebrated for and so conceited about; and so help me, I do believe that if ever the day comes that its honesty falls under great temptation, its grand reputation will go to ruin like a house of cards. There, now, I've made confession, and I feel better; I am a humbug, and I've been one all my life, without knowing it. Let no man call me honest again—I will not have it."

"I— Well, Mary, I feel a good deal as you do; I certainly do. It seems strange, too, so strange. I never could have believed it—never."

A long silence followed; both were sunk in thought. At last the wife looked up and said,

"I know what you are thinking, Edward."

Richards had the embarrassed look of a person who is caught.

"I am ashamed to confess it, Mary, but—"

"It's no matter, Edward, I was thinking the same question myself."

"I hope so. State it."

"You were thinking, if a body could only guess out *what the remark was* that Goodson made to the stranger."

"It's perfectly true. I feel guilty and ashamed. And you?"

"I'm past it. Let us make a pallet here; we've got to stand watch till the bank vault opens in the morning and admits the sack. . . . Oh, dear, oh, dear—if we hadn't made the mistake!"

The pallet was made, and Mary said:

"The open sesame — what could it have been? I do wonder what that remark could have been? But come; we will get to bed now."

"And sleep?"

"No; think."

"Yes, think."

By this time the Coxes too had completed their spat and their reconciliation, and were turning in —to think, to think, and toss, and fret, and worry over what the remark could possibly have been which Goodson made to the stranded derelict: that golden remark; that remark worth forty thousand dollars, cash.

The reason that the village telegraph-office was open later than usual that night was this: The foreman of Cox's paper was the local representative of the Associated Press. One might say its honorary representative, for it wasn't four times a year that he could furnish thirty words that would be accepted. But this time it was different. His despatch stating what he had caught got an instant answer:

" Send the whole thing—all the details—twelve hundred words."

A colossal order! The foreman filled the bill; and he was the proudest man in the State. By breakfast-time the next morning the name of Hadleyburg the Incorruptible was on every lip in America, from Montreal to the Gulf, from the glaciers of Alaska to the orange-groves of Florida; and millions and millions of people were discussing the stranger and his money-sack, and wondering if the right man would be found, and hoping some more news about the matter would come soon — right away.

II

Hadleyburg village woke up world-celebrated— astonished—happy—vain. Vain beyond imagination. Its nineteen principal citizens and their wives went about shaking hands with each other, and beaming, and smiling, and congratulating, and saying *this* thing adds a new word to the dictionary— *Hadleyburg*, synonym for *incorruptible* — destined to live in dictionaries forever! And the minor and unimportant citizens and their wives went around acting in much the same way. Everybody ran to

the bank to see the gold-sack; and before noon
grieved and envious crowds began to flock in from
Brixton and all neighboring towns; and that afternoon and next day reporters began to arrive from
everywhere to verify the sack and its history and
write the whole thing up anew, and make dashing
free-hand pictures of the sack, and of Richards's
house, and the bank, and the Presbyterian church,
and the Baptist church, and the public square, and
the town-hall where the test would be applied and
the money delivered; and damnable portraits of
the Richardses, and Pinkerton the banker, and Cox,
and the foreman, and Reverend Burgess, and the
postmaster—and even of Jack Halliday, who was
the loafing, good-natured, no-account, irreverent
fisherman, hunter, boys' friend, stray-dogs' friend,
typical "Sam Lawson" of the town. The little
mean, smirking, oily Pinkerton showed the sack to
all comers, and rubbed his sleek palms together
pleasantly, and enlarged upon the town's fine old
reputation for honesty and upon this wonderful
endorsement of it, and hoped and believed that
the example would now spread far and wide over
the American world, and be epoch-making in the
matter of moral regeneration. And so on, and so
on.

By the end of a week things had quieted down

again; the wild intoxication of pride and joy had sobered to a soft, sweet, silent delight — a sort of deep, nameless, unutterable content. All faces bore a look of peaceful, holy happiness.

Then a change came. It was a gradual change: so gradual that its beginnings were hardly noticed; maybe were not noticed at all, except by Jack Halliday, who always noticed everything; and always made fun of it, too, no matter what it was. He began to throw out chaffing remarks about people not looking quite so happy as they did a day or two ago; and next he claimed that the new aspect was deepening to positive sadness; next, that it was taking on a sick look; and finally he said that everybody was become so moody, thoughtful, and absent-minded that he could rob the meanest man in town of a cent out of the bottom of his breeches pocket and not disturb his revery.

At this stage — or at about this stage — a saying like this was dropped at bedtime—with a sigh, usually—by the head of each of the nineteen principal households:

"Ah, what *could* have been the remark that Goodson made!"

And straightway — with a shudder — came this, from the man's wife:

"Oh, *don't!* What horrible thing are you mulling in your mind? Put it away from you, for God's sake !"

But that question was wrung from those men again the next night — and got the same retort. But weaker.

And the third night the men uttered the question yet again—with anguish, and absently. This time — and the following night — the wives fidgeted feebly, and tried to say something. But didn't.

And the night after that they found their tongues and responded—longingly,

"Oh, if we *could* only guess !"

Halliday's comments grew daily more and more sparklingly disagreeable and disparaging. He went diligently about, laughing at the town, individually and in mass. But his laugh was the only one left in the village : it fell upon a hollow and mournful vacancy and emptiness. Not even a smile was find-able anywhere. Halliday carried a cigar-box around on a tripod, playing that it was a camera, and halted all passers and aimed the thing and said, " Ready ! — now look pleasant, please," but not even this capital joke could surprise the dreary faces into any softening.

So three weeks passed — one week was left. It was Saturday evening — after supper. Instead of the aforetime Saturday-evening flutter and bustle

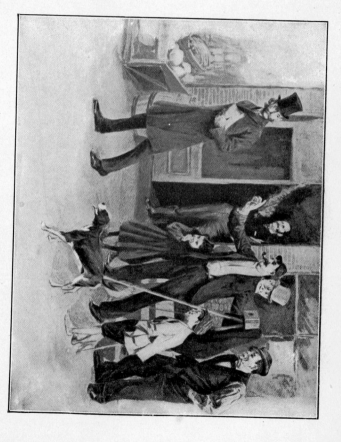

"READY!—NOW LOOK PLEASANT, PLEASE"

and shopping and larking, the streets were empty and desolate. Richards and his old wife sat apart in their little parlor—miserable and thinking. This was become their evening habit now: the life-long habit which had preceded it, of reading, knitting, and contented chat, or receiving or paying neighborly calls, was dead and gone and forgotten, ages ago—two or three weeks ago; nobody talked now, nobody read, nobody visited—the whole village sat at home, sighing, worrying, silent. Trying to guess out that remark.

The postman left a letter. Richards glanced listlessly at the superscription and the post-mark—unfamiliar, both—and tossed the letter on the table and resumed his might-have-beens and his hopeless dull miseries where he had left them off. Two or three hours later his wife got wearily up and was going away to bed without a good-night—custom now—but she stopped near the letter and eyed it awhile with a dead interest, then broke it open, and began to skim it over. Richards, sitting there with his chair tilted back against the wall and his chin between his knees, heard something fall. It was his wife. He sprang to her side, but she cried out:

"Leave me alone, I am too happy. Read the letter—read it!"

He did. He devoured it, his brain reeling. The letter was from a distant State, and it said:

"I am a stranger to you, but no matter: I have something to tell. I have just arrived home from Mexico, and learned about that episode. Of course you do not know who made that remark, but I know, and I am the only person living who does know. It was GOODSON. *I knew him well, many years ago. I passed through your village that very night, and was his guest till the midnight train came along. I overheard him make that remark to the stranger in the dark — it was in Hale Alley. He and I talked of it the rest of the way home, and while smoking in his house. He mentioned many of your villagers in the course of his talk — most of them in a very uncomplimentary way, but two or three favorably: among these latter yourself. I say 'favorably' — nothing stronger. I remember his saying he did not actually* LIKE *any person in the town — not one; but that you — I* THINK *he said you — am almost sure — had done him a very great service once, possibly without knowing the full value of it, and he wished he had a fortune, he would leave it to you when he died, and a curse apiece for the rest of the citizens. Now, then, if it was you that did him that service, you are his legitimate heir, and entitled to the sack of gold. I know that I can trust to your honor and honesty, for in a citizen of Hadleyburg these virtues are an unfailing inheritance, and so I am going to reveal to you the remark, well satisfied that if you are not the right man you will seek and find the right one and see that poor Goodson's debt of gratitude for the service referred to is paid. This is the remark:* 'YOU ARE FAR FROM BEING A BAD MAN: GO, AND REFORM.'*

*"*HOWARD L. STEPHENSON.*"*

"Oh, Edward, the money is ours, and I am so

grateful, *oh*, so grateful — kiss me, dear, it's forever since we kissed — and we needed it so — the money — and now you are free of Pinkerton and his bank, and nobody's slave any more; it seems to me I could fly for joy."

It was a happy half-hour that the couple spent there on the settee caressing each other; it was the old days come again—days that had begun with their courtship and lasted without a break till the stranger brought the deadly money. By-and-by the wife said :

" Oh, Edward, how lucky it was you did him that grand service, poor Goodson! I never liked him, but I love him now. And it was fine and beautiful of you never to mention it or brag about it." Then, with a touch of reproach, " But you ought to have told *me*, Edward, you ought to have told your wife, you know."

" Well, I—er—well, Mary, you see—"

" Now stop hemming and hawing, and tell me about it, Edward. I always loved you, and now I'm proud of you. Everybody believes there was only one good generous soul in this village, and now it turns out that you— Edward, why don't you tell me ?"

" Well—er—er— Why, Mary, I can't !"

" You *can't?* *Why* can't you ?"

"You see, he—well, he—he made me promise I wouldn't."

The wife looked him over, and said, very slowly,

"Made—you—promise? Edward, what do you tell me that for?"

"Mary, do you think I would lie?"

She was troubled and silent for a moment, then she laid her hand within his and said:

"No . . . no. We have wandered far enough from our bearings—God spare us that! In all your life you have never uttered a lie. But now—now that the foundations of things seem to be crumbling from under us, we—we—" She lost her voice for a moment, then said, brokenly, "Lead us not into temptation. . . . I think you made the promise, Edward. Let it rest so. Let us keep away from that ground. Now—that is all gone by; let us be happy again; it is no time for clouds."

Edward found it something of an effort to comply, for his mind kept wandering — trying to remember what the service was that he had done Goodson.

The couple lay awake the most of the night, Mary happy and busy, Edward busy, but not so happy. Mary was planning what she would do with the money. Edward was trying to recall that service. At first his conscience was sore on account of the lie he had told Mary—if it was a lie. After much reflection—suppose it *was* a lie? What then? Was it such a great matter? Aren't we always *acting* lies? Then why not *tell* them? Look at Mary —look what she had done. While he was hurrying off on his honest errand, what was she doing? Lamenting because the papers hadn't been destroyed and the money kept! Is theft better than lying?

That point lost its sting — the lie dropped into the background and left comfort behind it. The next point came to the front: *had* he rendered that service? Well, here was Goodson's own evidence as reported in Stephenson's letter; there could be no better evidence than that—it was even *proof* that he had rendered it. Of course. So that point was settled. . . . No, not quite. He recalled with a wince that this unknown Mr. Stephenson was just a trifle unsure as to whether the performer of it was Richards or some other—and, oh dear, he had put Richards on his honor! He must himself decide whither that money must go—and Mr. Stephenson was not doubting that if he was the wrong man he would go honorably and find the right one. Oh, it was odious to put a man in such a situation — ah, why couldn't Stephenson have left out that doubt! What did he want to intrude that for?

Further reflection. How did it happen that

Richards's name remained in Stephenson's mind as indicating the right man, and not some other man's name? That looked good. Yes, that looked very good. In fact, it went on looking better and better, straight along—until by-and-by it grew into positive *proof*. And then Richards put the matter at once out of his mind, for he had a private instinct that a proof once established is better left so.

He was feeling reasonably comfortable now, but there was still one other detail that kept pushing itself on his notice : of course he had done that service—that was settled ; but what *was* that service? He must recall it—he would not go to sleep till he had recalled it ; it would make his peace of mind perfect. And so he thought and thought. He thought of a dozen things— possible services, even probable services —but none of them seemed adequate, none of them seemed large enough, none of them seemed worth the money—worth the fortune Goodson had wished he could leave in his will. And besides, he couldn't remember having done them, anyway. Now, then—now, then—what *kind* of a service would it be that would make a man so inordinately grateful? Ah—the saving of his soul! That must be it. Yes, he could remember, now, how he once set himself the task of converting Goodson, and labored at it as much as — he was

going to say three months; but upon closer examination it shrunk to a month, then to a week, then
to a day, then to nothing. Yes, he remembered
now, and with unwelcome vividness, that Goodson
had told him to go to thunder and mind his own
business — *he* wasn't hankering to follow Hadleyburg to heaven!

So that solution was a failure — he hadn't saved
Goodson's soul. Richards was discouraged. Then
after a little came another idea: had he saved
Goodson's property? No, that wouldn't do — he
hadn't any. His life? That is it! Of course. Why,
he might have thought of it before. This time he
was on the right track, sure. His imagination-mill
was hard at work in a minute, now.

Thereafter during a stretch of two exhausting
hours he was busy saving Goodson's life. He saved
it in all kinds of difficult and perilous ways. In
every case he got it saved satisfactorily up to a
certain point; then, just as he was beginning to
get well persuaded that it had really happened, a
troublesome detail would turn up which made the
whole thing impossible. As in the matter of drowning, for instance. In that case he had swum out and
tugged Goodson ashore in an unconscious state with
a great crowd looking on and applauding, but when
he had got it all thought out and was just begin-

ning to remember all about it a whole swarm of disqualifying details arrived on the ground: the town would have known of the circumstance, Mary would have known of it, it would glare like a lime-light in his own memory instead of being an incon-spicuous service which he had possibly rendered " without knowing its full value." And at this point he remembered that he couldn't swim, any-way.

Ah—*there* was a point which he had been over-looking from the start: it had to be a service which he had rendered " possibly without knowing the full value of it." Why, really, that ought to be an easy hunt — much easier than those others. And sure enough, by-and-by he found it. Goodson, years and years ago, came near marrying a very sweet and pretty girl, named Nancy Hewitt, but in some way or other the match had been broken off; the girl died, Goodson remained a bachelor, and by-and-by became a soured one and a frank despiser of the human species. Soon after the girl's death the village found out, or thought it had found out, that she carried a spoonful of negro blood in her veins. Richards worked at these details a good while, and in the end he thought he remembered things concerning them which must have gotten mislaid in his memory through long neglect. He seemed to dimly remember that it was *he* that found out about the negro blood; that it was he that told the village; that the village told Goodson where they got it; that he thus saved Goodson from marrying the tainted girl; that he had done him this great service "without knowing the full value of it," in fact without knowing that he *was* doing it; but that Goodson knew the value of it, and what a narrow escape he had had, and so went to his grave grateful to his benefactor and wishing he had a fortune to leave him. It was all clear and simple now, and the more he went over it the more luminous and certain it grew; and at last, when he nestled to sleep satisfied and happy, he remembered the whole thing just as if it had been yesterday. In fact, he dimly remembered Goodson's *telling* him his gratitude once. Meantime Mary had spent six thousand dollars on a new house for herself and a pair of slippers for her pastor, and then had fallen peacefully to rest.

That same Saturday evening the postman had delivered a letter to each of the other principal citizens — nineteen letters in all. No two of the envelopes were alike, and no two of the superscriptions were in the same hand, but the letters inside were just like each other in every detail but one. They were exact copies of the letter received by

3

Richards—handwriting and all—and were all signed by Stephenson, but in place of Richard's name each receiver's own name appeared.

All night long eighteen principal citizens did what their caste-brother Richards was doing at the same time — they put in their energies trying to remember what notable service it was that they had unconsciously done Barclay Goodson. In no case was it a holiday job; still they succeeded.

And while they were at this work, which was difficult, their wives put in the night spending the money, which was easy. During that one night the nineteen wives spent an average of seven thousand dollars each out of the forty thousand in the sack —a hundred and thirty-three thousand altogether.

Next day there was a surprise for Jack Halliday. He noticed that the faces of the nineteen chief citizens and their wives bore that expression of peaceful and holy happiness again. He could not understand it, neither was he able to invent any remarks about it that could damage it or disturb it. And so it was his turn to be dissatisfied with life. His private guesses at the reasons for the happiness failed in all instances, upon examination. When he met Mrs. Wilcox and noticed the placid ecstasy in her face, he said to himself, " Her cat has had kittens "— and went and asked the cook; it was not so ; the cook had detected the happiness, but did not know the cause. When Halliday found the duplicate ecstasy in the face of " Shadbelly " Billson (village nickname), he was sure some neighbor of Billson's had broken his leg, but inquiry showed that this had not happened. The subdued ecstasy in Gregory Yates's face could mean but one thing — he was a mother-in-law short ; it was another mistake. "And Pinkerton — Pinkerton — he has collected ten cents that he thought he was going to lose." And so on, and so on. In some cases the guesses had to remain in doubt, in the others they proved distinct errors. In the end Halliday said to himself, " Anyway it foots up that there's nineteen Hadleyburg families temporarily in heaven : I don't know how it happened ; I only know Providence is off duty to-day."

An architect and builder from the next State had lately ventured to set up a small business in this unpromising village, and his sign had now been hanging out a week. Not a customer yet ; he was a discouraged man, and sorry he had come. But his weather changed suddenly now. First one and then another chief citizen's wife said to him privately :

"Come to my house Monday week — but say nothing about it for the present. We think of building."

He got eleven invitations that day. That night he wrote his daughter and broke off her match with her student. He said she could marry a mile higher than that.

Pinkerton the banker and two or three other well-to-do men planned country-seats—but waited. That kind don't count their chickens until they are hatched.

The Wilsons devised a grand new thing—a fancy-dress ball. They made no actual promises, but told all their acquaintanceship in confidence that they were thinking the matter over and thought they should give it—"and if we do, you will be invited, of course." People were surprised, and said, one to another, "Why, they are crazy, those poor Wilsons, they can't afford it." Several among the nineteen said privately to their husbands, "It is a good idea, we will keep still till their cheap thing is over, then *we* will give one that will make it sick."

The days drifted along, and the bill of future squanderings rose higher and higher, wilder and wilder, more and more foolish and reckless. It began to look as if every member of the nineteen would not only spend his whole forty thousand dollars before receiving-day, but be actually in debt by the time he got the money. In some cases light-headed people did not stop with planning to spend, they really spent — on credit. They bought land, mortgages, farms, speculative stocks, fine clothes, horses, and various other things, paid down the bonus, and made themselves liable for the rest—at ten days. Presently the sober second thought came, and Halliday noticed that a ghastly anxiety was beginning to show up in a good many faces. Again he was puzzled, and didn't know what to make of it. "The Wilcox kittens aren't dead, for they weren't born; nobody's broken a leg; there's no shrinkage in mother-in-laws; *nothing* has happened—it is an insolvable mystery."

There was another puzzled man, too — the Rev. Mr. Burgess. For days, wherever he went, people seemed to follow him or to be watching out for him; and if he ever found himself in a retired spot, a member of the nineteen would be sure to appear, thrust an envelope privately into his hand, whisper "To be opened at the town-hall Friday evening," then vanish away like a guilty thing. He was expecting that there might be one claimant for the sack—doubtful, however, Goodson being dead—but it never occurred to him that all this crowd might be claimants. When the great Friday came at last, he found that he had nineteen envelopes.

III

The town-hall had never looked finer. The platform at the end of it was backed by a showy draping of flags; at intervals along the walls were festoons of flags; the gallery fronts were clothed in flags; the supporting columns were swathed in flags; all this was to impress the stranger, for he would be there in considerable force, and in a large degree he would be connected with the press. The house was full. The 412 fixed seats were occupied; also the 68 extra chairs which had been packed into the aisles; the steps of the platform were occupied; some distinguished strangers were given seats on the platform; at the horseshoe of tables which fenced the front and sides of the platform sat a strong force of special correspondents who had come from everywhere. It was the best-dressed house the town had ever produced. There were some tolerably expensive toilets there, and in several cases the ladies who wore them had the look of being unfamiliar with that kind of clothes. At least the town thought they had that look, but the notion could have arisen from the town's knowledge of the fact that these ladies had never inhabited such clothes before.

The gold-sack stood on a little table at the front of the platform where all the house could see it. The bulk of the house gazed at it with a burning interest, a mouth-watering interest, a wistful and pathetic interest; a minority of nineteen couples gazed at it tenderly, lovingly, proprietarily, and the male half of this minority kept saying over to themselves the moving little impromptu speeches of thankfulness for the audience's applause and congratulations which they were presently going to get up and deliver. Every now and then one of these got a piece of paper out of his vest pocket and privately glanced at it to refresh his memory.

Of course there was a buzz of conversation going on—there always is; but at last when the Rev. Mr. Burgess rose and laid his hand on the sack he could hear his microbes gnaw, the place was so still. He related the curious history of the sack, then went on to speak in warm terms of Hadleyburg's old and well-earned reputation for spotless honesty, and of the town's just pride in this reputation. He said that this reputation was a treasure of priceless value; that under Providence its value had now become inestimably enhanced, for the recent episode had spread this fame far and wide, and thus had focussed the eyes of the American world upon this village, and made its name for all time, as he

hoped and believed, a synonym for commercial incorruptibility. (*Applause.*) "And who is to be the
guardian of this noble treasure—the community as
a whole? No! The responsibility is individual,
not communal. From this day forth each and every
one of you is in his own person its special guardian, and individually responsible that no harm
shall come to it. Do you—does each of you—ac-
cept this great trust? [*Tumultuous assent.*] Then
all is well. Transmit it to your children and to
your children's children. To-day your purity is
beyond reproach—see to it that it shall remain so.
To-day there is not a person in your community
who could be beguiled to touch a penny not his
own—see to it that you abide in this grace. ["*We
will! we will!*"] This is not the place to make
comparisons between ourselves and other commu-
nities—some of them ungracious toward us; they
have their ways, we have ours; let us be content.
[*Applause.*] I am done. Under my hand, my
friends, rests a stranger's eloquent recognition of
what we are; through him the world will always
henceforth know what we are. We do not know
who he is, but in your name I utter your gratitude,
and ask you to raise your voices in indorsement."

The house rose in a body and made the walls
quake with the thunders of its thankfulness for the

space of a long minute. Then it sat down, and
Mr. Burgess took an envelope out of his pocket.
The house held its breath while he slit the envelope open and took from it a slip of paper. He
read its contents—slowly and impressively—the
audience listening with tranced attention to this
magic document, each of whose words stood for an
ingot of gold :

"'*The remark which I made to the distressed
stranger was this : "You are very far from being a
bad man; go, and reform."'*" Then he continued :
"We shall know in a moment now whether the remark here quoted corresponds with the one concealed in the sack ; and if that shall prove to be so
—and it undoubtedly will—this sack of gold belongs to a fellow-citizen who will henceforth stand
before the nation as the symbol of the special virtue which has made our town famous throughout
the land—Mr. Billson !"

The house had gotten itself all ready to burst
into the proper tornado of applause ; but instead
of doing it, it seemed stricken with a paralysis ;
there was a deep hush for a moment or two, then
a wave of whispered murmurs swept the place—of
about this tenor : "*Billson !* oh, come, this is *too* thin !
Twenty dollars to a stranger—or *anybody—Billson !*
Tell it to the marines!" And now at this point the

house caught its breath all of a sudden in a new access of astonishment, for it discovered that whereas in one part of the hall Deacon Billson was standing up with his head meekly bowed, in another part of it Lawyer Wilson was doing the same. There was a wondering silence now for a while. Everybody was puzzled, and nineteen couples were surprised and indignant.

Billson and Wilson turned and stared at each other. Billson asked, bitingly,

"Why do *you* rise, Mr. Wilson?"

"Because I have a right to. Perhaps you will be good enough to explain to the house why *you* rise?"

"With great pleasure. Because I wrote that paper."

"It is an impudent falsity! I wrote it myself."

It was Burgess's turn to be paralyzed. He stood looking vacantly at first one of the men and then the other, and did not seem to know what to do. The house was stupefied. Lawyer Wilson spoke up, now, and said,

"I ask the Chair to read the name signed to that paper."

That brought the Chair to itself, and it read out the name,

"'John Wharton *Billson*.'"

" There !" shouted Billson, " what have you got to say for yourself, now? And what kind of apology are you going to make to me and to this insulted house for the imposture which you have attempted to play here ?"

" No apologies are due, sir ; and as for the rest of it, I publicly charge you with pilfering my note from Mr. Burgess and substituting a copy of it signed with your own name. There is no other way by which you could have gotten hold of the test-remark; I alone, of living men, possessed the secret of its wording."

There was likely to be a scandalous state of things if this went on ; everybody noticed with distress that the short-hand scribes were scribbling like mad ; many people were crying " Chair, Chair ! Order! order !" Burgess rapped with his gavel, and said :

" Let us not forget the proprieties due. There has evidently been a mistake somewhere, but surely that is all. If Mr. Wilson gave me an envelope —and I remember now that he did—I still have it."

He took one out of his pocket, opened it, glanced at it, looked surprised and worried, and stood silent a few moments. Then he waved his hand in a wandering and mechanical way, and made an effort or two to say something, then gave it up, despondently. Several voices cried out :

" Read it ! read it ! What is it ?"

So he began in a dazed and sleep-walker fashion :

" ' *The remark which I made to the unhappy stran-*
ger was this : "*You are far from being a bad man.*
[The house gazed at him, marvelling.] *Go, and re-*
form." ' [*Murmurs :* " Amazing ! what can this
mean ?"] This one," said the Chair, " is signed
Thurlow G. Wilson."

" There !" cried Wilson, " I reckon that settles
it ! I knew perfectly well my note was purloined."

" Purloined !" retorted Billson. " I'll let you
know that neither you nor any man of your kid-
ney must venture to—"

The Chair. " Order, gentlemen, order ! Take
your seats, both of you, please."

They obeyed, shaking their heads and grumbling
angrily. The house was profoundly puzzled ; it
did not know what to do with this curious emergency. Presently Thompson got up. Thompson
was the hatter. He would have liked to be a Nineteener ; but such was not for him ; his stock of hats
was not considerable enough for the position. He
said :

" Mr. Chairman, if I may be permitted to make a
suggestion, can both of these gentlemen be right ?
I put it to you, sir, can both have happened to say

the very same words to the stranger? It seems to me—"

The tanner got up and interrupted him. The tanner was a disgruntled man; he believed himself entitled to be a Nineteener, but he couldn't get recognition. It made him a little unpleasant in his ways and speech. Said he:

"Sho, *that's* not the point! *That* could happen — twice in a hundred years — but not the other thing. *Neither* of them gave the twenty dollars!" (*A ripple of applause.*)

Billson. "*I* did!'

Wilson. "*I* did!"

Then each accused the other of pilfering.

The Chair. "Order! Sit down, if you please —both of you. Neither of the notes has been out of my possession at any moment."

A Voice. "Good—that settles *that!*"

The Tanner. "Mr. Chairman, one thing is now plain: one of these men has been eavesdropping under the other one's bed, and filching family secrets. If it is not unparliamentary to suggest it, I will remark that both are equal to it. [*The Chair.* "Order! order!"] I withdraw the remark, sir, and will confine myself to suggesting that *if* one of them has overheard the other reveal the test-remark to his wife, we shall catch him now."

A Voice. " How ?"

The Tanner. "Easily. The two have not quoted the remark in exactly the same words. You would have noticed that, if there hadn't been a considerable stretch of time and an exciting quarrel inserted between the two readings."

A Voice. " Name the difference."

The Tanner. "The word *very* is in Billson's note, and not in the other."

Many Voices. " That's so—he's right !"

The Tanner. " And so, if the Chair will examine the test-remark in the sack, we shall know which of these two frauds—[*The Chair.* " Order !"]—which of these two adventurers — [*The Chair.* " Order ! order !"]—which of these two gentlemen—[*laughter and applause*]—is entitled to wear the belt as being the first dishonest blatherskite ever bred in this town—which he has dishonored, and which will be a sultry place for him from now out !" (*Vigorous applause.*)

Many Voices. " Open it !—open the sack !"

Mr. Burgess made a slit in the sack, slid his hand in and brought out an envelope. In it were a couple of folded notes. He said :

" One of these is marked, ' Not to be examined until all written communications which have been addressed to the Chair — if any — shall have been read.' The other is marked '*The Test.*' Allow me. It is worded—to wit :

"'I do not require that the first half of the remark which was made to me by my benefactor shall be quoted with exactness, for it was not striking, and could be forgotten ; but its closing fifteen words are quite striking, and I think easily rememberable ; unless *these* shall be accurately reproduced, let the applicant be regarded as an impostor. My benefactor began by saying he seldom gave advice to any one, but that it always bore the hall-mark of high value when he did give it. Then he said this —and it has never faded from my memory : "*You are far from being a bad man—*" ' "

Fifty Voices. "That settles it—the money's Wilson's ! Wilson ! Wilson ! Speech ! Speech !"

People jumped up and crowded around Wilson, wringing his hand and congratulating fervently— meantime the Chair was hammering with the gavel and shouting :

"Order, gentlemen ! Order ! Order ! Let me finish reading, please." When quiet was restored, the reading was resumed—as follows :

"' " *Go, and reform—or, mark my words—some day, for your sins, you will die and go to hell or Hadleyburg—*TRY AND MAKE IT THE FORMER." ' "

A ghastly silence followed. First an angry cloud

began to settle darkly upon the faces of the citizenship; after a pause the cloud began to rise, and a
tickled expression tried to take its place; tried so
hard that it was only kept under with great and
painful difficulty; the reporters, the Brixtonites,
and other strangers bent their heads down and
shielded their faces with their hands, and managed
to hold in by main strength and heroic courtesy.
At this most inopportune time burst upon the stillness the roar of a solitary voice—Jack Halliday's:

" *That's* got the hall-mark on it!"

Then the house let go, strangers and all.   Even
Mr. Burgess's gravity broke down presently, then
the audience considered itself officially absolved
from all restraint, and it made the most of its privilege.   It was a good long laugh, and a tempestu-
ously whole-hearted one, but it ceased at last—long
enough for Mr. Burgess to try to resume, and for
the people to get their eyes partially wiped; then
it broke out again; and afterward yet again; then
at last Burgess was able to get out these serious
words:

" It is useless to try to disguise the fact—we find
ourselves in the presence of a matter of grave import.   It involves the honor of your town, it strikes
at the town's good name.   The difference of a single
word between the test-remarks offered by Mr. Wil-

son and Mr. Billson was itself a serious thing, since it indicated that one or the other of these gentlemen had committed a theft—"

The two men were sitting limp, nerveless, crushed; but at these words both were electrified into movement, and started to get up—

"Sit down!" said the Chair, sharply, and they obeyed. "That, as I have said, was a serious thing. And it was — but for only one of them. But the matter has become graver; for the honor of *both* is now in formidable peril. Shall I go even further, and say in inextricable peril? *Both* left out the crucial fifteen words." He paused. During several moments he allowed the pervading stillness to gather and deepen its impressive effects, then added: "There would seem to be but one way whereby this could happen. I ask these gentlemen— Was there *collusion?—agreement?*"

A low murmer sifted through the house; its import was, "He's got them both."

Billson was not used to emergencies; he sat in a helpless collapse. But Wilson was a lawyer. He struggled to his feet, pale and worried, and said:

"I ask the indulgence of the house while I explain this most painful matter. I am sorry to say what I am about to say, since it must inflict irreparable injury upon Mr. Billson, whom I have always

4

esteemed and respected until now, and in whose invulnerability to temptation I entirely believed—as did you all. But for the preservation of my own honor I must speak—and with frankness. I confess with shame—and I now beseech your pardon for it —that I said to the ruined stranger all of the words contained in the test-remark, including the disparaging fifteen. [*Sensation.*] When the late publication was made I recalled them, and I resolved to claim the sack of coin, for by every right I was entitled to it. Now I will ask you to consider this point, and weigh it well: that stranger's gratitude to me that night knew no bounds; he said himself that he could find no words for it that were adequate, and that if he should ever be able he would repay me a thousandfold. Now, then, I ask you this: could I expect — could I believe — could I even remotely imagine—that, feeling as he did, he would do so ungrateful a thing as to add those quite unnecessary fifteen words to his test?—set a trap for me?—expose me as a slanderer of my own town before my own people assembled in a public hall? It was preposterous; it was impossible. His test would contain only the kindly opening clause of my remark. Of that I had no shadow of doubt. You would have thought as I did. You would not have expected a base betrayal from one whom you

had befriended and against whom you had committed no offence. And so, with perfect confidence,
perfect trust, I wrote on a piece of paper the opening words — ending with ' Go, and reform,' — and
signed it. When I was about to put it in an envelope I was called into my back office, and without thinking I left the paper lying open on my
desk." He stopped, turned his head slowly toward Billson, waited a moment, then added: " I
ask you to note this : when I returned, a little
later, Mr. Billson was retiring by my street door."
(*Sensation.*)

In a moment Billson was on his feet and shouting :
" It's a lie !   It's an infamous lie !"

The Chair. " Be seated, sir !   Mr. Wilson has the
floor."

Billson's friends pulled him into his seat and
quieted him, and Wilson went on :

" Those are the simple facts.   My note was now
lying in a different place on the table from where I
had left it.   I noticed that, but attached no importance to it, thinking a draught had blown it there.
That Mr. Billson would read a private paper was a
thing which could not occur to me ; he was an honorable man, and he would be above that.   If you
will allow me to say it, I think his extra word '*very*'
stands explained ; it is attributable to a defect of

memory. I was the only man in the world who could furnish here any detail of the test-mark—by *honorable* means. I have finished."

There is nothing in the world like a persuasive speech to fuddle the mental apparatus and upset the convictions and debauch the emotions of an audience not practised in the tricks and delusions of oratory. Wilson sat down victorious. The house submerged him in tides of approving applause; friends swarmed to him and shook him by the hand and congratulated him, and Billson was shouted down and not allowed to say a word. The Chair hammered and hammered with its gavel, and kept shouting,

" But let us proceed, gentlemen, let us proceed!"

At last there was a measurable degree of quiet, and the hatter said,

" But what is there to proceed with, sir, but to deliver the money?"

Voices. " That's it! That's it! Come forward, Wilson!"

The Hatter. " I move three cheers for Mr. Wilson, Symbol of the special virtue which—"

The cheers burst forth before he could finish; and in the midst of them—and in the midst of the clamor of the gavel also—some enthusiasts mounted Wilson on a big friend's shoulder and were going to fetch him in triumph to the platform. The Chair's voice now rose above the noise—

"Order! To your places! You forget that there is still a document to be read." When quiet had been restored he took up the document, and was going to read it, but laid it down again, saying, "I forgot; this is not to be read until all written communications received by me have first been read." He took an envelope out of his pocket, removed its enclosure, glanced at it—seemed astonished—held it out and gazed at it—stared at it.

Twenty or thirty voices cried out:

"What is it? Read it! read it!"

And he did—slowly, and wondering:

"'The remark which I made to the stranger— [*Voices*. "Hello! how's this?"]—was this: "You are far from being a bad man. [*Voices*. "Great Scott!"] Go, and reform."' [*Voice*. "Oh, saw my leg off!"] Signed by Mr. Pinkerton the banker."

The pandemonium of delight which turned itself loose now was of a sort to make the judicious weep. Those whose withers were unwrung laughed till the tears ran down; the reporters, in throes of laughter, set down disordered pot-hooks which would never in the world be decipherable; and a sleeping dog jumped up, scared out of its wits, and barked itself crazy at the turmoil. All manner of cries were

scattered through the din : "We're getting rich—
two Symbols of Incorruptibility !—without counting Billson !" " *Three !*—count Shadbelly in—we
can't have too many !" "All right—Billson's elected !" "Alas, poor Wilson—victim of *two* thieves!"

A Powerful Voice. "Silence ! The Chair's fished
up something more out of its pocket."

Voices. " Hurrah ! Is it something fresh ? Read
it ! read ! read !"

The Chair (*reading*). "' The remark which I
made,' etc. 'You are far from being a bad man.
Go,' etc. Signed, ' Gregory Yates.' "

Tornado of Voices. " Four Symbols !" "' 'Rah for
Yates !" " Fish again !"

The house was in a roaring humor now, and
ready to get all the fun out of the occasion that
might be in it. Several Nineteeners, looking pale
and distressed, got up and began to work their way
toward the aisles, but a score of shouts went up :

" The doors, the doors — close the doors ; no Incorruptible shall leave this place ! Sit down, everybody !"

The mandate was obeyed.

" Fish again ! Read ! read !

The Chair fished again, and once more the familiar words began to fall from its lips—"' You
are far from being a bad man—' "

"THE HOUSE WAS IN A ROARING HUMOR"

" Name ! name !   What's his name ?"

" ' L. Ingoldsby Sargent.' "

" Five elected !   Pile up the Symbols !   Go on, go on !"

" ' You are far from being a bad—' "

" Name ! name !"

" ' Nicholas Whitworth.' "

" Hooray ! hooray ! it's a symbolical day !"

Somebody wailed in, and began to sing this rhyme (leaving out " it's ") to the lovely " Mikado " tune of " When a man's afraid of a beautiful maid "; the audience joined in, with joy ; then, just in time, somebody contributed another line—

> " And don't you this forget—"

The house roared it out.   A third line was at once furnished—

> " Corruptibles far from Hadleyburg are—"

The house roared that one too.   As the last note died, Jack Halliday's voice rose high and clear, freighted with a final line—

> " But the Symbols are here, you bet !"

That was sung, with booming enthusiasm.   Then the happy house started in at the beginning and sang the four lines through twice, with immense swing and dash, and finished up with a crashing three-times-three and a tiger for " Hadleyburg the Incorruptible and all Symbols of it which we shall find worthy to receive the hall-mark to-night."

Then the shoutings at the Chair began again, all over the place :

" Go on ! go on ! Read ! read some more ! Read all you've got !"

" That's it — go on ! We are winning eternal celebrity !"

A dozen men got up now and began to protest. They said that this farce was the work of some abandoned joker, and was an insult to the whole community. Without a doubt these signatures were all forgeries—

" Sit down ! sit down ! Shut up ! You are confessing. We'll find *your* names in the lot."

" Mr. Chairman, how many of those envelopes have you got ?"

The Chair counted.

" Together with those that have been already examined, there are nineteen."

A storm of derisive applause broke out.

" Perhaps they all contain the secret. I move that you open them all and read every signature that is attached to a note of that sort — and read also the first eight words of the note."

" Second the motion !"

It was put and carried—uproariously. Then poor old Richards got up, and his wife rose and stood at his side. Her head was bent down, so that none might see that she was crying. Her husband gave her his arm, and so supporting her, he began to speak in a quavering voice :

" My friends, you have known us two—Mary and me — all our lives, and I think you have liked us and respected us—"

The Chair interrupted him :

" Allow me. It is quite true—that which you are saying, Mr. Richards ; this town *does* know you two ; it *does* like you ; it *does* respect you ; more—it honors you and *loves* you—"

Halliday's voice rang out :

" That's the hall-marked truth, too ! If the Chair is right, let the house speak up and say it. Rise ! Now, then—hip ! hip ! hip !—all together !"

The house rose in mass, faced toward the old couple eagerly, filled the air with a snow - storm of waving handkerchiefs, and delivered the cheers with all its affectionate heart.

The Chair then continued :

" What I was going to say is this : We know your good heart, Mr. Richards, but this is not a time for the exercise of charity toward offenders. [Shouts of " Right ! right !"] I see your generous purpose in your face, but I cannot allow you to plead for these men—"

" But I was going to—"

" Please take your seat, Mr. Richards. We must examine the rest of these notes—simple fairness to the men who have already been exposed requires this. As soon as that has been done — I give you my word for this—you shall be heard."

Many Voices. " Right ! — the Chair is right — no interruption can be permitted at this stage ! Go on ! — the names ! the names ! — according to the terms of the motion !"

The old couple sat reluctantly down, and the husband whispered to the wife, " It is pitifully hard to have to wait ; the shame will be greater than ever when they find we were only going to plead for *ourselves.*"

Straightway the jollity broke loose again with the reading of the names.

" ' You are far from being a bad man—' Signature, ' Robert J. Titmarsh.'

" ' You are far from being a bad man—' Signature, ' Eliphalet Weeks.'

" ' You are far from being a bad man—' Signature, ' Oscar B. Wilder.' "

At this point the house lit upon the idea of taking the eight words out of the Chairman's hands. He was not unthankful for that. Thenceforward he held up each note in its turn, and waited. The house droned out the eight words in a massed and measured and musical deep volume of sound (with a daringly close resemblance to a well-known church chant)—" You are f-a-r from being a b-a-a-a-d man.'" Then the Chair said, " Signature, ' Archibald Wilcox.'" And so on, and so on, name after name, and everybody had an increasingly and gloriously good time except the wretched Nineteen. Now and then, when a particularly shining name was called, the house made the Chair wait while it chanted the whole of the test-remark from the beginning to the closing words, " And go to hell or Hadleyburg— try and make it the for-or-m-e-r!" and in these special cases they added a grand and agonized and imposing " A-a-a-a-*men !*"

The list dwindled, dwindled, dwindled, poor old Richards keeping tally of the count, wincing when a name resembling his own was pronounced, and waiting in miserable suspense for the time to come when it would be his humiliating privilege to rise with Mary and finish his plea, which he was intending to word thus: " . . . for until now we have never done any wrong thing, but have gone our humble way unreproached. We are very poor, we are old, and have no chick nor child to help us; we were sorely tempted, and we fell. It was my purpose when I got up before to make confession and beg that my name might not be read out in this public place, for it seemed to us that we could not bear it; but I was prevented. It was just; it was our place to suffer with the rest. It has been hard for us. It is the first time we have ever heard our name fall from any one's lips—sullied. Be merciful —for the sake of the better days; make our shame as light to bear as in your charity you can." At this point in his revery Mary nudged him, perceiving that his mind was absent. The house was chanting, "You are f-a-r," etc.

"Be ready," Mary whispered. "Your name comes now; he has read eighteen."

The chant ended.

"Next! next! next!" came volleying from all over the house.

Burgess put his hand into his pocket. The old couple, trembling, began to rise. Burgess fumbled a moment, then said,

"I find I have read them all."

Faint with joy and surprise, the couple sank into their seats, and Mary whispered,

"Oh, bless God, we are saved!—he has lost ours —I wouldn't give this for a hundred of those sacks!"

The house burst out with its " Mikado " travesty, and sang it three times with ever-increasing enthusiasm, rising to its feet when it reached for the third time the closing line—

"But the Symbols are here, you bet!"

and finishing up with cheers and a tiger for " Hadleyburg purity and our eighteen immortal representatives of it."

Then Wingate, the saddler, got up and proposed cheers " for the cleanest man in town, the one solitary important citizen in it who didn't try to steal that money—Edward Richards."

They were given with great and moving heartiness; then somebody proposed that Richards be elected sole Guardian and Symbol of the now Sacred Hadleyburg Tradition, with power and right to stand up and look the whole sarcastic world in the face."

Passed, by acclamation; then they sang the " Mikado" again, and ended it with,

"And there's *one* Symbol left, you bet!"

There was a pause; then—

A Voice. " Now, then, who's to get the sack?"

The Tanner (*with bitter sarcasm*). " That's easy.

The money has to be divided among the eighteen Incorruptibles. They gave the suffering stranger twenty dollars apiece—and that remark—each in his turn—it took twenty-two minutes for the procession to move past. Staked the stranger—total contribution, $360. All they want is just the loan back—and interest—forty thousand dollars altogether."

Many Voices (*derisively*). "That's it! Divvy! divvy! Be kind to the poor—don't keep them waiting!"

The Chair. "Order! I now offer the stranger's remaining document. It says: 'If no claimant shall appear [*grand chorus of groans*], I desire that you open the sack and count out the money to the principal citizens of your town, they to take it in trust [*Cries of " Oh! Oh! Oh!"*], and use it in such ways as to them shall seem best for the propagation and preservation of your community's noble reputation for incorruptible honesty [*more cries*]—a reputation to which their names and their efforts will add a new and far-reaching lustre.' [*Enthusiastic outburst of sarcastic applause.*] That seems to be all. No— here is a postscript:

"'P.S.—CITIZENS OF HADLEYBURG: There *is* no test-remark—nobody made one. [*Great sensation.*] There wasn't any pauper stranger, nor any twenty-

dollar contribution, nor any accompanying benediction and compliment—these are all inventions.
[*General buzz and hum of astonishment and delight.*]
Allow me to tell my story—it will take but a word
or two. I passed through your town at a certain
time, and received a deep offence which I had not
earned. Any other man would have been content
to kill one or two of you and call it square, but to
me that would have been a trivial revenge, and inadequate; for the dead do not *suffer*. Besides, I
could not kill you all—and, anyway, made as I am,
even that would not have satisfied me. I wanted to
damage every man in the place, and every woman
—and not in their bodies or in their estate, but in
their vanity—the place where feeble and foolish
people are most vulnerable. So I disguised myself
and came back and studied you. You were easy
game. You had an old and lofty reputation for
honesty, and naturally you were proud of it—it was
your treasure of treasures, the very apple of your
eye. As soon as I found out that you carefully and
vigilantly kept yourselves and your children *out of
temptation*, I knew how to proceed. Why, you
simple creatures, the weakest of all weak things is
a virtue which has not been tested in the fire. I
laid a plan, and gathered a list of names. My project was to corrupt Hadleyburg the Incorruptible.

My idea was to make liars and thieves of nearly half a hundred smirchless men and women who had never in their lives uttered a lie or stolen a penny. I was afraid of Goodson. He was neither born nor reared in Hadleyburg. I was afraid that if I started to operate my scheme by getting my letter laid before you, you would say to yourselves, "Goodson is the only man among us who would give away twenty dollars to a poor devil"—and then you might not bite at my bait. But Heaven took Goodson; then I knew I was safe, and I set my trap and baited it. It may be that I shall not catch all the men to whom I mailed the pretended test secret, but I shall catch the most of them, if I know Hadleyburg nature. [*Voices*. "Right—he got every last one of them."] I believe they will even steal ostensible *gamble*-money, rather than miss, poor, tempted, and mistrained fellows. I am hoping to eternally and everlastingly squelch your vanity and give Hadleyburg a new renown—one that will *stick* —and spread far. If I have succeeded, open the sack and summon the Committee on Propagation and Preservation of the Hadleyburg Reputation.'"

A Cyclone of Voices. "Open it! Open it! The Eighteen to the front! Committee on Propagation of the Tradition! Forward—the Incorruptibles!"

The Chair ripped the sack wide, and gathered up

a handful of bright, broad, yellow coins, shook them together, then examined them—

" Friends, they are only gilded disks of lead !"

There was a crashing outbreak of delight over this news, and when the noise had subsided, the tanner called out :

" By right of apparent seniority in this business, Mr. Wilson is Chairman of the Committee on Propagation of the Tradition. I suggest that he step forward on behalf of his pals, and receive in trust the money."

A Hundred Voices. " Wilson ! Wilson ! Wilson ! Speech ! Speech !"

Wilson (*in a voice trembling with anger*). " You will allow me to say, and without apologies for my language, *damn* the money !"

A Voice. " Oh, and him a Baptist !"

A Voice. " Seventeen Symbols left ! Step up, gentlemen, and assume your trust !"

There was a pause—no response.

The Saddler. " Mr. Chairman, we've got *one* clean man left, anyway, out of the late aristocracy ; and he needs money, and deserves it. I move that you appoint Jack Halliday to get up there and auction off that sack of gilt twenty-dollar pieces, and give the result to the right man—the man whom Hadleyburg delights to honor—Edward Richards."

5

This was received with great enthusiasm, the dog taking a hand again ; the saddler started the bids at a dollar, the Brixton folk and Barnum's representative fought hard for it, the people cheered every jump that the bids made, the excitement climbed moment by moment higher and higher, the bidders got on their mettle and grew steadily more and more daring, more and more determined, the jumps went from a dollar up to five, then to ten, then to twenty, then fifty, then to a hundred, then—

At the beginning of the auction Richards whispered in distress to his wife: " Oh, Mary, can we allow it ?   It—it—you see, it is an honor-reward, a testimonial to purity of character, and—and—can we allow it ? Hadn't I better get up and— Oh, Mary, what ought we to do ? — what do you think we—" (*Halliday's voice. "Fifteen I'm bid! — fifteen for the sack! — twenty! — ah, thanks! — thirty—thanks again! Thirty, thirty, thirty!—do I hear forty?—forty it is! Keep the ball rolling, gentlemen, keep it rolling! — fifty! — thanks, noble Roman!—going at fifty, fifty, fifty! —seventy!—ninety!—splendid!—a hundred!—pile it up, pile it up!—hundred and twenty—forty!— just in time!—hundred and fifty!—*TWO *hundred! —superb! Do I hear two h— thanks!—two hundred and fifty!—"*)

"It is another temptation, Edward—I'm all in a tremble—but, oh, we've escaped *one* temptation, and that ought to warn us, to— [*"Six did I hear? —thanks!—six fifty, six f—* SEVEN *hundred!"*] And yet, Edward, when you think—nobody susp— [*"Eight hundred dollars!—hurrah!—make it nine! —Mr. Parsons, did I hear you say—thanks!—nine! —this noble sack of virgin lead going at only nine hundred dollars, gilding and all—come! do I hear— a thousand!—gratefully yours!—did some one say eleven?—a sack which is going to be the most cele- brated in the whole Uni—"*] Oh, Edward" (begin- ning to sob), "we are *so* poor!—but—but—do as you think best—do as you think best."

Edward fell—that is, he sat still; sat with a con- science which was not satisfied, but which was over- powered by circumstances.

Meantime a stranger, who looked like an ama- teur detective gotten up as an impossible English earl, had been watching the evening's proceedings with manifest interest, and with a contented ex- pression in his face; and he had been privately commenting to himself. He was now soliloquizing somewhat like this: "None of the Eighteen are bidding; that is not satisfactory; I must change that—the dramatic unities require it; they must buy the sack they tried to steal; they must pay a heavy price, too—some of them are rich. And another thing, when I make a mistake in Hadley-burg nature the man that puts that error upon me is entitled to a high honorarium, and some one must pay it. This poor old Richards has brought my judgment to shame; he is an honest man :—I don't understand it, but I acknowledge it. Yes, he saw my deuces-*and* with a straight flush, and by rights the pot is his. And it shall be a jack-pot, too, if I can manage it. He disappointed me, but let that pass."

He was watching the bidding. At a thousand, the market broke; the prices tumbled swiftly. He waited—and still watched. One competitor dropped out; then another, and another. He put in a bid or two, now. When the bids had sunk to ten dollars, he added a five; some one raised him a three ; he waited a moment, then flung in a fifty-dollar jump, and the sack was his—at $1282. The house broke out in cheers—then stopped; for he was on his feet, and had lifted his hand. He began to speak.

" I desire to say a word, and ask a favor. I am a speculator in rarities, and I have dealings with persons interested in numismatics all over the world. I can make a profit on this purchase, just as it stands; but there is a way, if I can get your approval, whereby I can make every one of these leaden twenty-dollar pieces worth its face in gold, and perhaps more. Grant me that approval, and I will give part of my gains to your Mr. Richards, whose invulnerable probity you have so justly and so cordially recognized to-night; his share shall be ten thousand dollars, and I will hand him the money to-morrow. [*Great applause from the house.* But the "invulnerable probity" made the Richardses blush prettily; however, it went for modesty, and did no harm.] If you will pass my proposition by a good majority—I would like a two-thirds vote —I will regard that as the town's consent, and that is all I ask. Rarities are always helped by any device which will rouse curiosity and compel remark. Now if I may have your permission to stamp upon the faces of each of these ostensible coins the names of the eighteen gentlemen who—"

Nine-tenths of the audience were on their feet in a moment—dog and all—and the proposition was carried with a whirlwind of approving applause and laughter.

They sat down, and all the Symbols except "Dr." Clay Harkness got up, violently protesting against the proposed outrage, and threatening to—

"I beg you not to threaten me," said the stranger, calmly. "I know my legal rights, and am not accustomed to being frightened at bluster." (*Applause.*) He sat down. "Dr." Harkness saw an opportunity here. He was one of the two very rich men of the place, and Pinkerton was the other. Harkness was proprietor of a mint; that is to say, a popular patent medicine. He was running for the Legislature on one ticket, and Pinkerton on the other. It was a close race and a hot one, and getting hotter every day. Both had strong appetites for money; each had bought a great tract of land, with a purpose; there was going to be a new railway, and each wanted to be in the Legislature and help locate the route to his own advantage; a single vote might make the decision, and with it two or three fortunes. The stake was large, and Harkness was a daring speculator. He was sitting close to the stranger. He leaned over while one or another of the other Symbols was entertaining the house with protests and appeals, and asked, in a whisper,

"What is your price for the sack?"

"Forty thousand dollars."

"I'll give you twenty."

"No."

"Twenty-five."

"No."

"Say thirty."

"The price is forty thousand dollars; not a penny less."

"All right, I'll give it. I will come to the hotel at ten in the morning. I don't want it known; will see you privately."

"Very good." Then the stranger got up and said to the house:

"I find it late. The speeches of these gentlemen are not without merit, not without interest, not without grace; yet if I may be excused I will take my leave. I thank you for the great favor which you have shown me in granting my petition. I ask the Chair to keep the sack for me until to-morrow, and to hand these three five-hundred-dollar notes to Mr. Richards." They were passed up to the Chair. "At nine I will call for the sack, and at eleven will deliver the rest of the ten thousand to Mr. Richards in person, at his home. Good-night."

Then he slipped out, and left the audience making a vast noise, which was composed of a mixture of cheers, the "Mikado" song, dog-disapproval, and the chant, "You are f-a-r from being a b-a-a-d man —a-a-a a-men!"

IV

At home the Richardses had to endure congratulations and compliments until midnight. Then they were left to themselves. They looked a little sad, and they sat silent and thinking. Finally Mary sighed and said,

" Do you think we are to blame, Edward—*much* to blame ?" and her eyes wandered to the accusing triplet of big bank-notes lying on the table, where the congratulators had been gloating over them and reverently fingering them. Edward did not answer at once ; then he brought out a sigh and said, hesitatingly :

" We — we couldn't help it, Mary. It —well, it was ordered. *All* things are."

Mary glanced up and looked at him steadily, but he didn't return the look. Presently she said :

" I thought congratulations and praises always tasted good. But — it seems to me, now— Edward ?"

" Well ?"

" Are you going to stay in the bank ?"

" N-no."

" Resign ?"

" In the morning—by note."

" It does seem best."

Richards bowed his head in his hands and muttered :

" Before, I was not afraid to let oceans of people's money pour through my hands, but— Mary, I am so tired, so tired—"

" We will go to bed."

At nine in the morning the stranger called for the sack and took it to the hotel in a cab. At ten Harkness had a talk with him privately. The stranger asked for and got five checks on a metropolitan bank — drawn to " Bearer,"—four for $1500 each, and one for $34,000. He put one of the former in his pocket-book, and the remainder, representing $38,500, he put in an envelope, and with these he added a note, which he wrote after Harkness was gone. At eleven he called at the Richards house and knocked. Mrs. Richards peeped through the shutters, then went and received the envelope, and the stranger disappeared without a word. She came back flushed and a little unsteady on her legs, and gasped out :

" I am sure I recognized him ! Last night it seemed to me that maybe I had seen him somewhere before."

" He is the man that brought the sack here ?"

" I am almost sure of it."

"Then he is the ostensible Stephenson too, and sold every important citizen in this town with his bogus secret. Now if he has sent checks instead of money, we are sold too, after we thought we had escaped. I was beginning to feel fairly comfortable once more, after my night's rest, but the look of that envelope makes me sick. It isn't fat enough; $8500 in even the largest bank-notes makes more bulk than that."

"Edward, why do you object to checks?"

"Checks signed by Stephenson! I am resigned to take the $8500 if it could come in bank-notes— for it does seem that it was so ordered, Mary—but I have never had much courage, and I have not the pluck to try to market a check signed with that disastrous name. It would be a trap. That man tried to catch me; we escaped somehow or other; and now he is trying a new way. If it is checks—"

"Oh, Edward, it is *too* bad!" and she held up the checks and began to cry.

"Put them in the fire! quick! we mustn't be tempted. It is a trick to make the world laugh at *us*, along with the rest, and— Give them to *me*, since you can't do it!" He snatched them and tried to hold his grip till he could get to the stove; but he was human, he was a cashier, and he stopped a moment to make sure of the signature. Then he came near to fainting.

"Fan me, Mary, fan me! They are the same as gold!"

"Oh, how lovely, Edward! Why?"

"Signed by Harkness. What can the mystery of that be, Mary?"

"Edward, do you think—"

"Look here—look at this! Fifteen—fifteen—fifteen — thirty-four. Thirty-eight thousand five hundred! Mary, the sack isn't worth twelve dollars, and Harkness—apparently—has paid about par for it."

"And does it all come to us, do you think—instead of the ten thousand?"

"Why, it looks like it. And the checks are made to 'Bearer,' too."

"Is that good, Edward? What is it for?"

"A hint to collect them at some distant bank, I reckon. Perhaps Harkness doesn't want the matter known. What is that—a note?"

"Yes. It was with the checks."

It was in the "Stephenson" handwriting, but there was no signature. It said:

"I am a disappointed man. Your honesty is beyond the reach of temptation. I had a different idea about it, but I wronged you in that, and I beg pardon, and do it sincerely. I

*honor you—and that is sincere, too. This town is not worthy
to kiss the hem of your garment. Dear sir, I made a square
bet with myself that there were nineteen debauchable men in
your self-righteous community. I have lost. Take the whole
pot, you are entitled to it."*

Richards drew a deep sigh, and said:

"It seems written with fire—it burns so. Mary
—I am miserable again."

"I, too. Ah, dear, I wish—"

"To think, Mary—he *believes* in me."

"Oh, don't, Edward—I can't bear it."

"If those beautiful words were deserved, Mary—
and God knows I believed I deserved them once—
I think I could give the forty thousand dollars for
them. And I would put that paper away, as representing more than gold and jewels, and keep it always. But now— We could not live in the shadow
of its accusing presence, Mary."

He put it in the fire.

A messenger arrived and delivered an envelope.
Richards took from it a note and read it; it was
from Burgess.

*"You saved me, in a difficult time. I saved you last night.
It was at cost of a lie, but I made the sacrifice freely, and out
of a grateful heart. None in this village knows so well as I
know how brave and good and noble you are. At bottom you
cannot respect me, knowing as you do of that matter of which*

*I am accused, and by the general voice condemned; but I beg
that you will at least believe that I am a grateful man; it
will help me to bear my burden.*

[*Signed*] " BURGESS."

" Saved, once more. And on such terms !" He
put the note in the fire. " I—I wish I were dead,
Mary, I wish I were out of it all."

" Oh, these are bitter, bitter days, Edward. The
stabs, through their very generosity, are so deep—
and they come so fast !"

Three days before the election each of two thousand voters suddenly found himself in possession of
a prized memento — one of the renowned bogus
double-eagles. Around one of its faces was stamped
these words : " THE REMARK I MADE TO THE POOR
STRANGER WAS —" Around the other face was
stamped these : " GO, AND REFORM. [SIGNED] PIN-
KERTON." Thus the entire remaining refuse of the
renowned joke was emptied upon a single head, and
with calamitous effect. It revived the recent vast
laugh and concentrated it upon Pinkerton; and
Harkness's election was a walk-over.

Within twenty-four hours after the Richardses
had received their checks their consciences were
quieting down, discouraged ; the old couple were
learning to reconcile themselves to the sin which
they had committed. But they were to learn, now,

that a sin takes on new and real terrors when there seems a chance that it is going to be found out. This gives it a fresh and most substantial and important aspect. At church the morning sermon was of the usual pattern; it was the same old things said in the same old way; they had heard them a thousand times and found them innocuous, next to meaningless, and easy to sleep under; but now it was different: the sermon seemed to bristle with accusations; it seemed aimed straight and specially at people who were concealing deadly sins. After church they got away from the mob of congratulators as soon as they could, and hurried homeward, chilled to the bone at they did not know what— vague, shadowy, indefinite fears. And by chance they caught a glimpse of Mr. Burgess as he turned a corner. He paid no attention to their nod of recognition! He hadn't seen it; but they did not know that. What could his conduct mean? It might mean — it might mean — oh, a dozen dreadful things. Was it possible that he knew that Richards could have cleared him of guilt in that bygone time, and had been silently waiting for a chance to even up accounts? At home, in their distress they got to imagining that their servant might have been in the next room listening when Richards revealed the secret to his wife that he knew of Burgess's innocence; next, Richards began to imagine that he had heard the swish of a gown in there at that time; next, he was sure he *had* heard it. They would call Sarah in, on a pretext, and watch her face: if she had been betraying them to Mr. Burgess, it would show in her manner. They asked her some questions—questions which were so random and incoherent and seemingly purposeless that the girl felt sure that the old people's minds had been affected by their sudden good fortune; the sharp and watchful gaze which they bent upon her frightened her, and that completed the business. She blushed, she became nervous and confused, and to the old people these were plain signs of guilt —guilt of some fearful sort or other—without doubt she was a spy and a traitor. When they were alone again they began to piece many unrelated things together and get horrible results out of the combination. When things had got about to the worst, Richards was delivered of a sudden gasp, and his wife asked,

"Oh, what is it?—what is it?"

"The note—Burgess's note! Its language was sarcastic, I see it now." He quoted: "'At bottom you cannot respect me, *knowing*, as you do, of *that matter* of which I am accused'—oh, it is perfectly plain, now, God help me! He knows that I know!"

You see the ingenuity of the phrasing. It was a trap — and like a fool, I walked into it. And Mary—?"

"Oh, it is dreadful—I know what you are going to say—he didn't return your transcript of the pretended test-remark."

"No—kept it to destroy us with. Mary, he has exposed us to some already. I know it—I know it well. I saw it in a dozen faces after church. Ah, he wouldn't answer our nod of recognition — *he* knew what he had been doing!"

In the night the doctor was called. The news went around in the morning that the old couple were rather seriously ill—prostrated by the exhausting excitement growing out of their great windfall, the congratulations, and the late hours, the doctor said. The town was sincerely distressed ; for these old people were about all it had left to be proud of, now.

Two days later the news was worse. The old couple were delirious, and were doing strange things. By witness of the nurses, Richards had exhibited checks—for $8500? No—for an amazing sum— $38,500! What could be the explanation of this gigantic piece of luck?

The following day the nurses had more news— and wonderful. They had concluded to hide the checks, lest harm come to them; but when they searched they were gone from under the patient's pillow—vanished away. The patient said:

"Let the pillow alone; what do you want?'

"We thought it best that the checks—"

"You will never see them again—they are destroyed. They came from Satan. I saw the hell-brand on them, and I knew they were sent to betray me to sin." Then he fell to gabbling strange and dreadful things which were not clearly understandable, and which the doctor admonished them to keep to themselves.

Richards was right; the checks were never seen again.

A nurse must have talked in her sleep, for within two days the forbidden gabblings were the property of the town; and they were of a surprising sort. They seemed to indicate that Richards had been a claimant for the sack himself, and that Burgess had concealed that fact and then maliciously betrayed it.

Burgess was taxed with this and stoutly denied it. And he said it was not fair to attach weight to the chatter of a sick old man who was out of his mind. Still, suspicion was in the air, and there was much talk.

After a day or two it was reported that Mrs.

6

Richards's delirious deliveries were getting to be duplicates of her husband's. Suspicion flamed up into conviction, now, and the town's pride in the purity of its one undiscredited important citizen began to dim down and flicker toward extinction.

Six days passed, then came more news. The old couple were dying. Richards's mind cleared in his latest hour, and he sent for Burgess. Burgess said :

"Let the room be cleared. I think he wishes to say something in privacy."

"No !" said Richards ; "I want witnesses. I want you all to hear my confession, so that I may die a man, and not a dog. I was clean—artificially—like the rest ; and like the rest I fell when temptation came. I signed a lie, and claimed the miserable sack. Mr. Burgess remembered that I had done him a service, and in gratitude (and ignorance) he suppressed my claim and saved me. You know the thing that was charged against Burgess years ago. My testimony, and mine alone, could have cleared him, and I was a coward, and left him to suffer disgrace—"

"No—no—Mr. Richards, you—"

"My servant betrayed my secret to him—"

"No one has betrayed anything to me—"

—" and then he did a natural and justifiable thing ,

he repented of the saving kindness which he had done me, and he *exposed* me—as I deserved—"

" Never!—I make oath—"

" Out of my heart I forgive him."

Burgess's impassioned protestations fell upon deaf ears; the dying man passed away without knowing that once more he had done poor Burgess a wrong. The old wife died that night.

The last of the sacred Nineteen had fallen a prey to the fiendish sack; the town was stripped of the last rag of its ancient glory. Its mourning was not showy, but it was deep.

By act of the Legislature — upon prayer and pe- tition—Hadleyburg was allowed to change its name to (never mind what—I will not give it away), and leave one word out of the motto that for many gen- erations had graced the town's official seal.

It is an honest town once more, and the man will have to rise early that catches it napping again.

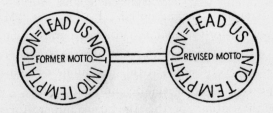

MY DÉBUT AS A LITERARY PERSON

IN those early days I had already published one
little thing ("The Jumping Frog") in an Eastern
paper, but I did not consider that that counted. In my view, a person who published things in
a mere newspaper could not properly claim recognition as a Literary Person: he must rise away
above that; he must appear in a magazine. He
would then be a Literary Person; also, he would
be famous — right away. These two ambitions
were strong upon me. This was in 1866. I prepared my contribution, and then looked around for
the best magazine to go up to glory in. I selected the most important one in New York. The
contribution was accepted. I signed it " MARK
TWAIN "; for that name had some currency on the
Pacific coast, and it was my idea to spread it all
over the world, now, at this one jump. The article
appeared in the December number, and I sat up a
month waiting for the January number; for that
one would contain the year's list of contributors,

my name would be in it, and I should be famous and could give the banquet I was meditating.

I did not give the banquet. I had not written the "MARK TWAIN" distinctly; it was a fresh name to Eastern printers, and they put it "Mike Swain" or "MacSwain," I do not remember which. At any rate, I was not celebrated, and I did not give the banquet. I was a Literary Person, but that was all—a buried one; buried alive.

My article was about the burning of the clipper-ship *Hornet* on the line, May 3, 1866. There were thirty-one men on board at the time, and I was in Honolulu when the fifteen lean and ghostly survivors arrived there after a voyage of forty-three days in an open boat, through the blazing tropics, on *ten days' rations* of food. A very remarkable trip; but it was conducted by a captain who was a remarkable man, otherwise there would have been no survivors. He was a New-Englander of the best sea-going stock of the old capable times— Captain Josiah Mitchell.

I was in the islands to write letters for the weekly edition of the Sacramento *Union*, a rich and influential daily journal which hadn't any use for them, but could afford to spend twenty dollars a week for nothing. The proprietors were lovable and well-beloved men: long ago dead, no doubt, but in me there is at least one person who still holds them in grateful remembrance ; for I dearly wanted to see the islands, and they listened to me and gave me the opportunity when there was but slender likelihood that it could profit them in any way.

I had been in the islands several months when the survivors arrived. I was laid up in my room at the time, and unable to walk. Here was a great occasion to serve my journal, and I not able to take advantage of it. Necessarily I was in deep trouble. But by good luck his Excellency Anson Burlingame was there at the time, on his way to take up his post in China, where he did such good work for the United States. He came and put me on a stretcher and had me carried to the hospital where the shipwrecked men were, and I never needed to ask a question. He attended to all of that himself, and I had nothing to do but make the notes. It was like him to take that trouble. He was a great man and a great American, and it was in his fine nature to come down from his high office and do a friendly turn whenever he could.

We got through with this work at six in the evening. I took no dinner, for there was no time to spare if I would beat the other correspondents. I spent four hours arranging the notes in their proper order, then wrote all night and beyond it ; with this result: that I had a very long and de- tailed account of the *Hornet* episode ready at nine in the morning, while the correspondents of the San Francisco journals had nothing but a brief outline report—for they didn't sit up. The now- and - then schooner was to sail for San Francisco about nine ; when I reached the dock she was free forward and was just casting off her stern-line. My fat envelope was thrown by a strong hand, and fell on board all right, and my victory was a safe thing. All in due time the ship reached San Francisco, but it was my complete report which made the stir and was telegraphed to the New York papers, by Mr. Cash ; he was in charge of the Pacific bureau of the New York *Herald* at the time.

When I returned to California by-and-by, I went up to Sacramento and presented a bill for general correspondence at twenty dollars a week. It was paid. Then I presented a bill for " special " service on the *Hornet* matter of three columns of solid non- pareil at *a hundred dollars a column*. The cashier didn't faint, but he came rather near it. He sent for the proprietors, and they came and never uttered a protest. They only laughed in their jolly fashion, and said it was robbery, but no mat- ter; it was a grand " scoop " (the bill or my *Hornet* report, I didn't know which); "pay it. It's all right." The best men that ever owned a newspaper.

The *Hornet* survivors reached the Sandwich Islands the 15th of June. They were mere skinny skeletons; their clothes hung limp about them and fitted them no better than a flag fits the flag-staff in a calm. But they were well nursed in the hospital; the people of Honolulu kept them supplied with all the dainties they could need; they gathered strength fast, and were presently nearly as good as new. Within a fortnight the most of them took ship for San Francisco; that is, if my dates have not gone astray in my memory. I went in the same ship, a sailing-vessel. Captain Mitchell of the *Hornet* was along; also the only passengers the *Hornet* had carried. These were two young men from Stamford, Connecticut—brothers: Samuel Ferguson, aged twenty-eight, a graduate of Trinity College, Hartford, and Henry Ferguson, aged eighteen, a student of the same college. The elder brother had had some trouble with his lungs, which induced his physician to prescribe a long sea-voyage for him. This terrible disaster, however, developed the disease which later ended fatally. The younger brother is still living, and is fifty years old this year (1898). The *Hor-*

net was a clipper of the first class and a fast sailer; the young men's quarters were roomy and comfortable, and were well stocked with books, and also with canned meats and fruits to help out the ship-fare with; and when the ship cleared from New York harbor in the first week of January there was promise that she would make quick and pleasant work of the fourteen or fifteen thousand miles in front of her. As soon as the cold latitudes were left behind and the vessel entered summer weather, the voyage became a holiday picnic. The ship flew southward under a cloud of sail which needed no attention, no modifying or change of any kind, for days together. The young men read, strolled the ample deck, rested and drowsed in the shade of the canvas, took their meals with the captain; and when the day was done they played dummy whist with him till bedtime. After the snow and ice and tempests of the Horn, the ship bowled northward into summer weather again, and the trip was a picnic once more.

Until the early morning of the 3d of May. Computed position of the ship 112° 10′ west longitude; latitude 2° above the equator; no wind, no sea— dead calm; temperature of the atmosphere, tropical, blistering, unimaginable by one who has not been roasted in it. There was a cry of fire. An unfaithful sailor had disobeyed the rules and gone into the booby-hatch with an open light to draw some varnish from a cask. The proper result followed, and the vessel's hours were numbered.

There was not much time to spare, but the captain made the most of it. The three boats were launched—long-boat and two quarter-boats. That the time was very short and the hurry and excitement considerable is indicated by the fact that in launching the boats a hole was stove in the side of one of them by some sort of collision, and an oar driven through the side of another. The captain's first care was to have four sick sailors brought up and placed on deck out of harm's way — among them a "Portyghee." This man had not done a day's work on the voyage, but had lain in his hammock four months nursing an abscess. When we were taking notes in the Honolulu hospital and a sailor told this to Mr. Burlingame, the third mate, who was lying near, raised his head with an effort, and in a weak voice made this correction — with solemnity and feeling:

"*Raising* abscesses! He had a family of them. He done it to keep from standing his watch."

Any provisions that lay handy were gathered up by the men and the two passengers and brought and dumped on the deck where the "Portyghee" lay; then they ran for more. The sailor who was telling this to Mr. Burlingame added:

"We pulled together thirty-two days' rations for the thirty-one men that way."

The third mate lifted his head again and made another correction—with bitterness:

"The Portyghee et twenty-two of them while he was soldiering there and nobody noticing. A damned hound."

The fire spread with great rapidity. The smoke and flame drove the men back, and they had to stop their incomplete work of fetching provisions, and take to the boats with only ten days' rations secured.

Each boat had a compass, a quadrant, a copy of Bowditch's *Navigator*, and a nautical almanac, and the captain's and chief mate's boats had chronometers. There were thirty-one men all told. The captain took an account of stock, with the following result: four hams, nearly thirty pounds of salt pork, half-box of raisins, one hundred pounds of bread, twelve two-pound cans of oysters, clams, and assorted meats, a keg containing four pounds of butter, twelve gallons of water in a forty-gallon "scuttle-butt," four one-gallon demijohns full of water, three bottles of brandy (the property of passengers), some pipes, matches, and a hundred pounds of tobacco. No medicines. Of course the whole party had to go on short rations at once.

The captain and the two passengers kept diaries. On our voyage to San Francisco we ran into a calm in the middle of the Pacific, and did not move a rod during fourteen days; this gave me a chance to copy the diaries. Samuel Ferguson's is the fullest; I will draw upon it now. When the following paragraph was written the ship was about one hundred and twenty days out from port, and all hands were putting in the lazy time about as usual, as no one was forecasting disaster.

May 2. Latitude 1° 28' N., longitude 111° 38' W. Another hot and sluggish day; at one time, however, the clouds promised wind, and there came a slight breeze—just enough to keep us going. The only thing to chronicle to-day is the quantities of fish about; nine bonitos were caught this forenoon, and some large albacores seen. After dinner the first mate hooked a fellow which he could not hold, so he let the line go to the captain, who was on the bow. He, holding on, brought the fish to with a jerk, and snap went the line, hook and all. We also saw astern, swimming lazily after us, an enormous shark, which must have been nine or ten feet long. We tried him with all sorts of lines and a piece of pork, but he declined to take hold. I suppose he had appeased his appetite on the heads and other remains of the bonitos we had thrown overboard.

Next day's entry records the disaster. The three boats got away, retired to a short distance, and

stopped. The two injured ones were leaking badly; some of the men were kept busy bailing, others
patched the holes as well as they could. The captain, the two passengers, and eleven men were in
the long-boat, with a share of the provisions and
water, and with no room to spare, for the boat was
only twenty-one feet long, six wide, and three deep.
The chief mate and eight men were in one of the
small boats, the second mate and seven men in the
other. The passengers had saved no clothing but
what they had on, excepting their overcoats. The
ship, clothed in flame and sending up a vast column
of black smoke into the sky, made a grand picture
in the solitudes of the sea, and hour after hour the
outcasts sat and watched it. Meantime the captain ciphered on the immensity of the distance that
stretched between him and the nearest available
land, and then scaled the rations down to meet the
emergency: half a biscuit for breakfast; one biscuit and some canned meat for dinner; half a biscuit for tea; a few swallows of water for each meal.
And so hunger began to gnaw while the ship was
still burning.

*May 4. The ship burned all night very brightly, and hopes
are that some ship has seen the light and is bearing down upon
us. None seen, however, this forenoon, so we have determined
to go together north and a little west to some islands in 18° or*

*19° north latitude and 114° to 115° west longitude, hoping in
the meantime to be picked up by some ship. The ship sank
suddenly at about 5 A.M. We find the sun very hot and scorching, but all try to keep out of it as much as we can.*

They did a quite natural thing now : waited several hours for that possible ship that might have
seen the light to work her slow way to them through
the nearly dead calm. Then they gave it up and set
about their plans. If you will look at the map you will
say that their course could be easily decided. Albemarle Island (Galapagos group) lies straight east-
ward nearly a thousand miles ; the islands referred
to in the diary indefinitely as " some islands " (Revillagigedo Islands) lie, as they think, in some wide-
ly uncertain region northward about one thousand
miles and westward one hundred or one hundred
and fifty miles. Acapulco, on the Mexican coast, lies
about northeast something short of one thousand
miles. You will say random rocks in the ocean are
not what is wanted; let them strike for Acapulco
and the solid continent. That does look like the
rational course, but one presently guesses from the
diaries that the thing would have been wholly ir-
rational—indeed, suicidal. If the boats struck for
Albemarle they would be in the doldrums all the
way ; and that means a watery perdition, with winds
which are wholly crazy, and blow from all points of

the compass at once and also perpendicularly. If the boats tried for Acapulco they would get out of the doldrums when half-way there — in case they ever got half-way—and then they would be in lamentable case, for there they would meet the northeast trades coming down in their teeth, and these boats were so rigged that they could not sail within eight points of the wind. So they wisely started northward, with a slight slant to the west. They had but ten days' short allowance of food; the long-boat was towing the others; they could not depend on making any sort of definite progress in the doldrums, and they had four or five hundred miles of doldrums in front of them yet. *They* are the real equator, a tossing, roaring, rainy belt, ten or twelve hundred miles broad, which girdles the globe.

It rained hard the first night, and all got drenched, but they filled up their water-butt. The brothers were in the stern with the captain, who steered. The quarters were cramped; no one got much sleep. "Kept on our course till squalls headed us off."

Stormy and squally the next morning, with drenching rains. A heavy and dangerous "cobbling" sea. One marvels how such boats could live in it. It is called a feat of desperate daring when one man and a dog cross the Atlantic in a boat the size of a long-boat, and indeed it is ; but this long-boat was over-loaded with men and other plunder, and was only three feet deep. "We naturally thought often of all at home, and were glad to remember that it was Sacrament Sunday, and that prayers would go up from our friends for us, although they know not our peril."

The captain got not even a cat-nap during the first three days and nights, but he got a few winks of sleep the fourth night. "The worst sea yet." About ten at night the captain changed his course and headed east-northeast, hoping to make Clipper-ton Rock. If he failed, no matter ; he would be in a better position to make those other islands. I will mention here that he did not find that rock.

On the 8th of May no wind all day ; sun blister-ing hot ; they take to the oars. Plenty of dolphins, but they couldn't catch any. "I think we are all beginning to realize more and more the awful sit-uation we are in." "It often takes a ship a week to get through the doldrums ; how much longer, then, such a craft as ours." "We are so crowded that we cannot stretch ourselves out for a good sleep, but have to take it any way we can get it."

Of course this feature will grow more and more trying, but it will be human nature to cease to set it down ; there will be five weeks of it yet—we must try to remember that for the diarist; it will make our beds the softer.

The 9th of May the sun gives him a warning: "Looking with both eyes, the horizon crossed thus +." "Henry keeps well, but broods over our troubles more than I wish he did." They caught two dolphins; they tasted well. "The captain believed the compass out of the way, but the long-invisible north star came out—a welcome sight—and endorsed the compass."

May 10, "latitude 7° 0′ 3″ N., longitude 111° 32′ W." So they have made about three hundred miles of northing in the six days since they left the region of the lost ship. "Drifting in calms all day." And baking hot, of course; I have been down there, and I remember that detail. "Even as the captain says, all romance has long since vanished, and I think the most of us are beginning to look the fact of our awful situation full in the face." "We are making but little headway on our course." Bad news from the rearmost boat: the men are improvident; "they have eaten up all of the canned meats brought from the ship, and are now growing discontented." Not so with the chief mate's people—they are evidently under the eye of a *man*.

Under date of May 11: "Standing still! or worse; we lost more last night than we made yesterday."

7

In fact, they have lost three miles of the three hundred of northing they had so laboriously made. "The cock that was rescued and pitched into the boat while the ship was on fire still lives, and crows with the breaking of dawn, cheering us a good deal." What has he been living on for a week? Did the starving men feed him from their dire poverty? "The second mate's boat out of water again, showing that they overdrink their allowance. The captain spoke pretty sharply to them." It is true: I have the remark in my old note-book; I got it of the third mate in the hospital at Honolulu. But there is not room for it here, and it is too combustible, anyway. Besides, the third mate admired it, and what he admired he was likely to enhance.

They were still watching hopefully for ships. The captain was a thoughtful man, and probably did not disclose to them that that was substantially a waste of time. "In this latitude the horizon is filled with little upright clouds that look very much like ships." Mr. Ferguson saved three bottles of brandy from his private stores when he left the ship, and the liquor came good in these days. "The captain serves out two table-spoonfuls of brandy and water —half and half—to our crew." He means the watch that is on duty; they stood regular watches—four hours on and four off. The chief mate was an excellent officer—a self-possessed, resolute, fine, all-round man. The diarist makes the following note—there is character in it : " I offered one bottle of brandy to the chief mate, but he declined, saying he could keep the after-boat quiet, and we had not enough for all."

HENRY FERGUSON'S DIARY TO DATE, GIVEN IN FULL

May 4, 5, 6, doldrums. May 7, 8, 9, doldrums. May 10, 11, 12, doldrums. Tells it all. Never saw, never felt, never heard, never experienced such heat, such darkness, such lightning and thunder, and wind and rain, in my life before.

That boy's diary is of the economical sort that a person might properly be expected to keep in such circumstances — and be forgiven for the economy, too. His brother, perishing of consumption, hunger, thirst, blazing heat, drowning rains, loss of sleep, lack of exercise, was persistently faithful and circumstantial with his diary from the first day to the last—an instance of noteworthy fidelity and resolution. In spite of the tossing and plunging boat he wrote it close and fine, in a hand as easy to read as print. They can't seem to get north of $7°$ N.; they are still there the next day:

May 12. A good rain last night, and we caught a good deal, though not enough to fill up our tank, pails, etc. Our object is to get out of these doldrums, but it seems as if we

cannot do it. To-day we have had it very variable, and hope
we are on the northern edge, though we are not much above
7°. This morning we all thought we had made out a sail;
but it was one of those deceiving clouds. Rained a good deal
to-day, making all hands wet and uncomfortable; we filled
up pretty nearly all our water-pots, however. I hope we
may have a fine night, for the captain certainly wants rest,
and while there is any danger of squalls, or danger of any
kind, he is always on hand. I never would have believed
that open boats such as ours, with their loads, could live in
some of the seas we have had.

During the night, 12th–13th, " the cry of *A ship !*
brought us to our feet." It seemed to be the glim-
mer of a vessel's signal-lantern rising out of the
curve of the sea. There was a season of breath-
less hope while they stood watching, with their
hands shading their eyes, and their hearts in their
throats ; then the promise failed : the light was a
rising star. It is a long time ago, — thirty-two
years,—and it doesn't matter now, yet one is sorry
for their disappointment. " Thought often of those
at home to-day, and of the disappointment they
will feel next Sunday at not hearing from us by
telegraph from San Francisco." It will be many
weeks yet before the telegram is received, and it
will come as a thunder-clap of joy then, and with
the seeming of a miracle, for it will raise from the
grave men mourned as dead. " To-day our rations

were reduced to a quarter of a biscuit a meal, with about half a pint of water." This is on the 13th of May, with more than a month of voyaging in front of them yet! However, as they do not know that, "we are all feeling pretty cheerful."

In the afternoon of the 14th there was a thunderstorm, "which toward night seemed to close in around us on every side, making it very dark and squally." "Our situation is becoming more and more desperate," for they were making very little northing, "and every day diminishes our small stock of provisions." They realize that the boats must soon separate, and each fight for its own life. Towing the quarter-boats is a hindering business.

That night and next day, light and baffling winds and but little progress. Hard to bear, that persistent standing still, and the food wasting away. "Everything in a perfect sop; and all so cramped, and no change of clothes." Soon the sun comes out and roasts them. "Joe caught another dolphin to-day; in his maw we found a flying-fish and two skipjacks." There is an event, now, which rouses an enthusiasm of hope: a land-bird arrives! It rests on the yard for awhile, and they can look at it all they like, and envy it, and thank it for its message. As a subject of talk it is beyond price—a fresh, new topic for tongues tired to death of talking upon a single theme : Shall we ever see the land again ; and when ? Is the bird from Clipperton Rock ? They hope so ; and they take heart of grace to believe so. As it turned out, the bird had no message ; it merely came to mock.

May 16, " the cock still lives, and daily carols forth His praise." It will be a rainy night, " but I do not care if we can fill up our water-butts."

On the 17th one of those majestic spectres of the deep, a water-spout, stalked by them, and they trembled for their lives. Young Henry set it down in his scanty journal with the judicious comment that "it might have been a fine sight from a ship."

From Captain Mitchell's log for this day : " *Only half a bushel of bread-crumbs left.*" (And a month to wander the seas yet.)

It rained all night and all day ; everybody uncomfortable. Now came a sword-fish chasing a bonito ; and the poor thing, seeking help and friends, took refuge under the rudder. The big sword-fish kept hovering around, scaring everybody badly. The men's mouths watered for him, for he would have made a whole banquet ; but no one dared to touch him, of course, for he would sink a boat promptly if molested. Providence protected the poor bonito from the cruel sword-fish. This was just and right. Providence next befriended the shipwrecked sailors : they got the bonito. This was also just and right. But in the distribution of mercies the sword-fish himself got overlooked. He now went away; to muse over these subtleties, probably. "The men in all the boats seem pretty well; the feeblest of the sick ones (not able for a long time to stand his watch on board the ship) is wonderfully recovered." This is the third mate's detested "Portyghee" that raised the family of abscesses.

Passed a most awful night. Rained hard nearly all the time, and blew in squalls, accompanied by terrific thunder and lightning, from all points of the compass.—Henry's Log.

Most awful night I ever witnessed.—Captain's Log.

Latitude, May 18, 11° 11'. So they have averaged but forty miles of northing a day during the fortnight. Further talk of separating. "Too bad, but it must be done for the safety of the whole." "At first I never dreamed, but now hardly shut my eyes for a cat-nap without conjuring up something or other—to be accounted for by weakness, I suppose." But for their disaster they think they would be arriving in San Francisco about this time. " I should have liked to send B—— the telegram for her birthday." This was a young sister.

On the 19th the captain called up the quarter-boats and said one would have to go off on its own hook. The long-boat could no longer tow both of them. The second mate refused to go, but the chief mate was ready; in fact, he was always ready when there was a man's work to the fore. He took the second mate's boat; six of its crew elected to remain, and two of his own crew came with him (nine in the boat, now, including himself). He sailed away, and toward sunset passed out of sight. The diarist was sorry to see him go. It was natural; one could have better spared the "Portyghee." After thirty-two years I find my prejudice against this "Portyghee" reviving. His very looks have long passed out of my memory; but no matter, I am coming to hate him as religiously as ever. "Water will now be a scarce article, for as we get out of the doldrums we shall get showers only now and then in the trades. This life is telling severely on my strength. Henry holds out first-rate." Henry did not start well, but under hardships he improved straight along.

Latitude, Sunday, May 20, 12° 0′ 9″. They ought to be well out of the doldrums now, but they are not. No breeze—the longed-for trades still missing. They are still anxiously watching for a sail, but they have only "visions of ships that come to naught — the shadow without the substance." The second mate catches a booby this afternoon, a bird which consists mainly of feathers; "but as they have no other meat, it will go well."

May 21, they strike the trades at last! The second mate catches three more boobies, and gives the long-boat one. Dinner "half a can of mince-meat divided up and served around, which strengthened us somewhat." They have to keep a man bailing all the time; the hole knocked in the boat when she was launched from the burning ship was never efficiently mended. "Heading about northwest now." They hope they have easting enough to make some of those indefinite isles. Failing that, they think they will be in a better position to be picked up. It was an infinitely slender chance, but the captain probably refrained from mentioning that.

The next day is to be an eventful one.

May 22. Last night wind headed us off, so that part of the time we had to steer east-southeast and then west-north-west, and so on. This morning we were all startled by a cry of "SAIL HO!" Sure enough, we could see it! And for a time we cut adrift from the second mate's boat, and steered so as to attract its attention. This was about half-past five A.M. After sailing in a state of high excitement for almost twenty minutes we made it out to be the chief mate's boat. Of course we were glad to see them and have them report all well; but still it was a bitter disappointment to us all. Now that we are in the trades it seems impossible to make northing enough to strike the isles. We have determined to do the best we can, and get in the route of vessels. Such being the determination, it became necessary to cast off the other boat, which, after a good deal of unpleasantness, was done, we again dividing water and stores, and taking Cox into our boat. This makes our number fifteen. The second mate's crew wanted to all get in with us and cast the other boat adrift. It was a very painful separation.

So those isles that they have struggled for so long and so hopefully have to be given up. What with lying birds that come to mock, and isles that are but a dream, and " visions of ships that come to naught," it is a pathetic time they are having, with much heartbreak in it. It was odd that the vanished boat, three days lost to sight in that vast solitude, should appear again. But it brought Cox—we can't be certain why. But if it hadn't, the diarist would never have seen the land again.

Our chances as we go west increase in regard to being picked up, but each day our scanty fare is so much reduced. Without the fish, turtle, and birds sent us, I do not know how we should have got along. The other day I offered to read prayers morning and evening for the captain, and last night commenced. The men, although of various nationalities and religions, are very attentive, and always uncovered. May God grant my weak endeavor its issue.

Latitude, May 24, 14° 18′ N. Five oysters apiece for dinner and three spoonfuls of juice, a gill of water, and a piece of biscuit the size of a silver dollar. "We are plainly getting weaker—God have mercy upon us all!" That night heavy seas break over the weather side and make everybody wet and uncomfortable, besides requiring constant bailing.

Next day "nothing particular happened." Perhaps some of us would have regarded it differently. "Passed a spar, but not near enough to see what it was." They saw some whales blow; there were flying-fish skimming the seas, but none came aboard. Misty weather, with fine rain, very penetrating.

Latitude, May 26, 15° 50′. They caught a flying-fish and a booby, but had to eat them raw. "The men grow weaker, and, I think, despondent; they say very little, though." And so, to all the other imaginable and unimaginable horrors, silence is added—the muteness and brooding of coming despair. "It seems our best chance to get in the track of ships, with the hope that some one will run near enough to our speck to see it." He hopes the other boats stood west and have been picked up. (They will never be heard of again in this world.)

Sunday, May 27. Latitude 16° 0′ 5″; longitude, by chronometer, 117° 22′. Our fourth Sunday! When we left *the ship we reckoned on having about ten days' supplies, and now we hope to be able, by rigid economy, to make them last another week if possible.* Last night the sea was comparatively quiet, but the wind headed us off to about west-north-west, which has been about our course all day to-day. Another flying-fish came aboard last night, and one more to-day—both small ones. No birds. A booby is a great catch, and a good large one makes a small dinner for the fifteen of us—that is, of course, as dinners go in the "Hornet's" long-boat. Tried this morning to read the full service to myself, with the communion, but found it too much ; am too weak, and get sleepy, and cannot give strict attention ; so I put off half till this afternoon. I trust God will hear the prayers gone up for us at home to-day, and graciously answer them by sending us succor and help in this our season of deep distress.*

The next day was "a good day for seeing a ship." But none was seen. The diarist "still feels pretty well," though very weak ; his brother Henry "bears up and keeps his strength the best of any on board." "I do not feel despondent at all, for I fully trust that the Almighty will hear our and the home prayers, and He who suffers not a sparrow to fall sees and cares for us, His creatures."

Considering the situation and circumstances, the record for next day, May 29, is one which has a surprise in it for those dull people who think that

---

* There are nineteen days of voyaging ahead yet.—M. T.

nothing but medicines and doctors can cure the sick. A little starvation can really do more for the average sick man than can the best medicines and the best doctors. I do not mean a restricted diet; I mean *total abstention from food for one or two days*. I speak from experience; starvation has been my cold and fever doctor for fifteen years, and has accomplished a cure in all instances. The third mate told me in Honolulu that the " Porty-ghee " had lain in his hammock for months, raising his family of abscesses and feeding like a cannibal. We have seen that in spite of dreadful weather, deprivation of sleep, scorching, drenching, and all manner of miseries, thirteen days of starvation " wonderfully recovered " him. There were four sailors down sick when the ship was burned. Twenty-five days of pitiless starvation have followed, and now we have this curious record: "*All the men are hearty and strong; even the ones that were down sick are well*, except poor Peter." When I wrote an article some months ago urging temporary abstention from food as a remedy for an inactive appetite and for disease, I was accused of jesting, but I was in earnest. "*We are all wonderfully well and strong, comparatively speaking*." On this day the starvation regimen drew its belt a couple of buckle-holes tighter: the bread ration

was reduced from the usual piece of cracker the
size of a silver dollar *to the half of that, and one
meal was abolished from the daily three*. This will
weaken the men physically, but if there are any
diseases of an ordinary sort left in them they will
disappear.

*Two quarts bread-crumbs left, one-third of a ham, three
small cans of oysters, and twenty gallons of water.*—Captain's Log.

The hopeful tone of the diaries is persistent. It
is remarkable. Look at the map and see where
the boat is: latitude 16° 44′, longitude 119° 20′.
It is more than two hundred miles west of the
Revillagigedo Islands, so they are quite out of the
question against the trades, rigged as this boat is.
The nearest land available for such a boat is the
American group, *six hundred and fifty miles away*
westward; still, there is no note of surrender, none
even of discouragement! Yet, May 30, "we have
now left: *one can of oysters; three pounds of raisins;
one can of soup; one-third of a ham; three pints of
biscuit-crumbs*." And fifteen starved men to live
on it while they creep and crawl six hundred and
fifty miles. "Somehow I feel much encouraged
by this change of course (west by north) which we
have made to-day." Six hundred and fifty mile

on a hatful of provisions. Let us be thankful,
even after thirty-two years, that they are mercifully
ignorant of the fact that it isn't six hundred and
fifty that they must creep on the hatful, but *twenty-
two hundred!*

Isn't the situation romantic enough just as it
stands? No. Providence added a startling detail: pulling an oar in that boat, for common sea-
man's wages, was *a banished duke*—Danish. We
hear no more of him; just that mention, that is all,
with the simple remark added that " he is one of
our best men "—a high enough compliment for a
duke or any other man in those manhood-testing
circumstances. With that little glimpse of him at
his oar, and that fine word of praise, he vanishes
out of our knowledge for all time. For all time,
unless he should chance upon this note and reveal
himself.

The last day of May is come. And now there
is a disaster to report: think of it, reflect upon it,
and try to understand how much it means, when
you sit down with your family and pass your eye
over your breakfast-table. Yesterday there were
three pints of bread-crumbs; this morning the
little bag is found open and *some of the crumbs
missing.* " We dislike to suspect any one of such
a rascally act, but there is no question that this

grave crime has been committed. Two days will certainly finish the remaining morsels. God grant us strength to reach the American group!" The third mate told me in Honolulu that in these days the men remembered with bitterness that the "Portyghee" had devoured twenty-two days' rations while he lay waiting to be transferred from the burning ship, and that now they cursed him and swore an oath that if it came to cannibalism he should be the first to suffer for the rest.

The captain has lost his glasses, and therefore he cannot read our pocket prayer-books as much as I think he would like, though he is not familiar with them.

Further of the captain: " He is a good man, and has been most kind to us—almost fatherly. He says that if he had been offered the command of the ship sooner he should have brought his two daughters with him." It makes one shudder yet to think how narrow an escape it was.

The two meals (rations) a day are as follows: fourteen raisins and a piece of cracker the size of a cent, for tea ; a gill of water, and a piece of ham and a piece of bread, each the size of a cent, for breakfast.—Captain's Log.

He means a cent in *thickness* as well as in circumference. Samuel Ferguson's diary says th ham was shaved "about as thin as it could be cut."

June 1. Last night and to-day sea very high and cobbling, breaking over and making us all wet and cold. Weather squally, and there is no doubt that only careful management —with God's protecting care—preserved us through both the night and the day; and really it is most marvellous how every morsel that passes our lips is blessed to us. It makes me think daily of the miracle of the loaves and fishes. Henry keeps up wonderfully, which is a great consolation to me. I somehow have great confidence, and hope that our afflictions will soon be ended, though we are running rapidly across the track of both outward and inward bound vessels, and away from them; our chief hope is a whaler, man-of-war, or some Australian ship. The isles we are steering for are put down in Bowditch, but on my map are said to be doubtful. God grant they may be there!

Hardest day yet.—Captain's Log.

Doubtful! It was worse than that. A week later *they sailed straight over them.*

June 2. Latitude 18° 9'. Squally, cloudy, a heavy sea. . . . I cannot help thinking of the cheerful and comfortable time we had aboard the "Hornet."

Two days' scanty supplies left—ten rations of water apiece and a little morsel of bread. BUT THE SUN SHINES, AND GOD IS MERCIFUL.—Captain's Log.

Sunday, June 3. Latitude 17° 54'. Heavy sea all night, and from 4 A.M. very wet, the sea breaking over us in frequent sluices, and soaking everything aft, particularly. All day

8

the sea has been very high, and it is a wonder that we are not swamped. Heaven grant that it may go down this evening! Our suspense and condition are getting terrible. I managed this morning to crawl, more than step, to the forward end of the boat, and was surprised to find that I was so weak, especially in the legs and knees. The sun has been out again, and I have dried some things, and hope for a better night.

June 4. Latitude 17° 6', longitude 131° 30'. Shipped hardly any seas last night, and to-day the sea has gone down somewhat, although it is still too high for comfort, as we have an occasional reminder that water is wet. The sun has been out all day, and so we have had a good drying. I have been trying for the last ten or twelve days to get a pair of drawers dry enough to put on, and to-day at last succeeded. I mention this to show the state in which we have lived. If our chronometer is anywhere near right, we ought to see the American Isles to-morrow or next day. If they are not there, we have only the chance, for a few days, of a stray ship, for we cannot eke out the provisions more than five or six days longer, and our strength is failing very fast. I was much surprised to-day to note how my legs have wasted away above my knees : they are hardly thicker than my upper arm used to be. Still, I trust in God's infinite mercy, and feel sure he will do what is best for us. To survive, as we have done, thirty-two days in an open boat, with only about ten days' fair provisions for thirty-one men in the first place, and these divided twice subsequently, is more than mere unassisted HUMAN *art and strength could have accomplished and endured.*

Bread and raisins all gone.—Captain's Log.

Men growing dreadfully discontented, and awful grumbling and unpleasant talk is arising. God save us from all strife of men ; and if we must die now, take us himself, and not embitter our bitter death still more.—Henry's Log.

June 5.   Quiet night and pretty comfortable day, though our sail and block show signs of failing, and need taking down—which latter is something of a job, as it requires the climbing of the mast.   We also had news from forward, there being discontent and some threatening complaints of unfair allowances, etc., all as unreasonable as foolish ; still, these things bid us be on our guard.   I am getting miserably weak, but try to keep up the best I can.   If we cannot find those isles we can only try to make northwest and get in the track of Sandwich Island bound vessels, living as best we can in the meantime.   To-day we changed to one meal, and that at about noon, with a small ration of water at 8 or 9 A.M., another at 12 M., and a third at 5 or 6 P.M.

Nothing left but a little piece of ham and a gill of water, all around.—Captain's Log.

They are down to *one* meal a day now,—such as it is,—and *fifteen hundred miles to crawl yet!* And now the horrors deepen, and though they escaped actual mutiny, the attitude of the men became alarming. Now we seem to see why that curious accident happened, so long ago: I mean Cox's return, after he had been far away and out of sight several days in the chief mate's boat. If he had not come back the captain and the two young passengers might have been slain, now, by these sailors, who were becoming crazed through their sufferings.

NOTE SECRETLY PASSED BY HENRY TO HIS BROTHER

Cox told me last night that there is getting to be a good deal of ugly talk among the men against the captain and us *aft. They say that the captain is the cause of all; that he did not try to save the ship at all, nor to get provisions, and even would not let the men put in some they had; and that partiality is shown us in apportioning our rations aft. * * * * asked Cox the other day if he would starve first or eat human flesh. Cox answered he would starve. * * * * then told him he would only be killing himself. If we do not find these islands we would do well to prepare for anything. * * * * * is the loudest of all.*

REPLY

*We can depend on * * * * *, I think, and * * * * *, and Cox, can we not?*

SECOND NOTE

*I guess so, and very likely on * * * * *; but there is no telling. * * * * * * and Cox are certain. There is nothing definite said or hinted as yet, as I understand Cox; but starving men are the same as maniacs. It would be well to keep a watch on your pistol, so as to have it and the cartridges safe from theft.*

Henry's Log, *June 5. Dreadful forebodings. God spare us from all such horrors! Some of the men getting to talk a good deal. Nothing to write down. Heart very sad.*

Henry's Log, *June 6. Passed some sea-weed and something that looked like the trunk of an old tree, but no birds; beginning to be afraid islands not there. To-day it was said to the captain, in the hearing of all, that some of the men would not shrink, when a man was dead, from using the flesh, though they would not kill. Horrible! God give us all full use of our reason, and spare us from such things! " From plague, pestilence, and famine; from battle and murder, and from sudden death, good Lord, deliver us!"*

June 6. Latitude 16° 30', longitude (chron.) 134°. Dry night, and wind steady enough to require no change in sail; but this A.M. an attempt to lower it proved abortive. First the third mate tried and got up to the block, and fastened a temporary arrangement to reeve the halyards through, but had to come down, weak and almost fainting, before finishing; then Joe tried, and after twice ascending, fixed it and brought down the block; but it was very exhausting work, and afterward he was good for nothing all day. The clue-iron which we are trying to make serve for the broken block works, however, very indifferently, and will, I am afraid, soon cut the rope. It is very necessary to get everything connected with the sail in good, easy running order before we get too weak to do anything with it.

Only three meals left.—Captain's Log.

June 7. Latitude 16° 35' N., longitude 136° 30' W. Night wet and uncomfortable. To-day shows us pretty conclusively that the American Isles are not there, though we have had some signs that looked like them. At noon we decided to abandon looking any farther for them, and to-night haul a little more northerly, so as to get in the way of Sandwich Island vessels, which fortunately come down pretty well this way—say to latitude 19° to 20° to get the benefit of the trade-winds. Of course all the westing we have made is gain, and I hope the chronometer is wrong in our favor, for I do not see how any such delicate instrument can keep good time with the constant jarring and thumping we get from the sea. With the strong trade we have, I hope that a week from Sunday will put us in sight of the Sandwich Islands, if we are not safe by that time by being picked up.

It is twelve hundred miles to the Sandwich Islands; the provisions are virtually exhausted, but not the perishing diarist's pluck.

June 8. My cough troubled me a good deal last night, and therefore I got hardly any sleep at all. Still, I make out pretty well, and should not complain. Yesterday the third mate mended the block, and this P.M. the sail, after some difficulty, was got down, and Harry got to the top of the mast and rove the halyards through after some hardship, so that it now works easy and well. This getting up the mast is no easy matter at any time with the sea we have, and is very exhausting in our present state. We could only reward Harry by an extra ration of water. We have made good time and course to-day. Heading her up, however, makes the boat ship seas and keeps us all wet; however, it cannot be helped. Writing is a rather precarious thing these times. Our meal to-day for the fifteen consists of half a can of "soup and boullie"; the other half is reserved for to-morrow. Henry still keeps up grandly, and is a great favorite. God grant he may be spared!

A better feeling prevails among the men.—Captain's Log.

June 9. Latitude 17° 53'. Finished to-day, I may say, our whole stock of provisions.* We have only left a lower end of a ham-bone, with some of the outer rind and skin on. In regard to the water, however, I think we have got ten days' supply at our present rate of allowance. This, with what nourishment we can get from boot-legs and such chewable matter, we hope will enable us to weather it out till we get to the Sandwich Islands, or, sailing in the meantime in the track of vessels thither bound, be picked up. My hope is

---

* Six days to sail yet, nevertheless.—M. T.

in the latter, for in all human probability I cannot stand the other. Still, we have been marvellously protected, and God, I hope, will preserve us all in his own good time and way. The men are getting weaker, but are still quiet and orderly.

Sunday, June 10. Latitude 18° 40', longitude 142° 34'. A pretty good night last night, with some wettings, and again another beautiful Sunday. I cannot but think how we should all enjoy it at home, and what a contrast is here! How terrible their suspense must begin to be! God grant that it may be relieved before very long, and he certainly seems to be with us in everything we do, and has preserved this boat miraculously; for since we left the ship we have sailed considerably over three thousand miles, which, taking into consideration our meagre stock of provisions, is almost unprecedented. As yet I do not feel the stint of food so much as I do that of water. Even Henry, who is naturally a good water-drinker, can save half of his allowance from time to time, when I cannot. My diseased throat may have something to do with that, however.

Nothing is now left which by any flattery can be called food. But they must manage somehow for five days more, for at noon they have still eight hundred miles to go. It is a race for life now.

This is no time for comments or other interruptions from me—every moment is valuable. I will take up the boy brother's diary at this point, and clear the seas before it and let it fly.

HENRY FERGUSON'S LOG

Sunday, June 10. Our ham-bone has given us a taste of food to-day, and we have got left a little meat and the re-

mainder of the bone for to-morrow. Certainly, never was there such a sweet knuckle-bone, or one that was so thoroughly appreciated. . . . I do not know that I feel any worse than I did last Sunday, notwithstanding the reduction of diet; and I trust that we may all have strength given us to sustain the sufferings and hardships of the coming week. We estimate that we are within seven hundred miles of the Sandwich Islands, and that our average, daily, is somewhat over a hundred miles, so that our hopes have some foundation in reason. Heaven send we may all live to see land!

June 11. Ate the meat and rind of our ham-bone, and have the bone and the greasy cloth from around the ham left to eat to-morrow. God send us birds or fish, and let us not perish of hunger, or be brought to the dreadful alternative of feeding on human flesh! As I feel now, I do not think anything could persuade me; but you cannot tell what you will do when you are reduced by hunger and your mind wandering. I hope and pray we can make out to reach the islands before we get to this strait; but we have one or two desperate men aboard, though they are quiet enough now. IT IS MY FIRM TRUST AND BELIEF THAT WE ARE GOING TO BE SAVED.

All food gone.—Captain's Log.*

June 12. Stiff breeze, and we are fairly flying — dead ahead of it — and toward the islands. Good hope, but the prospects of hunger are awful. Ate ham-bone to-day. It is the captain's birthday; he is fifty-four years old.

June 13. The ham-rags are not quite all gone yet, and the boot-legs, we find, are very palatable after we get the salt out

---

* It was at this time discovered that the crazed sailors had gotten the delusion that the captain had *a million dollars* in gold concealed aft, and they were conspiring to kill him and the two passengers and seize it.—M. T.

of them. A little smoke, I think, does some little good ; but I don't know.

June 14. Hunger does not pain us much, but we are dreadfully weak. Our water is getting frightfully low. God grant we may see land soon! NOTHING TO EAT, *but feel better than I did yesterday. Toward evening saw a magnificent rainbow—* THE FIRST WE HAD SEEN. *Captain said, " Cheer up, boys ; it's a prophecy—*IT'S THE BOW OF PROMISE!"

June 15. God be forever praised for his infinite mercy! LAND IN SIGHT! *Rapidly neared it and soon were* SURE *of it . . . . Two noble Kanakas swam out and took the boat ashore. We were joyfully received by two white men— Mr. Jones and his steward Charley—and a crowd of native men, women, and children. They treated us splendidly—aided us, and carried us up the bank, and brought us water, poi, bananas, and green cocoanuts ; but the white men took care of us and prevented those who would have eaten too much from doing so. Everybody overjoyed to see us, and all sympathy expressed in faces, deeds, and words. We were then helped up to the house ; and help we needed. Mr. Jones and Charley are the only white men here. Treated us splendidly. Gave us first about a teaspoonful of spirits in water, and then to each a cup of warm tea, with a little bread. Takes* EVERY *care of us. Gave us later another cup of tea, and bread the same, and then let us go to rest.* IT IS THE HAPPIEST DAY OF MY LIFE. . . . *God in his mercy has heard our prayer. . . . Everybody is so kind. Words cannot tell.*

June 16. Mr. Jones gave us a delightful bed, and we surely had a good night's rest ; but not sleep—we were too happy to sleep ; would keep the reality and not let it turn to a delusion—dreaded that we might wake up and find ourselves in the boat again.

It is an amazing adventure. There is nothing of

its sort in history that surpasses it in impossibilities made possible. In one extraordinary detail—the survival of *every person* in the boat—it probably stands alone in the history of adventures of its kind. Usually merely a part of a boat's company survive—officers, mainly, and other educated and tenderly reared men, unused to hardship and heavy labor; the untrained, roughly reared hard workers succumb. But in this case even the rudest and roughest stood the privations and miseries of the voyage almost as well as did the college-bred young brothers and the captain. I mean, physically. The minds of most of the sailors broke down in the fourth week and went to temporary ruin, but physically the endurance exhibited was astonishing. Those men did not survive by any merit of their own, of course, but by merit of the character and intelligence of the captain; they lived by the mastery of his spirit. Without him they would have been children without a nurse; they would have exhausted their provisions in a week, and their pluck would not have lasted even as long as the provisions.

The boat came near to being wrecked at the last. As it approached the shore the sail was let go, and came down with a run; then the captain saw that he was drifting swiftly toward an ugly reef, and an effort was made to hoist the sail again: but it could not be done; the men's strength was wholly exhausted; they could not even pull an oar. They were helpless, and death imminent. It was then that they were discovered by the two Kanakas who achieved the rescue. They swam out and manned the boat and piloted her through a narrow and hardly noticeable break in the reef—the only break in it in a stretch of thirty-five miles! The spot where the landing was made was the only one in that stretch where footing could have been found on the shore; everywhere else precipices came sheer down into forty fathoms of water. Also, in all that stretch this was the only spot where anybody lived.

Within ten days after the landing all the men but one were up and creeping about. Properly, they ought to have killed themselves with the "food" of the last few days—some of them, at any rate—men who had freighted their stomachs with strips of leather from old boots and with chips from the butter-cask; a freightage which they did not get rid of by digestion, but by other means. The captain and the two passengers did not eat strips and chips, as the sailors did, but *scraped* the boot-leather and the wood, and made a pulp of the scrapings by moistening them with water. The third mate told me that the boots were old and full of holes; then added thoughtfully, "but the holes digested the best." Speaking of digestion, here is a remarkable thing, and worth noting: during this strange voyage, and for a while afterward on shore, the bowels of some of the men virtually ceased from their functions; in some cases there was no action for twenty and thirty days, and in one case for forty-four! Sleeping also came to be rare. Yet the men did very well without it. During many days the captain did not sleep at all—twenty-one, I think, on one stretch.

When the landing was made, all the men were successfully protected from overeating except the " Portyghee "; he escaped the watch and ate an incredible number of bananas: a hundred and fifty-two, the third mate said, but this was undoubtedly an exaggeration; I think it was a hundred and fifty-one. He was already nearly full of leather; it was hanging out of his ears. (I do not state this on the third mate's authority, for we have seen what sort of person he was; I state it on my own.) The " Portyghee " ought to have died, of course, and even now it seems a pity that he didn't; but he got well, and as early as any of them; and all full of leather, too, the way he was, and butter-timber and handkerchiefs and bananas. Some of the men did eat handkerchiefs in those last days, also socks; and he was one of them.

It is to the credit of the men that they did not kill the rooster that crowed so gallantly mornings. He lived eighteen days, and then stood up and stretched his neck and made a brave, weak effort to do his duty once more, and died in the act. It is a picturesque detail; and so is that rainbow, too,— the only one seen in the forty-three days,—raising its triumphal arch in the skies for the sturdy fighters to sail under to victory and rescue.

With ten days' provisions Captain Josiah Mitchell performed this memorable voyage of forty-three days and eight hours in an open boat, sailing four thousand miles in reality and thirty-three hundred and sixty by direct courses, and brought every man safe to land. A bright, simple-hearted, unassuming, plucky, and most companionable man. I walked the deck with him twenty-eight days,— when I was not copying diaries,—and I remember him with reverent honor. If he is alive he is eighty-six years old now.

If I remember rightly, Samuel Ferguson died soon after we reached San Francisco. I do not think he lived to see his home again; his disease had been seriously aggravated by his hardships.

For a time it was hoped that the two quarter-

boats would presently be heard of, but this hope
suffered disappointment. They went down with
all on board, no doubt, not even sparing that
knightly chief mate.

The authors of the diaries allowed me to copy
them exactly as they were written, and the ex-
tracts that I have given are without any smoothing
over or revision. These diaries are finely modest
and unaffected, and with unconscious and uninten-
tional art they rise toward the climax with gradu-
ated and gathering force and swing and dramatic
intensity; they sweep you along with a cumulative
rush, and when the cry rings out at last, " Land in
sight!" your heart is in your mouth, and for a moment you think it is you that have been saved.
The last two paragraphs are not improvable by
anybody's art; they are literary gold; and their
very pauses and uncompleted sentences have in
them an eloquence not reachable by any words.

The interest of this story is unquenchable; it is
of the sort that time cannot decay. I have not
looked at the diaries for thirty-two years, but I find
that they have lost nothing in that time. Lost?
They have gained; for by some subtile law all
tragic human experiences gain in pathos by the
perspective of time. We realize this when in
Naples we stand musing over the poor Pompeian

mother, lost in the historic storm of volcanic ashes eighteen centuries ago, who lies with her child gripped close to her breast, trying to save it, and whose despair and grief have been preserved for us by the fiery envelope which took her life but eternalized her form and features. She moves us, she haunts us, she stays in our thoughts for many days, we do not know why, for she is nothing to us, she has been nothing to any one for eighteen centuries; whereas of the like case to-day we should say, "Poor thing! it is pitiful," and forget it in an hour.

FROM THE "LONDON TIMES"
OF 1904

I

Correspondence of the " London Times "

CHICAGO, *April* 1, 1894.

I RESUME by cable-telephone where I left off
yesterday. For many hours, now, this vast city
—along with the rest of the globe, of course—
has talked of nothing but the extraordinary episode
mentioned in my last report. In accordance with
your instructions, I will now trace the romance from
its beginnings down to the culmination of yesterday—or to-day ; call it which you like. By an odd
chance, I was a personal actor in a part of this
drama myself. The opening scene plays in Vienna.
Date, one o'clock in the morning, March 31, 1898.
I had spent the evening at a social entertainment.
About midnight I went away, in company with the
military attachés of the British, Italian, and Ameri-

can embassies, to finish with a late smoke. This
function had been appointed to take place in the
house of Lieutenant Hillyer, the third attaché
mentioned in the above list. When we arrived
there we found several visitors in the room: young
Szczepanik;* Mr. K., his financial backer; Mr. W.,
the latter's secretary; and Lieutenant Clayton of
the United States army. War was at that time
threatening between Spain and our country, and
Lieutenant Clayton had been sent to Europe on
military business. I was well acquainted with
young Szczepanik and his two friends, and I knew
Mr. Clayton slightly. I had met him at West
Point years before, when he was a cadet. It was
when General Merritt was superintendent. He
had the reputation of being an able officer, and
also of being quick-tempered and plain-spoken.

This smoking-party had been gathered together
partly for business. This business was to consider
the availability of the telelectroscope for military
service. It sounds oddly enough now, but it is
nevertheless true that at that time the invention
was not taken seriously by any one except its inventor. Even his financial supporter regarded it
merely as a curious and interesting toy. Indeed,

* Pronounced (approximately) Ze*pan*nik.

9

he was so convinced of this that he had actually postponed its use by the general world to the end of the dying century by granting a two years' exclusive lease of it to a syndicate, whose intent was to exploit it at the Paris World's Fair. When we entered the smoking-room we found Lieutenant Clayton and Szczepanik engaged in a warm talk over the telelectroscope in the German tongue. Clayton was saying:

"Well, you know *my* opinion of it, anyway!" and he brought his fist down with emphasis upon the table.

"And I do not value it," retorted the young inventor, with provoking calmness of tone and manner.

Clayton turned to Mr. K., and said:

"*I* cannot see why you are wasting money on this toy. In my opinion, the day will never come when it will do a farthing's worth of real service for any human being."

"That may be; yes, that may be; still, I have put the money in it, and am content. I think, myself, that it is only a toy; but Szczepanik claims more for it, and I know him well enough to believe that he can see farther than I can—either with his telelectroscope or without it."

The soft answer did not cool Clayton down; it

seemed only to irritate him the more; and he repeated and emphasized his conviction that the invention would never do any man a farthing's worth
of real service. He even made it a "brass" farthing, this time. Then he laid an English farthing
on the table, and added:

"Take that, Mr. K., and put it away; and if
ever the telelectroscope does any man an actual
service—mind, a *real* service—please mail it to me
as a reminder, and I will take back what I have
been saying. Will you?"

"I will"; and Mr. K. put the coin in his pocket.

Mr. Clayton now turned toward Szczepanik, and
began with a taunt—a taunt which did not reach a
finish; Szczepanik interrupted it with a hardy retort, and followed this with a blow. There was a
brisk fight for a moment or two; then the attachés
separated the men.

The scene now changes to Chicago. Time, the
autumn of 1901. As soon as the Paris contract re-
leased the telelectroscope, it was delivered to public use, and was soon connected with the telephonic
systems of the whole world. The improved "lim-
itless-distance" telephone was presently introduced, and the daily doings of the globe made
visible to everybody, and audibly discussable, too,
by witnesses separated by any number of leagues.

By-and-by Szczepanik arrived in Chicago. Clayton (now captain) was serving in that military department at the time. The two men resumed the
Viennese quarrel of 1898. On three different occasions they quarreled, and were separated by witnesses. Then came an interval of two months,
during which time Szczepanik was not seen by
any of his friends, and it was at first supposed
that he had gone off on a sight-seeing tour and
would soon be heard from. But no ; no word came
from him. Then it was supposed that he had returned to Europe. Still, time drifted on, and he
was not heard from. Nobody was troubled, for
he was like most inventors and other kinds of
poets, and went and came in a capricious way,
and often without notice.

Now comes the tragedy. On the 29th of December, in a dark and unused compartment of the
cellar under Captain Clayton's house, a corpse was
discovered by one of Clayton's maid-servants. It
was easily identified as Szczepanik's. The man had
died by violence. Clayton was arrested, indicted,
and brought to trial, charged with this murder.
The evidence against him was perfect in every detail, and absolutely unassailable. Clayton admitted
this himself. He said that a reasonable man could
not examine this testimony with a dispassionate

mind and not be convinced by it; yet the man would be in error, nevertheless. Clayton swore that he did not commit the murder, and that he had had nothing to do with it.

As your readers will remember, he was condemned to death. He had numerous and powerful friends, and they worked hard to save him, for none of them doubted the truth of his assertion. I did what little I could to help, for I had long since become a close friend of his, and thought I knew that it was not in his character to inveigle an enemy into a corner and assassinate him. During 1902 and 1903 he was several times reprieved by the governor; he was reprieved once more in the beginning of the present year, and the execution day postponed to March 31.

The governor's situation has been embarrassing, from the day of the condemnation, because of the fact that Clayton's wife is the governor's niece. The marriage took place in 1899, when Clayton was thirty-four and the girl twenty-three, and has been a happy one. There is one child, a little girl three years old. Pity for the poor mother and child kept the mouths of grumblers closed at first; but this could not last forever,—for in America politics has a hand in everything,—and by-and-by the governor's political opponents began to call attention to his delay in allowing the law to take its course. These hints have grown more and more frequent of late, and more and more pronounced. As a natural result, his own party grew nervous. Its leaders began to visit Springfield and hold long private conferences with him. He was now between two fires. On the one hand, his niece was imploring him to pardon her husband; on the other were the leaders, insisting that he stand to his plain duty as chief magistrate of the State, and place no further bar to Clayton's execution. Duty won in the struggle, and the governor gave his word that he would not again respite the condemned man. This was two weeks ago. Mrs. Clayton now said :

"Now that you have given your word, my last hope is gone, for I know you will never go back from it. But you have done the best you could for John, and I have no reproaches for you. You love him, and you love me, and both know that if you could honorably save him, you would do it. I will go to him now, and be what help I can to him, and get what comfort I may out of the few days that are left to us before the night comes which will have no end for me in life. You will be with me that day? You will not let me bear it alone?"

" I will take you to him myself, poor child, and I will be near you to the last."

By the governor's command, Clayton was now allowed every indulgence he might ask for which could interest his mind and soften the hardships of his imprisonment. His wife and child spent the days with him; I was his companion by night. He was removed from the narrow cell which he had occupied during such a dreary stretch of time, and given the chief warden's roomy and comfortable quarters. His mind was always busy with the catastrophe of his life, and with the slaughtered inventor, and he now took the fancy that he would like to have the telelectroscope and divert his mind with it. He had his wish. The connection was made with the international telephone-station, and day by day, and night by night, he called up one corner of the globe after another, and looked upon its life, and studied its strange sights, and spoke with its people, and realized that by grace of this marvellous instrument he was almost as free as the birds of the air, although a prisoner under locks and bars. He seldom spoke, and I never interrupted him when he was absorbed in this amusement. I sat in his parlor and read and smoked, and the nights were very quiet and re-posefully sociable, and I found them pleasant.

Now and then I would hear him say, "Give me Yedo"; next, "Give me Hong-Kong"; next "Give me Melbourne." And I smoked on, and read in comfort, while he wandered about the remote under-world, where the sun was shining in the sky, and the people were at their daily work. Sometimes the talk that came from those far regions through the microphone attachment interested me, and I listened.

Yesterday—I keep calling it yesterday, which is quite natural, for certain reasons—the instrument remained unused, and that, also, was natural, for it was the eve of the execution day. It was spent in tears and lamentations and farewells. The governor and the wife and child remained until a quarter past eleven at night, and the scenes I witnessed were pitiful to see. The execution was to take place at four in the morning. A little after eleven a sound of hammering broke out upon the still night, and there was a glare of light, and the child cried out, "What is that, papa?" and ran to the window before she could be stopped, and clapped her small hands and said, "Oh, come and see, mamma—such a pretty thing they are making!" The mother knew—and fainted. It was the gallows!

She was carried away to her lodging, poor

woman, and Clayton and I were alone—alone, and thinking, brooding, dreaming. We might have been statues, we sat so motionless and still. It was a wild night, for winter was come again for a moment, after the habit of this region in the early spring. The sky was starless and black, and a strong wind was blowing from the lake. The silence in the room was so deep that all outside sounds seemed exaggerated by contrast with it. These sounds were fitting ones; they harmonized with the situation and the conditions: the boom and thunder of sudden storm - gusts among the roofs and chimneys, then the dying down into moanings and wailings about the eaves and angles; now and then a gnashing and lashing rush of sleet along the window-panes; and always the muffled and uncanny hammering of the gallows-builders in the court-yard. After an age of this, another sound—far off, and coming smothered and faint through the riot of the tempest—a bell tolling twelve! Another age, and it was tolled again. By-and-by, again. A dreary, long interval after this, then the spectral sound floated to us once more—one, two, three; and this time we caught our breath; sixty minutes of life left!

Clayton rose, and stood by the window, and looked up into the black sky, and listened to the

thrashing sleet and the piping wind ; then he said :
" That a dying man's last of earth should be—
this !" After a little he said : "I must see the
sun again—the sun !" and the next moment he
was feverishly calling : " China ! Give me China—
Peking !"

I was strangely stirred, and said to myself : " To
think that it is a mere human being who does this
unimaginable miracle—turns winter into summer,
night into day, storm into calm, gives the freedom
of the great globe to a prisoner in his cell, and the
sun in his naked splendor to a man dying in
Egyptian darkness !"

I was listening.

" What light ! what brilliancy ! what radiance !
. . . This is Peking ?"

" Yes."

" The time ?"

" Mid-afternoon."

" What is the great crowd for, and in such gor-
geous costumes ? What masses and masses of
rich color and barbaric magnificence ! And how
they flash and glow and burn in the flooding sun-
light ! What *is* the occasion of it all ?"

." The coronation of our new emperor—the Czar."

" But I thought that that was to take place yesterday."

"This *is* yesterday—to you."

"Certainly it is. But my mind is confused, these days; there are reasons for it. . . . Is this the beginning of the procession?"

"Oh, no; it began to move an hour ago."

"Is there much more of it still to come?"

"Two hours of it. Why do you sigh?"

"Because I should like to see it all."

"And why can't you?"

"I have to go—presently."

"You have an engagement?"

After a pause, softly: "Yes." After another pause: "Who are these in the splendid pavilion?"

"The imperial family, and visiting royalties from here and there and yonder in the earth."

"And who are those in the adjoining pavilions to the right and left?"

"Ambassadors and their families and suites to the right; unofficial foreigners to the left."

"If you will be so good, I—"

Boom! That distant bell again, tolling the half-hour faintly through the tempest of wind and sleet. The door opened, and the governor and the mother and child entered—the woman in widow's weeds! She fell upon her husband's breast in a passion of sobs, and I—I could not stay; I could not bear it. I went into the bedchamber, and closed the door.

I sat there waiting—waiting—waiting, and listening to the rattling sashes and the blustering of the storm. After what seemed a long, long time, I heard a rustle and movement in the parlor, and knew that the clergyman and the sheriff and the guard were come. There was some low-voiced talking; then a hush; then a prayer, with a sound of sobbing; presently, footfalls—the departure for the gallows; then the child's happy voice: "Don't cry *now*, mamma, when we've got papa again, and taking him home."

The door closed; they were gone. I was ashamed: I was the only friend of the dying man that had no spirit, no courage. I stepped into the room, and said I would be a man and would follow. But we are made as we are made, and we cannot help it. I did not go.

I fidgeted about the room nervously, and presently went to the window, and softly raised it,—drawn by that dread fascination which the terrible and the awful exert,—and looked down upon the court-yard. By the garish light of the electric lamps I saw the little group of privileged witnesses, the wife crying on her uncle's breast, the condemned man standing on the scaffold with the halter around his neck, his arms strapped to his body, the black cap on his head, the sheriff at his side with his hand

on the drop, the clergyman in front of him with bare
head and his book in his hand.

"*I am the resurrection and the life—*"

I turned away. I could not listen; I could not
look. I did not know whither to go or what to
do. Mechanically, and without knowing it, I put
my eye to that strange instrument, and there was
Peking and the Czar's procession! The next moment I was leaning out of the window, gasping,
suffocating, trying to speak, but dumb from the
very imminence of the necessity of speaking. The
preacher could speak, but I, who had such need of
words—

"*And may God have mercy upon your soul.
Amen.*"

The sheriff drew down the black cap, and laid
his hand upon the lever. I got my voice.

"Stop, for God's sake! The man is innocent.
Come here and see Szczepanik face to face!"

Hardly three minutes later the governor had my
place at the window, and was saying:

"Strike off his bonds and set him free!"

Three minutes later all were in the parlor again.
The reader will imagine the scene; I have no need
to describe it. It was a sort of mad orgy of joy.

A messenger carried word to Szczepanik in the
pavilion, and one could see the distressed amaze-

ment dawn in his face as he listened to the tale. Then he came to his end of the line, and talked with Clayton and the governor and the others; and the wife poured out her gratitude upon him for saving her husband's life, and in her deep thankfulness she kissed him at twelve thousand miles' range.

The telelectrophonoscopes of the globe were put to service now, and for many hours the kings and queens of many realms (with here and there a reporter) talked with Szczepanik, and praised him; and the few scientific societies which had not already made him an honorary member conferred that grace upon him.

How had he come to disappear from among us? It was easily explained. He had not grown used to being a world-famous person, and had been forced to break away from the lionizing that was robbing him of all privacy and repose. So he grew a beard, put on colored glasses, disguised himself a little in other ways, then took a fictitious name, and went off to wander about the earth in peace.

Such is the tale of the drama which began with an inconsequential quarrel in Vienna in the spring of 1898, and came near ending as a tragedy in the spring of 1904.

II

Correspondence of the " London Times"

CHICAGO, *April* 5, 1904.

To-day, by a clipper of the Electric Line, and the latter's Electric Railway connections, arrived an envelope from Vienna, for Captain Clayton, containing an English farthing. The receiver of it was a good deal moved. He called up Vienna, and stood face to face with Mr. K., and said :

" I do not need to say anything; you can see it all in my face. My wife has the farthing. Do not be afraid—she will not throw it away.

III

Correspondence of the " London Times"

CHICAGO, *April* 23, 1904.

Now that the after developments of the Clayton case have run their course and reached a finish, I will sum them up. Clayton's romantic escape from a shameful death steeped all this region in an enchantment of wonder and joy — during the proverbial nine days. Then the sobering process followed, and men began to take thought, and to say : " But *a man was killed*, and Clayton killed him." Others replied: "That is true: we have been overlooking that important detail; we have been led away by excitement."

The feeling soon became general that Clayton ought to be tried again. Measures were taken accordingly, and the proper representations conveyed to Washington; for in America, under the new paragraph added to the Constitution in 1889, second trials are not State affairs, but national, and must be tried by the most august body in the land—the Supreme Court of the United States. The justices were therefore summoned to sit in Chicago. The session was held day before yesterday, and was opened with the usual impressive formalities, the nine judges appearing in their black robes, and the new chief justice (Lemaitre) presiding. In opening the case, the chief justice said:

"It is my opinion that this matter is quite simple. The prisoner at the bar was charged with murdering the man Szczepanik; he was tried for murdering the man Szczepanik; he was fairly tried, and justly condemned and sentenced to death for murdering the man Szczpanik. It turns out that the man Szczepanik was not murdered at all. By the decision of the French courts in the Dreyfus matter, it is established beyond cavil or question that the decisions of courts are permanent and cannot be revised. We are obliged to respect and adopt this precedent. It is upon precedents that the enduring edifice of jurisprudence is reared. The prisoner at the bar has been fairly and righteously condemned to death for the murder of the man Szczepanik, and, in my opinion, there is but one course to pursue in the matter: he must be hanged."

Mr. Justice Crawford said:

"But, your Excellency, he was pardoned on the scaffold for that."

"The pardon is not valid, and cannot stand, because he was pardoned for killing a man whom he had not killed. A man cannot be pardoned for a crime which he has not committed; it would be an absurdity."

"But, your Excellency, he did kill a man."

"That is an extraneous detail; we have nothing to do with it. The court cannot take up this crime until the prisoner has expiated the other one."

Mr. Justice Halleck said:

"If we order his execution, your Excellency, we shall bring about a miscarriage of justice; for the governor will pardon him again."

"He will not have the power. He cannot pardon a man for a crime which he has not committed. As I observed before, it would be an absurdity."

10

After a consultation, Mr. Justice Wadsworth said:

"Several of us have arrived at the conclusion, your Excellency, that it would be an error to hang the prisoner for killing Szczepanik, but only for killing the other man, since it is proven that he did not kill Szczepanik."

"On the contrary, it is proven that he *did* kill Szczepanik. By the French precedent, it is plain that we must abide by the finding of the court."

"But Szczepanik is still alive."

"So is Dreyfus."

In the end it was found impossible to ignore or get around the French precedent. There could be but one result: Clayton was delivered over to the executioner. It made an immense excitement; the State rose as one man and clamored for Clayton's pardon and retrial. The governor issued the pardon, but the Supreme Court was in duty bound to annul it, and did so, and poor Clayton was hanged yesterday. The city is draped in black, and, indeed, the like may be said of the State. All America is vocal with scorn of "French justice," and of the malignant little soldiers who invented it and inflicted it upon the other Christian lands.

AT THE APPETITE-CURE

I

THIS establishment's name is Hochberghaus. It is in Bohemia, a short day's journey from Vienna, and being in the Austrian empire is of course a health resort. The empire is made up of health resorts; it distributes health to the whole world. Its waters are all medicinal. They are bottled and sent throughout the earth; the natives themselves drink beer. This is self-sacrifice, apparently—but outlanders who have drunk Vienna beer have another idea about it. Particularly the Pilsner which one gets in a small cellar up an obscure back lane in the First Bezirk—the name has escaped me, but the place is easily found: You inquire for the Greek church; and when you get to it, go right along by—the next house is that little beer-mill. It is remote from all traffic and all noise; it is always Sunday there. There are two small rooms, with low ceilings supported by massive arches; the arches and ceilings are whitewashed, otherwise the rooms would pass for cells in the dungeons of a bastile. The furniture is plain and cheap, there is no ornamentation anywhere; yet it is a heaven for the self-sacrificers, for the beer there is incomparable; there is nothing like it elsewhere in the world. In the first room you will find twelve or fifteen ladies and gentlemen of civilian quality; in the other one a dozen generals and ambassadors. One may live in Vienna many months and not hear of this place; but having once heard of it and sampled it, the sampler will afterward infest it.

However, this is all incidental—a mere passing note of gratitude for blessings received — it has nothing to do with my subject. My subject is health resorts. All unhealthy people ought to domicile themselves in Vienna, and use that as a base, making flights from time to time to the outlying resorts, according to need. A flight to Marienbad to get rid of fat; a flight to Carlsbad to get rid of rheumatism; a flight to Kaltenleutgeben to take the water cure and get rid of the rest of the diseases. It is all so handy. You can stand in Vienna and toss a biscuit into Kaltenleutgeben, with a twelve-inch gun. You can run out thither

at any time of the day; you go by the phenom-
enally slow trains, and yet inside of an hour you
have exchanged the glare and swelter of the city
for wooded hills, and shady forest paths, and soft
cool airs, and the music of birds, and the repose
and peace of paradise.

And there are plenty of other health resorts at
your service and convenient to get at from Vienna;
charming places, all of them; Vienna sits in the
centre of a beautiful world of mountains with now
and then a lake and forests; in fact, no other city
is so fortunately situated.

There are abundance of health resorts, as I have
said. Among them this place—Hochberghaus. It
stands solitary on the top of a densely wooded
mountain, and is a building of great size. It is
called the Appetite Anstallt, and people who have
lost their appetites come here to get them restored.
When I arrived I was taken by Professor Haimberger to his consulting-room and questioned :

" It is six o'clock. When did you eat last."

"At noon."

"What did you eat ?"

"Next to nothing."

"What was on the table ?"

" The usual things."

"Chops, chickens, vegetables, and so on ?"

"Yes; but don't mention them—I can't bear it."

"Are you tired of them?"

"Oh, utterly. I wish I might never hear of them again."

"The mere sight of food offends you, does it?"

"More, it revolts me."

The doctor considered awhile, then got out a long menu and ran his eye slowly down it.

"I think," said he, "that what you need to eat is—but here, choose for yourself."

I glanced at the list, and my stomach threw a hand-spring. Of all the barbarous layouts that were ever contrived, this was the most atrocious. At the top stood "tough, underdone, overdue tripe, garnished with garlic"; half-way down the bill stood "young cat; old cat; scrambled cat"; at the bottom stood "sailor-boots, softened with tallow — served raw." The wide intervals of the bill were pack-ed with dishes calculated to insult a cannibal. I said:

"Doctor, it is not fair to joke over so serious a case as mine. I came here to get an appetite, not to throw away the remnant that's left."

He said gravely: "I am not joking; why should I joke?"

"But I can't eat these horrors."

"Why not?"

He said it with a naïveté that was admirable, whether it was real or assumed.

"Why not? Because—why, doctor, for months I have seldom been able to endure anything more substantial than omelettes and custards. These unspeakable dishes of yours—"

"Oh, you will come to like them. They are very good. And you *must* eat them. It is the rule of the place, and is strict. I cannot permit any departure from it."

I said, smiling: "Well, then, doctor, you will have to permit the departure of the patient. I am going."

He looked hurt, and said in a way which changed the aspect of things:

"I am sure you would not do me that injustice. I accepted you in good faith—you will not shame that confidence. This appetite-cure is my whole living. If you should go forth from it with the sort of appetite which you now have, it could become known, and you can see, yourself, that people would say my cure failed in your case and hence can fail in other cases. You will not go; you will not do me this hurt."

I apologized and said I would stay.

"That is right. I was sure you would not go; it would take the food from my family's mouths."

"Would they mind that? Do they eat these fiendish things?"

"They? My family?" His eyes were full of gentle wonder. "Of course not."

"Oh, they don't! Do you?"

"Certainly not."

"I see. It's another case of a physician who doesn't take his own medicine."

"I don't need it. It is six hours since you lunched. Will you have supper now—or later?"

"I am not hungry, but now is as good a time as any, and I would like to be done with it and have it off my mind. It is about my usual time, and regularity is commanded by all the authorities. Yes, I will try to nibble a little now—I wish a light horsewhipping would answer instead."

The professor handed me that odious menu.

"Choose—or will you have it later?"

"Oh, dear me, show me to my room; I forgot your hard rule."

"Wait just a moment before you finally decide. There is another rule. If you choose now, the order will be filled at once; but if you wait, you will have to await my pleasure. You cannot get a dish from that entire bill until I consent."

"All right. Show me to my room, and send the cook to bed; there is not going to be any hurry."

The professor took me up one flight of stairs and showed me into a most inviting and comfortable apartment consisting of parlor, bedchamber, and bathroom.

The front windows looked out over a far-reaching spread of green glades and valleys, and tumbled hills clothed with forests — a noble solitude unvexed by the fussy world. In the parlor were many shelves filled with books. The professor said he would now leave me to myself; and added:

"Smoke and read as much as you please, drink all the water you like. When you get hungry, ring and give your order, and I will decide whether it shall he filled or not. Yours is a stubborn, bad case, and I think the first fourteen dishes in the bill are each and all too delicate for its needs. I ask you as a favor to restrain yourself and not call for them."

"Restrain myself, is it? Give yourself no uneasiness. You are going to save money by me. The idea of coaxing a sick man's appetite back with this buzzard-fare is clear insanity."

I said it with bitterness, for I felt outraged by this calm, cold talk over these heartless new engines of assassination. The doctor looked grieved, but not offended. He laid the bill of fare on the commode at my bed's head, "so that it would be handy," and said :

"Yours is not the worst case I have encountered, by any means; still it is a bad one and requires robust treatment; therefore I shall be gratified if you will restrain yourself and skip down to No. 15 and begin with that."

Then he left me and I began to undress, for I was dog-tired and very sleepy. I slept fifteen hours and woke up finely refreshed at ten the next morning. Vienna coffee! It was the first thing I thought of — that unapproachable luxury — that sumptuous coffee-house coffee, compared with which all other European coffee and all American hotel coffee is mere fluid poverty. I rang, and ordered it; also Vienna bread, that delicious invention. The servant spoke through the wicket in the door and said—but you know what he said. He referred me to the bill of fare. I allowed him to go—I had no further use for him.

After the bath I dressed and started for a walk, and got as far as the door. It was locked on the outside. I rang and the servant came and explained that it was another rule. The seclusion of the patient was required until after the first meal. I had not been particularly anxious to get out before; but it was different now. Being locked in makes a person wishful to get out. I soon began to find it difficult to put in the time. At two o'clock I had been twenty-six hours without food. I had been growing hungry for some time ; I recognized that I was not only hungry now, but hungry with a strong adjective in front of it. Yet I was not hungry enough to face the bill of fare.

I must put in the time somehow. I would read and smoke. I did it ; hour by hour. The books were all of one breed—shipwrecks ; people lost in deserts ; people shut up in caved-in mines ; people starving in besieged cities. I read about all the revolting dishes that ever famishing men had stayed their hunger with. During the first hours these things nauseated me : hours followed in which they did not so affect me ; still other hours followed in which I found myself smacking my lips over some tolerably infernal messes. When I had been without food forty-five hours I ran eagerly to the bell and ordered the second dish in the bill, which was a sort of dumplings containing a compost made of caviar and tar.

It was refused me. During the next fifteen hours I visited the bell every now and then and ordered a dish that was further down the list. Always a refusal. But I was conquering prejudice after prejudice, right along ; I was making sure progress; I was creeping up on No. 15 with deadly certainty, and my heart beat faster and faster, my hopes rose higher and higher.

At last when food had not passed my lips for sixty hours, victory was mine, and I ordered No. 15:

"Soft-boiled spring chicken—in the egg; six dozen, hot and fragrant!"

In fifteen minutes it was there; and the doctor along with it, rubbing his hands with joy. He said with great excitement:

"It's a cure, it's a cure! I knew I could do it. Dear sir, my grand system never fails — never. You've got your appetite back—you know you have; say it and make me happy."

"Bringing on your carrion—I can eat anything in the bill!"

"Oh, this is noble, this is splendid—but I knew I could do it, the system never fails. How are the birds?"

"Never was anything so delicious in the world; and yet as a rule I don't care for game. But don't interrupt me, don't—I can't spare my mouth, I really can't."

Then the doctor said:

"The cure is perfect. There is no more doubt nor danger. Let the poultry alone; I can trust you with a beefsteak, now."

The beefsteak came—as much as a basketful of it—with potatoes, and Vienna bread and coffee; and I ate a meal then that was worth all the costly preparation I had made for it. And dripped tears of gratitude into the gravy all the time—gratitude to the doctor for putting a little plain common-sense into me when I had been empty of it so many, many years.

II

Thirty years ago Haimberger went off on a long voyage in a sailing-ship. There were fifteen passengers on board. The table-fare was of the regulation pattern of the day: At 7 in the morning, a cup of bad coffee in bed; at 9, breakfast: bad coffee, with condensed milk; soggy rolls, crackers, salt fish; at 1 P.M., luncheon: cold tongue, cold ham, cold corned beef, soggy cold rolls, crackers; 5 P.M., dinner: thick pea soup, salt fish, hot corned beef and sour kraut, boiled pork and beans, pudding; 9 till 11 P.M., supper: tea, with condensed milk, cold tongue, cold ham, pickles, sea-biscuit, pickled oysters, pickled pig's feet, grilled bones, golden buck.

At the end of the first week eating had ceased, nibbling had taken its place. The passengers came

to the table, but it was partly to put in the time,
and partly because the wisdom of the ages commanded them to be regular in their meals. They
were tired of the coarse and monotonous fare,
and took no interest in it, had no appetite for it.
All day and every day they roamed the ship half
hungry, plagued by their gnawing stomachs, moody,
untalkative, miserable. Among them were three
confirmed dyspeptics. These became shadows in
the course of three weeks. There was also a bed-
ridden invalid; he lived on boiled rice; he could
not look at the regular dishes.

Now came shipwreck and life in open boats, with
the usual paucity of food. Provisions ran lower
and lower. The appetites improved, then. When
nothing was left but raw ham and the ration of
that was down to two ounces a day per person, the
appetites were perfect. At the end of fifteen days
the dyspeptics, the invalid, and the most delicate
ladies in the party were chewing sailor-boots in
ecstasy, and only complaining because the supply
of them was limited. Yet these were the same
people who couldn't endure the ship's tedious
corned beef and sour kraut and other crudities.
They were rescued by an English vessel. Within
ten days the whole fifteen were in as good condition as they had been when the shipwreck occurred.

"They had suffered no damage by their adventure," said the professor. "Do you note that?"

"Yes."

"Do you note it well?"

"Yes—I think I do."

"But you don't. You hesitate. You don't rise to the importance of it. I will say it again—with emphasis—*not one of them suffered any damage.*"

"Now I begin to see. Yes, it was indeed remarkable."

"Nothing of the kind. It was perfectly natural. There was no reason why they should suffer damage. They were undergoing Nature's Appetite Cure, the best and wisest in the world."

"Is that where you got your idea?"

"That is where I got it."

"It taught those people a valuable lesson."

"What makes you think that?"

"Why shouldn't I? You seem to think it taught you one."

"That is nothing to the point. I am not a fool."

"I see. Were they fools?"

"They were human beings."

"Is it the same thing?"

"Why do you ask? You know it yourself. As regards his health—and the rest of the things—the average man is what his environment and his superstitions have made him; and their function is to make him an ass. He can't add up three or four new circumstances together and perceive what they mean; it is beyond him. He is not capable of observing for himself; he has to get everything at second-hand. If what are miscalled the lower animals were as silly as man is, they would all perish from the earth in a year."

"Those passengers learned no lesson, then?"

"Not a sign of it. They went to their regular meals in the English ship, and pretty soon they were nibbling again—nibbling, appetiteless, disgusted with the food, moody, miserable, half hungry, their outraged stomachs cursing and swearing and whining and supplicating all day long. And in vain, for they were the stomachs of fools."

"Then, as I understand it, your scheme is—"

"Quite simple. Don't eat till you are hungry. If the food fails to taste good, fails to satisfy you, rejoice you, comfort you, don't eat again until you are *very* hungry. Then it will rejoice you—and do you good, too."

"And I observe no regularity, as to hours?"

"When you are conquering a bad appetite—no. After it is conquered, regularity is no harm, so long as the appetite remains good. As soon as

the appetite wavers, apply the corrective again—
which is starvation, long or short according to the
needs of the case."

"The best diet, I suppose—I mean the whole-
somest—"

"All diets are wholesome. Some are wholesomer
than others, but all the ordinary diets are wholesome enough for the people who use them. Whether the food be fine or coarse it will taste good and
it will nourish if a watch be kept upon the appetite
and a little starvation introduced every time it
weakens. Nansen was used to fine fare, but when
his meals were restricted to bear-meat months at
a time he suffered no damage and no discomfort,
because his appetite was kept at par through the
difficulty of getting his bear-meat regularly."

"But doctors arrange carefully considered and
delicate diets for invalids."

"They can't help it. The invalid is full of in-
herited superstitions and won't starve himself. He
believes it would certainly kill him."

"It would weaken him, wouldn't it?"

"Nothing to hurt. Look at the invalids in our
shipwreck. They lived fifteen days on pinches of
raw ham, a suck at sailor-boots, and general starvation. It weakened them, but it didn't hurt them.
It put them in fine shape to eat heartily of hearty

food and build themselves up to a condition of robust health. But they do not perceive that; they lost their opportunity; they remained invalids; it served them right. Do you know the tricks that the health-resort doctors play?"

"What is it?"

"My system disguised—covert starvation. Grape-cure, bath-cure, mud-cure—it is all the same. The grape and the bath and the mud make a show and do a trifle of the work—the real work is done by the surreptitious starvation. The patient accustomed to four meals and late hours—at both ends of the day—now consider what he has to do at a health resort. He gets up at 6 in the morning. Eats one egg. Tramps up and down a promenade two hours with the other fools. Eats a butterfly. Slowly drinks a glass of filtered sewage that smells like a buzzard's breath. Promenades another two hours, but alone; if you speak to him he says anxiously, 'My water!—I am walking off my water!— please don't interrupt,' and goes stumping along again. Eats a candied rose-leaf. Lies at rest in the silence and solitude of his room for hours; mustn't read, mustn't smoke. The doctor comes and feels of his heart, now, and his pulse, and thumps his breast and his back and his stomach, and listens for results through a penny flageolet; then orders the man's bath—half a degree, Reamur, cooler than yesterday. After the bath another egg. A glass of sewage at 3 or 4 in the afternoon, and promenade solemnly with the other freaks. Dinner at 6—half a doughnut and a cup of tea. Walk again. Half-past 8, supper—more butterfly; at 9, to bed. Six weeks of this régime—think of it. It starves a man out and puts him in splendid condition. It would have the same effect in London, New York, Jericho—anywhere."

"How long does it take to put a person in condition here?"

"It ought to take but a day or two; but in fact it takes from one to six weeks, according to the character and mentality of the patient."

"How is that?"

"Do you see that crowd of women playing football, and boxing, and jumping fences yonder? They have been here six or seven weeks. They were spectral poor weaklings when they came. They were accustomed to nibbling at dainties and delicacies at set hours four times a day, and they had no appetite for anything. I questioned them, and then locked them into their rooms—the frailest ones to starve nine or ten hours, the others twelve or fifteen. Before long they began to beg; and indeed they suffered a good deal. They complained of nausea, headache, and so on. It was good to see them eat when the time was up. They could not remember when the devouring of a meal had afforded them such rapture—that was their word. Now, then, that ought to have ended their cure, but it didn't. They were free to go to any meals in the house, and they chose their accustomed four. Within a day or two I had to interfere. Their appetites were weakening. I made them knock out a meal. That set them up again. Then they resumed the four. I begged them to learn to knock out a meal themselves, without waiting for me. Up to a fortnight ago they couldn't; they really hadn't manhood enough; but they were gaining it, and now I think they are safe. They drop out a meal every now and then of their own accord. They are in fine condition now, and they might safely go home, I think, but their confidence is not quite perfect yet, so they are waiting awhile."

"Other cases are different?"

"Oh yes. Sometimes a man learns the whole trick in a week. Learns to regulate his appetite and keep it in perfect order. Learns to drop out a meal with frequency and not mind it."

"But why drop the entire meal out? Why not a part of it?"

"It's a poor device, and inadequate. If the stomach doesn't call vigorously — with a shout, as you may say — it is better not to pester it but just give it a real rest. Some people can eat more meals than others, and still thrive. There are all sorts of people, and all sorts of appetites. I will show you a man presently who was accustomed to nibble at eight meals a day. It was beyond the proper gait of his appetite by two. I have got him down to six a day, now, and he is all right, and enjoys life. How many meals do you affect per day?"

"Formerly — for twenty-two years — a meal and a half; during the past two years, two and a half: coffee and a roll at 9, luncheon at 1, dinner at 7.30 or 8."

"Formerly a meal and a half — that is, coffee and a roll at 9, dinner in the evening, nothing between — is that it?"

"Yes."

"Why did you add a meal?"

"It was the family's idea. They were uneasy. They thought I was killing myself."

"You found a meal and a half per day enough, all through the twenty-two years?"

"Plenty."

"Your present poor condition is due to the extra meal. Drop it out. You are trying to eat oftener than your stomach demands. You don't gain, you lose. You eat less food now, in a day, on two and a half meals, than you formerly ate on one and a half."

"True—a good deal less; for in those old days my dinner was a very sizable thing."

"Put yourself on a single meal a day, now—dinner—for a few days, till you secure a good, sound, regular, trustworthy appetite, then take to your one and a half permanently, and don't listen to the family any more. When you have any ordinary ailment, particularly of a feverish sort, eat nothing at all during twenty-four hours. That will cure it. It will cure the stubbornest cold in the head, too. No cold in the head can survive twenty-four hours' unmodified starvation."

"I know it. I have proved it many a time."

MY FIRST LIE, AND HOW I GOT OUT OF IT

A S I understand it, what you desire is information about "my first lie, and how I got out
of it." I was born in 1835; I am well along,
and my memory is not as good as it was. If you
had asked about my first truth it would have been
easier for me and kinder of you, for I remember
that fairly well; I remember it as if it were last
week. The family think it was week before, but
that is flattery and probably has a selfish project
back of it. When a person has become seasoned
by experience and has reached the age of sixty-
four, which is the age of discretion, he likes a family compliment as well as ever, but he does not
lose his head over it as in the old innocent days.

I do not remember my first lie, it is too far back;
but I remember my second one very well. I was
nine days old at the time, and had noticed that if
a pin was sticking in me and I advertised it in the
usual fashion, I was lovingly petted and coddled

and pitied in a most agreeable way and got a ration between meals besides.

It was human nature to want to get these riches, and I fell. I lied about the pin — advertising one when there wasn't any. You would have done it ; George Washington did it, anybody would have done it. During the first half of my life I never knew a child that was able to rise above that temptation and keep from telling that lie. Up to 1867 all the civilized children that were ever born into the world were liars—including George. Then the safety-pin came in and blocked the game. But is that reform worth anything? No ; for it is reform by force and has no virtue in it; it merely stops that form of lying, it doesn't impair the disposition to lie, by a shade. It is the cradle application of conversion by fire and sword, or of the temperance principle through prohibition.

To return to that early lie. They found no pin and they realized that another liar had been added to the world's supply. For by grace of a rare inspiration a quite commonplace but seldom noticed fact was borne in upon their understandings—that almost all lies are acts, and speech has no part in them. Then, if they examined a little further they recognized that all people are liars from the cradle onward, without exception, and that they begin to lie as soon as they wake in the morning, and keep it up without rest or refreshment until they go to sleep at night. If they arrived at that truth it probably grieved them—did, if they had been heedlessly and ignorantly educated by their books and teachers; for why should a person grieve over a thing which by the eternal law of his make he cannot help? He didn't invent the law; it is merely his business to obey it and keep still; join the universal conspiracy and keep so still that he shall deceive his fellow-conspirators into imagining that he doesn't know that the law exists. It is what we all do—we that know. I am speaking of the lie of silent assertion; we can tell it without saying a word, and we all do it—we that know. In the magnitude of its territorial spread it is one of the most majestic lies that the civilizations make it their sacred and anxious care to guard and watch and propagate.

For instance. It would not be possible for a humane and intelligent person to invent a rational excuse for slavery; yet you will remember that in the early days of the emancipation agitation in the North the agitators got but small help or countenance from any one. Argue and plead and pray as they might, they could not break the universal stillness that reigned, from pulpit and press all the way down to the bottom of society—the clammy stillness created and maintained by the lie of silent assertion—the silent assertion that there wasn't anything going on in which humane and intelligent people were interested.

From the beginning of the Dreyfus case to the end of it all France, except a couple of dozen moral paladins, lay under the smother of the silent-assertion lie that no wrong was being done to a persecuted and unoffending man. The like smother was over England lately, a good half of the population silently letting on that they were not aware that Mr. Chamberlain was trying to manufacture a war in South Africa and was willing to pay fancy prices for the materials.

Now there we have instances of three prominent ostensible civilizations working the silent-assertion lie. Could one find other instances in the three countries? I think so. Not so very many, perhaps, but say a billion — just so as to keep within bounds. Are those countries working that kind of lie, day in and day out, in thousands and thousands of varieties, without ever resting? Yes, we know that to be true. The universal conspiracy of the silent-assertion lie is hard at work always and everywhere, and always in the interest of a stupidity or a sham, never in the interest of a thing fine or respectable.

Is it the most timid and shabby of all lies? It seems to have the look of it. For ages and ages it has mutely labored in the interest of despotisms and aristocracies and chattel slaveries, and military slaveries, and religious slaveries, and has kept them alive; keeps them alive yet, here and there and yonder, all about the globe; and will go on keeping them alive until the silent-assertion lie retires from business—the silent assertion that nothing is going on which fair and intelligent men are aware of and are engaged by their duty to try to stop.

What I am arriving at is this: When whole races and peoples conspire to propagate gigantic mute lies in the interest of tyrannies and shams, why should we care anything about the trifling lies told by individuals? Why should we try to make it appear that abstention from lying is a virtue? Why should we want to beguile ourselves in that way? Why should we without shame help the nation lie, and then be ashamed to do a little lying on our own account? Why shouldn't we be honest and honorable, and lie every time we get a chance? That is to say, why shouldn't we be consistent, and either lie all the time or not at all? Why should we help the nation lie the whole day long and then object to telling one little individual private lie in our own interest to go to bed on? Just for the refreshment of it, I mean, and to take the rancid taste out of our mouth.

Here in England they have the oddest ways. They won't tell a spoken lie—nothing can persuade them. Except in a large moral interest, like politics or religion, I mean. To tell a spoken lie to get even the poorest little personal advantage out of it is a thing which is impossible to them. They make me ashamed of myself sometimes, they are so bigoted. They will not even tell a lie for the fun of it; they will not tell it when it hasn't even a suggestion of damage or advantage in it for any one. This has a restraining influence upon me in spite of reason, and I am always getting out of practice.

Of course, they tell all sorts of little unspoken lies, just like anybody; but they don't notice it until their attention is called to it. They have got me so that sometimes I never tell a verbal lie now except in a modified form; and even in the modified form they don't approve of it. Still, that is as far as I can go in the interest of the growing friendly relations between the two countries; I must keep some of my self-respect—and my health. I can live on a pretty low diet, but I can't get along on no sustenance at all.

Of course, there are times when these people

have to come out with a spoken lie, for that is a thing which happens to everybody once in a while, and would happen to the angels if they came down here much. Particularly to the angels, in fact, for the lies I speak of are self-sacrificing ones told for a generous object, not a mean one; but even when these people tell a lie of that sort it seems to scare them and unsettle their minds. It is a wonderful thing to see, and shows that they are all insane. In fact, it is a country which is full of the most interesting superstitions.

I have an English friend of twenty-five years' standing, and yesterday when we were coming down-town on top of the 'bus I happened to tell him a lie—a modified one, of course; a half-breed, a mulatto; I can't seem to tell any other kind now, the market is so flat. I was explaining to him how I got out of an embarrassment in Austria last year. I do not know what might have become of me if I hadn't happened to remember to tell the police that I belonged to the same family as the Prince of Wales. That made everything pleasant and they let me go; and apologized, too, and were ever so kind and obliging and polite, and couldn't do too much for me, and explained how the mistake came to be made, and promised to hang the officer that did it, and hoped I would let bygones be bygones and not say anything about it; and I said they could depend on me. My friend said, austerely:

"You call it a modified lie? Where is the modification?"

I explained that it lay in the form of my statement to the police.

"I didn't say I belonged to the royal family; I only said I belonged to the same family as the Prince — meaning the human family, of course; and if those people had had any penetration they would have known it. I can't go around furnishing brains to the police; it is not to be expected."

"How did you feel after that performance?"

"Well, of course I was distressed to find that the police had misunderstood me, but as long as I had not told any lie I knew there was no occasion to sit up nights and worry about it."

My friend struggled with the case several minutes, turning it over and examining it in his mind, then he said that so far as he could see the modification was itself a lie, it being a misleading reservation of an explanatory fact, and so I had told two lies instead of only one.

"I wouldn't have done it," said he; "I have never told a lie, and I should be very sorry to do such a thing."

Just then he lifted his hat and smiled a basketful of surprised and delighted smiles down at a gentleman who was passing in a hansom.

" Who was that, G—— ?"

" I don't know."

" Then why did you do that ?"

" Because I saw he thought he knew me and was expecting it of me. If I hadn't done it he would have been hurt. I didn't want to embarrass him before the whole street."

"Well, your heart was right, G——, and your act was right. What you did was kindly and courteous and beautiful; I would have done it myself; but it was a lie."

"A lie? I didn't say a word. How do you make it out?"

"I know you didn't speak, still you said to him very plainly and enthusiastically in dumb show, ' Hello! you in town? Awful glad to see you, old fellow; when did you get back?' Concealed in your actions was what you have called ' a misleading reservation of an explanatory fact'—the fact that you had never seen him before. You expressed joy in encountering him — a lie; and you made that reservation—another lie. It was my pair over again. But don't be troubled—we all do it."

Two hours later, at dinner, when quite other matters were being discussed, he told how he happened along once just in the nick of time to do a great service for a family who were old friends of his. The head of it had suddenly died in circumstances and surroundings of a ruinously disgraceful character. If known the facts would break the hearts of the innocent family and put upon them a load of unendurable shame. There was no help but in a giant lie, and he girded up his loins and told it.

"The family never found out, G——?"

"Never. In all these years they have never suspected. They were proud of him and always had reason to be; they are proud of him yet, and to them his memory is sacred and stainless and beautiful."

"They had a narrow escape, G——."

"Indeed they had."

"For the very next man that came along might have been one of these heartless and shameless truth-mongers. You have told the truth a million times in your life, G——, but that one golden lie atones for it all. Persevere."

Some may think me not strict enough in my morals, but that position is hardly tenable. There are many kinds of lying which I do not approve. I do not like an injurious lie, except when it injures somebody else; and I do not like the lie of bravado, nor the lie of virtuous ecstasy; the latter was affected by Bryant, the former by Carlyle.

Mr. Bryant said, "Truth crushed to earth will rise again." I have taken medals at thirteen world's fairs, and may claim to be not without capacity, but I never told as big a one as that Mr. Bryant was playing to the gallery; we all do it. Carlyle said, in substance, this — I do not remember the exact words: "This gospel is eternal — that a lie shall not live." I have a reverent affection for Carlyle's books, and have read his *Revolution* eight times; and so I prefer to think he was not entirely at himself when he told that one. To me it is plain that he said it in a moment of excitement, when chasing Americans out of his back-yard with brickbats. They used to go there and worship. At bottom he was probably fond of them, but he was always able to conceal it. He kept bricks for them, but he was not a good shot, and it is matter of history that when he fired they dodged, and carried off the brick; for as a nation we like relics, and so long as we get them we do not much care what the reliquary thinks about it. I am quite sure that when he told that large one about a lie not being able to live he had just missed an American and was over-excited. He told it above thirty years ago, but it is alive yet; alive, and very healthy and hearty, and

12

likely to outlive any fact in history. Carlyle was truthful when calm, but give him Americans enough and bricks enough and he could have taken medals himself.

As regards that time that George Washington told the truth, a word must be said, of course. It is the principal jewel in the crown of America, and it is but natural that we should work it for all it is worth, as Milton says in his "Lay of the Last Minstrel." It was a timely and judicious truth, and I should have told it myself in the circumstances. But I should have stopped there. It was a stately truth, a lofty truth—a Tower; and I think it was a mistake to go on and distract attention from its sublimity by building another Tower alongside of it fourteen times as high. I refer to his remark that he "could not lie." I should have fed that to the marines; or left it to Carlyle; it is just in his style. It would have taken a medal at any European fair, and would have got an Honorable Mention even at Chicago if it had been saved up. But let it pass; the Father of his Country was excited. I have been in those circumstances, and I recollect.

With the truth he told I have no objection to offer, as already indicated. I think it was not premeditated, but an inspiration. With his fine military mind, he had probably arranged to let his brother Edward in for the cherry-tree results, but by an inspiraton he saw his opportunity in time and took advantage of it. By telling the truth he could astonish his father; his father would tell the neighbors; the neighbors would spread it; it would travel to all firesides; in the end it would make him President, and not only that, but First President. He was a far-seeing boy and would be likely to think of these things. Therefore, to my mind, he stands justified for what he did. But not for the other Tower; it was a mistake. Still, I don't know about that; upon reflection I think perhaps it wasn't. For indeed it is that Tower that makes the other one live. If he hadn't said "I cannot tell a lie" there would have been no convulsion. That was the earthquake that rocked the planet. That is the kind of statement that lives forever, and a fact barnacled to it has a good chance to share its immortality.

To sum up, on the whole I am satisfied with things the way they are. There is a prejudice against the spoken lie, but none against any other, and by examination and mathematical computation I find that the proportion of the spoken lie to the other varities is as 1 to 22,894. Therefore the spoken lie is of no consequence, and it is not worth while to go around fussing about it and trying to make believe that it is an important matter. The silent colossal National Lie that is the support and confederate of all the tyrannies and shams and in-equalities and unfairnesses that afflict the peoples —that is the one to throw bricks and sermons at. But let us be judicious and let somebody else begin.

And then— But I have wandered from my text. How did I get out of my second lie? I think I got out with honor, but I cannot be sure, for it was a long time ago and some of the details have faded out of my memory. I recollect that I was reversed and stretched across some one's knee, and that something happened, but I cannot now remember what it was. I think there was music; but it is all dim now and blurred by the lapse of time, and this may be only a senile fancy.

IS HE LIVING OR IS HE DEAD?

I WAS spending the month of March, 1892, at Mentone, in the Riviera. At this retired spot one has all the advantages, privately, which are to be had at Monte Carlo and Nice, a few miles farther along, publicly. That is to say, one has the flooding sunshine, the balmy air, and the brilliant blue sea, without the marring additions of human pow-wow and fuss and feathers and display. Mentone is quiet, simple, restful, unpretentious; the rich and the gaudy do not come there. As a rule, I mean, the rich do not come there. Now and then a rich man comes, and I presently got acquainted with one of these. Partially to disguise him I will call him Smith. One day, in the Hôtel des Anglais, at the second breakfast, he exclaimed:

"Quick! Cast your eye on the man going out at the door. Take in every detail of him."

"Why?"

"Do you know who he is?"

"Yes. He spent several days here before you came. He is an old, retired, and very rich silk manufacturer from Lyons, they say, and I guess he is alone in the world, for he always looks sad and dreamy, and doesn't talk with anybody. His name is Theophile Magnan."

I supposed that Smith would now proceed to justify the large interest which he had shown in Monsieur Magnan, but, instead, he dropped into a brown study, and was apparently lost to me and to the rest of the world during some minutes. Now and then he passed his fingers through his flossy white hair, to assist his thinking, and meantime he allowed his breakfast to go on cooling. At last he said :

"No, it's gone ; I can't call it back."

"Can't call what back ?"

"It's one of Hans Andersen's beautiful little stories. But it's gone from me. Part of it is like this : A child has a caged bird, which it loves, but thoughtlessly neglects. The bird pours out its song unheard and unheeded ; but, in time, hunger and thirst assail the creature, and its song grows plaintive and feeble and finally ceases — the bird dies. The child comes, and is smitten to the heart with remorse ; then, with bitter tears and lamentations, it calls its mates, and they bury the bird with elaborate pomp and the tenderest grief, without knowing, poor things, that it isn't children only who starve poets to death and then spend enough on their funerals and monuments to have kept them alive and made them easy and comfortable. Now—"

But here we were interrupted. About ten that evening I ran across Smith, and he asked me up to his parlor to help him smoke and drink hot Scotch. It was a cosy place, with its comfortable chairs, its cheerful lamps, and its friendly open fire of seasoned olive-wood. To make everything perfect, there was the muffled booming of the surf outside. After the second Scotch and much lazy and contented chat, Smith said:

"Now we are properly primed—I to tell a curious history, and you to listen to it. It has been a secret for many years—a secret between me and three others; but I am going to break the seal now. Are you comfortable?"

"Perfectly. Go on."

Here follows what he told me:

"A long time ago I was a young artist—a very young artist, in fact—and I wandered about the country parts of France, sketching here and sketching there, and was presently joined by a couple of darling young Frenchmen who were at the same kind of thing that I was doing. We were as happy as we were poor, or as poor as we were happy — phrase it to suit yourself. Claude Frère and Carl Boulanger—these are the names of those boys; dear, dear fellows, and the sunniest spirits that ever laughed at poverty and had a noble good time in all weathers.

"At last we ran hard aground in a Breton village, and an artist as poor as ourselves took us in and literally saved us from starving—François Millet—

"'What! the *great* François Millet?'

"Great? He wasn't any greater than we were, then. He hadn't any fame, even in his own village; and he was so poor that he hadn't anything to feed us on but turnips, and even the turnips failed us sometimes. We four became fast friends, doting friends, inseparables. We painted away together with all our might, piling up stock, piling up stock, but very seldom getting rid of any of it. We had lovely times together; but, O my soul! how we were pinched now and then!

"For a little over two years this went on. At last, one day, Claude said:

"'Boys, we've come to the end. Do you understand that?—absolutely to the end. Everybody has struck—there's a league formed against us. I've been all around the village and it's just as I

tell you. They refuse to credit us for another centime until all the odds and ends are paid up.'

"This struck us cold. Every face was blank with
dismay. We realized that our circumstances were
desperate, now. There was a long silence. Finally,
Millet said, with a sigh :

"'Nothing occurs to me — nothing. Suggest
something, lads.'

"There was no response, unless a mournful silence may be called a response. Carl got up,
and walked nervously up and down a while, then
said :

"'It's a shame ! Look at these canvases:
stacks and stacks of as good pictures as anybody
in Europe paints — I don't care who he is. Yes,
and plenty of lounging strangers have said the
same—or nearly that, anyway.'

"'But didn't buy,' Millet said.

"'No matter, they said it ; and it's true, too.
Look at your "Angelus" there ! Will anybody
tell me—'

"'Pah, Carl—my "Angelus" ! I was offered five
francs for it.'

"'When ?'

"'Who offered it ?'

"'Where is he ?'

"'Why didn't you take it ?'

"'Come—don't all speak at once. I thought he would give more—I was sure of it—he looked it—so I asked him eight.'

"'Well—and then?'

"'He said he would call again.'

"'Thunder and lightning! Why, François—'

"'Oh, I know—I know! It was a mistake, and I was a fool. Boys, I meant for the best; you'll grant me that, and I—'

"'Why, certainly, we know that, bless your dear heart; but don't you be a fool again.'

"'I? I wish somebody would come along and offer us a cabbage for it—you'd see!'

"'A cabbage! Oh, don't name it—it makes my mouth water. Talk of things less trying.'

"'Boys,' said Carl, '*do* these pictures lack merit? Answer me that.'

"'No!'

"'Aren't they of very great and high merit? Answer me that.'

"'Yes.'

"'Of such great and high merit that, if an illustrious name were attached to them, they would sell at splendid prices. Isn't it so?'

"'Certainly it is. Nobody doubts that.'

"'But—I'm not joking—*isn't* it so?'

"'Why, of course it's so—and *we* are not joking.

But what of it? What of it? How does that concern us?'

" ' In this way, comrades—we'll *attach* an illustrious name to them !'

" The lively conversation stopped. The faces were turned inquiringly upon Carl. What sort of riddle might this be? Where was an illustrious name to be borrowed? And who was to borrow it?

"Carl sat down, and said :

" ' Now, I have a perfectly serious thing to propose. I think it is the only way to keep us out of the almshouse, and I believe it to be a perfectly sure way. I base this opinion upon certain multitudinous and long - established facts in human history. I believe my project will make us all rich.'

" ' Rich ! You've lost your mind.'

" ' No, I haven't.'

" ' Yes, you have—you've lost your mind. What do you *call* rich ?'

" ' A hundred thousand francs apiece.'

" ' He *has* lost his mind. I knew it.'

" ' Yes, he has. Carl, privation has been too much for you, and—'

" ' Carl, you want to take a pill and get right to bed.'

" ' Bandage him first — bandage his head, and then—'

" ' No, bandage his heels; his brains have been settling for weeks—I've noticed it.'

" ' Shut up !' said Millet, with ostensible severity, ' and let the boy say his say. Now, then—come out with your project, Carl. What is it ?'

" ' Well, then, by way of preamble I will ask you to note this fact in human history : that the merit of many a great artist has never been acknowledged until after he was starved and dead. This has happened so often that I make bold to found a law upon it. This law : that the merit of *every* great unknown and neglected artist must and will be recognized, and his pictures climb to high prices after his death. My project is this : we must cast lots—one of us must die.'

" The remark fell so calmly and so unexpectedly that we almost forgot to jump. Then there was a wild chorus of advice again—medical advice—for the help of Carl's brain ; but he waited patiently for the hilarity to calm down, then went on again with his project :

" ' Yes, one of us must die, to save the others— and himself. We will cast lots. The one chosen shall be illustrious, all of us shall be rich. Hold still, now—hold still ; don't interrupt—I tell you I know what I am talking about. Here is the idea. During the next three months the one who is to die shall paint with all his might, enlarge his stock all he can—not pictures, *no!* skeleton sketches, studies, parts of studies, fragments of studies, a dozen dabs of the brush on each—meaningless, of course, but *his*, with his cipher on them ; turn out fifty a day, each to contain some peculiarity or mannerism easily detectable as his—*they're* the things that sell, you know, and are collected at fabulous prices for the world's museums, after the great man is gone ; we'll have a ton of them ready—a ton ! And all that time the rest of us will be busy supporting the moribund, and working Paris and the dealers—preparations for the coming event, you know ; and when everything is hot and just right, we'll spring the death on them and have the notorious funeral. You get the idea ?'

" ' N–o ; at least, not qu—'

" ' Not quite ? Don't you see ? The man doesn't really die ; he changes his name and vanishes ; we bury a dummy, and cry over it, with all the world to help. And I—'

"But he wasn't allowed to finish. Everybody broke out into a rousing hurrah of applause ; and all jumped up and capered about the room and fell on each other's necks in transports of gratitude and joy. For hours we talked over the great plan, without ever feeling hungry ; and at last, when all the details had been arranged satisfactorily, we cast lots and Millet was elected—elected to die, as we called it. Then we scraped together those things which one never parts with until he is betting them against future wealth—keepsake trinkets and such-like—and these we pawned for enough to furnish us a frugal farewell supper and breakfast, and leave us a few francs over for travel, and a stake of turnips and such for Millet to live on for a few days.

"Next morning, early, the three of us cleared out, straightway after breakfast—on foot, of course. Each of us carried a dozen of Millet's small pictures, purposing to market them. Carl struck for Paris, where he would start the work of building up Millet's fame against the coming great day. Claude and I were to separate, and scatter abroad over France.

"Now, it will surprise you to know what an easy and comfortable thing we had. I walked two days before I began business. Then I began to sketch a villa in the outskirts of a big town—because I saw the proprietor standing on an upper veranda. He came down to look on—I thought he would. I worked swiftly, intending to keep him interested. Occasionally he fired off a little ejaculation of approbation, and by-and-by he spoke up with enthusiasm, and said I was a master!

"I put down my brush, reached into my satchel, fetched out a Millet, and pointed to the cipher in the corner. I said, proudly:

"'I suppose you recognize *that?* Well, he taught me! I should *think* I ought to know my trade!'

"The man looked guiltily embarrassed, and was silent. I said, sorrowfully:

"'You don't mean to intimate that you don't know the cipher of François Millet!'

"Of course he didn't know that cipher; but he was the gratefullest man you ever saw, just the same, for being let out of an uncomfortable place on such easy terms. He said:

"'No! Why, it *is* Millet's, sure enough! I don't know what I could have been thinking of. Of course I recognize it now.'

"Next, he wanted to buy it; but I said that although I wasn't rich I wasn't *that* poor. However, at last, I let him have it for eight hundred francs."

"Eight hundred!"

"Yes. Millet would have sold it for a pork chop. Yes, I got eight hundred francs for that little thing. I wish I could get it back for eighty thousand. But that time's gone by. I made a very nice picture of that man's house, and I wanted to offer it to him for ten francs, but that wouldn't answer, seeing I was the pupil of such a master, so I sold it to him for a hundred. I sent the eight hundred francs straight back to Millet from that town and struck out again next day.

"But I didn't walk—no. I rode. I have ridden ever since. I sold one picture every day, and never tried to sell two. I always said to my customer:

"'I am a fool to sell a picture of François Millet's at all, for that man is not going to live three months, and when he dies his pictures can't be had for love or money.'

"I took care to spread that little fact as far as I could, and prepare the world for the event.

"I take credit to myself for our plan of selling the pictures—it was mine. I suggested it that last evening when we were laying out our campaign, and all three of us agreed to give it a good fair trial before giving it up for some other. It succeeded with all of us. I walked only two days, Claude walked two — both of us afraid to make Millet celebrated too close to home — but Carl walked only half a day, the bright, conscienceless rascal, and after that he travelled like a duke.

" Every now and then we got in with a country editor and started an item around through the press ; not an item announcing that a new painter had been discovered, but an item which let on that everybody knew François Millet ; not an item praising him in any way, but merely a word concerning the present condition of the " master "— sometimes hopeful, sometimes despondent, but always tinged with fears for the worst. We always marked these paragraphs, and sent the papers to all the people who had bought pictures of us.

"Carl was soon in Paris, and he worked things with a high hand. He made friends with the correspondents, and got Millet's condition reported to England and all over the continent, and America, and everywhere.

"At the end of six weeks from the start, we three met in Paris and called a halt, and stopped sending back to Millet for additional pictures. The boom was so high, and everything so ripe, that we saw that it would be a mistake not to strike now, right away, without waiting any longer. So we wrote Millet to go to bed and begin to waste away pretty fast, for we should like him to die in ten days if he could get ready.

" Then we figured up and found that among us

13

we had sold eighty-five small pictures and studies, and had sixty-nine thousand francs to show for it. Carl had made the last sale and the most brilliant one of all. He sold the 'Angelus' for twenty-two hundred francs. How we did glorify him! — not foreseeing that a day was coming by-and-by when France would struggle to own it and a stranger would capture it for five hundred and fifty thousand, cash.

"We had a wind-up champagne supper that night, and next day Claude and I packed up and went off to nurse Millet through his last days and keep busybodies out of the house and send daily bulletins to Carl in Paris for publication in the papers of several continents for the information of a waiting world. The sad end came at last, and Carl was there in time to help in the final mournful rites.

"You remember that great funeral, and what a stir it made all over the globe, and how the illustrious of two worlds came to attend it and testify their sorrow. We four—still inseparable— carried the coffin, and would allow none to help. And we were right about that, because it hadn't anything in it but a wax figure, and any other coffin-bearers would have found fault with the weight. Yes, we same old four, who had lovingly shared privation together in the old hard times now gone forever, carried the cof—"

"Which four?"

"*We* four — for Millet helped to carry his own coffin. In disguise, you know. Disguised as a relative—distant relative."

"Astonishing!"

"But true, just the same. Well, you remember how the pictures went up. Money? We didn't know what to do with it. There's a man in Paris to-day who owns seventy Millet pictures. He paid us two million francs for them. And as for the bushels of sketches and studies which Millet shovelled out during the six weeks that we were on the road, well, it would astonish you to know the figure we sell them at nowadays — that is, when we consent to let one go!"

"It is a wonderful history, perfectly wonderful!"

"Yes—it amounts to that."

"Whatever became of Millet?"

"Can you keep a secret?"

"I can."

"Do you remember the man I called your attention to in the dining-room to-day? *That was François Millet.*"

"Great—"

"Scott! Yes. For once they didn't starve a

genius to death and then put into other pockets the rewards he should have had himself. *This* song-bird was not allowed to pipe out its heart unheard and then be paid with the cold pomp of a big funeral. We looked out for that."

THE ESQUIMAU MAIDEN'S ROMANCE

"YES, I will tell you anything about my life that you would like to know, Mr. Twain," she said, in her soft voice, and letting her honest eyes rest placidly upon my face, "for it is kind and good of you to like me and care to know about me."

She had been absently scraping blubber-grease from her cheeks with a small bone-knife and transferring it to her fur sleeve, while she watched the Aurora Borealis swing its flaming streamers out of the sky and wash the lonely snow-plain and the templed icebergs with the rich hues of the prism, a spectacle of almost intolerable splendor and beauty ; but now she shook off her reverie and prepared to give me the humble little history I had asked for. She settled herself comfortably on the block of ice which we were using as a sofa, and I made ready to listen.

She was a beautiful creature. I speak from the Esquimaux point of view. Others would have thought her a trifle over-plump. She was just twenty years old, and was held to be by far the most bewitching girl in her tribe. Even now, in the open air, with her cumbersome and shapeless fur coat and trousers and boots and vast hood, the beauty of her face was at least apparent; but her figure had to be taken on trust. Among all the guests who came and went, I had seen no girl at her father's hospitable trough who could be called her equal. Yet she was not spoiled. She was sweet and natural and sincere, and if she was aware that she was a belle, there was nothing about her ways to show that she possessed that knowledge.

She had been my daily comrade for a week now, and the better I knew her the better I liked her. She had been tenderly and carefully brought up, in an atmosphere of singularly rare refinement for the polar regions, for her father was the most important man of his tribe and ranked at the top of Esquimau cultivation. I made long dog - sledge trips across the mighty ice-floes with Lasca—that was her name — and found her company always pleasant and her conversation agreeable. I went fishing with her, but not in her perilous boat: I merely followed along on the ice and watched her strike her game with her fatally accurate spear. We went sealing together; several times I stood by while she and the family dug blubber from a stranded whale, and once I went part of the way when she was hunting a bear, but turned back before the finish, because at bottom I am afraid of bears.

However, she was ready to begin her story, now, and this is what she said :

"Our tribe had always been used to wander about from place to place over the frozen seas, like the other tribes, but my father got tired of that, two years ago, and built this great mansion of frozen snow-blocks—look at it; it is seven feet high and three or four times as long as any of the others—and here we have stayed ever since. He was very proud of his house, and that was reasonable, for if you have examined it with care you must have noticed how much finer and completer it is than houses usually are.   But if you have not, you must, for you will find it has luxurious appointments that are quite beyond the common.   For instance, in that end of it which you have called the 'parlor,' the raised platform for the accommodation of guests and the family at meals is the largest you have ever seen in any house—is it not so?"

"Yes, you are quite right, Lasca ; it is the largest; we have nothing resembling it in even the finest houses in the United States."   This admission made her eyes sparkle with pride and pleasure. I noted that, and took my cue.

"I thought it must have surprised you," she said. "And another thing: it is bedded far deeper in furs than is usual; all kinds of furs — seal, sea - otter, silver-gray fox, bear, marten, sable—every kind of fur in profusion; and the same with the ice-block sleeping-benches along the walls, which you call 'beds.' Are your platforms and sleeping-benches better provided at home?"

"Indeed, they are not, Lasca—they do not begin to be." That pleased her again. All she was thinking of was the *number* of furs her æsthetic father took the trouble to keep on hand, not their value. I could have told her that those masses of rich furs constituted wealth—or would in my country — but she would not have understood that; those were not the kind of things that ranked as riches with her people. I could have told her that the clothes she had on, or the every-day clothes of the commonest person about her, were worth twelve or fifteen hundred dollars, and that I was not acquainted with anybody at home who wore twelve-hundred dollar toilets to go fishing in; but she would not have understood it, so I said nothing. She resumed:

"And then the slop-tubs. We have two in the

parlor, and two in the rest of the house. It is very seldom that one has two in the parlor. Have you two in the parlor at home?"

The memory of those tubs made me gasp, but I recovered myself before she noticed, and said with effusion :

" Why, Lasca, it is a shame of me to expose my country, and you must not let it go further, for I am speaking to you in confidence ; but I give you my word of honor that not even the richest man in the city of New York has two slop-tubs in his drawing-room."

She clapped her fur-clad hands in innocent delight, and exclaimed :

" Oh, but you cannot mean it, you cannot *mean* it !"

" Indeed, I am in earnest, dear. There is Vanderbilt. Vanderbilt is almost the richest man in the whole world. Now, if I were on my dying bed, I could say to you that not even he has two in his drawing-room. Why, he hasn't even *one*—I wish I may die in my tracks if it isn't true."

Her lovely eyes stood wide with amazement, and she said, slowly, and with a sort of awe in her voice :

" How strange—how incredible—one is not able to realize it. Is he penurious ?"

"No—it isn't that. It isn't the expense he minds, but—er—well, you know, it would look like showing off. Yes, that is it, that is the idea ; he is a plain man in his way, and shrinks from display."

"Why, that humility is right enough," said Lasca, " if one does not carry it too far—but what does the place *look* like ?"

" Well, necessarily it looks pretty barren and unfinished, but—"

" I should think so ! I never heard anything like it.   Is it a fine house—that is, otherwise?"

" Pretty fine, yes.   It is very well thought of."

The girl was silent awhile, and sat dreamily gnawing a candle-end, apparently trying to think the thing out. At last she gave her head a little toss and spoke out her opinion with decision :

" Well, to my mind there's a breed of humility which is *itself* a species of showing-off, when you get down to the marrow of it ; and when a man is able to afford two slop-tubs in his parlor, and don't do it, it *may* be that he is truly humble-minded, but it's a hundred times more likely that he is just trying to strike the public eye. In my judgment, your Mr. Vanderbilt knows what he is about."

I tried to modify this verdict, feeling that a double slop-tub standard was not a fair one to try everybody by, although a sound enough one in its own habitat ; but the girl's head was set, and she was not to be persuaded. Presently she said :

" Do the rich people, with you, have as good sleeping-benches as ours, and made out of as nice broad ice-blocks ?"

" Well, they are pretty good — good enough— but they are not made of ice-blocks."

" I want to know ! *Why* aren't they made of ice-blocks ?"

I explained the difficulties in the way, and the expensiveness of ice in a country where you have to keep a sharp eye on your ice-man or your ice-bill will weigh more than your ice. Then she cried out :

" Dear me, do you *buy* your ice ?"

" We most surely do, dear."

She burst into a gale of guileless laughter, and said :

" Oh, I *never* heard of anything so silly ! My, there's plenty of it—it isn't worth anything. Why, there is a hundred miles of it in sight, right now. I wouldn't give a fish-bladder for the whole of it."

" Well, it's because you don't know how to value it, you little provincial muggins. If you had it in

New York in midsummer, you could buy all the whales in the market with it."

She looked at me doubtfully, and said :

" Are you speaking true ?"

" Absolutely.   I take my oath to it."

This made her thoughful.   Presently she said, with a little sigh :

" I wish *I* could live there."

I had merely meant to furnish her a standard of values which she could understand ; but my purpose had miscarried.   I had only given her the impression that whales were cheap and plenty in New York, and set her mouth to watering for them.   It seemed best to try to mitigate the evil which I had done, so I said :

" But you wouldn't care for whale-meat if you lived there.   Nobody does."

" What !"

" Indeed they don't."

" *Why* don't they ?"

" Wel-1-1, I hardly know.   It's prejudice, I think.   Yes, that is it—just prejudice.   I reckon somebody that hadn't anything better to do started a prejudice against it, some time or other, and once you get a caprice like that fairly going, you know, it will last no end of time."

" That is true—*perfectly* true," said the girl, re-

flectively. " Like our prejudice against soap, here—
our tribes had a prejudice against soap at first, you
know."

I glanced at her to see if she was in earnest.
Evidently she was. I hesitated, then said, cautiously :

" But pardon me. They *had* a prejudice against
soap ? Had ?"—with falling inflection.

" Yes—but that was only at first ; nobody would
eat it."

" Oh—I understand. I didn't get your idea before."

She resumed :

" It was just a prejudice. The first time soap
came here from the foreigners, nobody liked it ;
but as soon as it got to be fashionable, everybody
liked it, and now everybody has it that can afford
it. Are you fond of it ?"

" Yes, indeed ; I should die if I couldn't have
it—especially here. Do you like it ?"

" I just *adore* it ! Do you like candles ?"

" I regard them as an absolute necessity. Are
you fond of them ?"

Her eyes fairly danced, and she exclaimed :

" Oh ! Don't mention it ! Candles ! — and
soap !—"

" And fish-interiors !—"

" And train-oil !—"

" And slush !—"

" And whale-blubber !—"

" And carrion ! and sour-krout ! and beeswax !
and tar ! and turpentine ! and molasses ! and—"

" Don't — oh, don't — I shall expire with ecstasy !—"

" And then serve it all up in a slush-bucket, and
invite the neighbors and sail in !"

But this vision of an ideal feast was too much for
her, and she swooned away, poor thing.   I rubbed
snow in her face and brought her to, and after
a while got her excitement cooled down.   By-and-
by she drifted into her story again:

" So we began to live here, in the fine house.
But I was not happy.   The reason was this : I was
born for love ; for me there could be no true happiness without it.   I wanted to be loved for myself
alone.   I wanted an idol, and I wanted to be my
idol's idol ; nothing less than mutual idolatry would
satisfy my fervent nature.   I had suitors in plenty—
in over - plenty, indeed — but in each and every
case they had a fatal defect ; sooner or later I discovered that defect — not one of them failed to
betray it — it was not me they wanted, but my
wealth."

" Your wealth ?"

"Yes; for my father is much the richest man in this tribe—or in any tribe in these regions."

I wondered what her father's wealth consisted of. It couldn't be the house—anybody could build its mate. It couldn't be the furs — they were not valued. It couldn't be the sledge, the dogs, the harpoons, the boat, the bone fish-hooks and needles, and such things—no, these were not wealth. Then what could it be that made this man so rich and brought this swarm of sordid suitors to his house? It seemed to me, finally, that the best way to find out would be to ask. So I did it. The girl was so manifestly gratified by the question that I saw she had been aching to have me ask it. She was suffering fully as much to tell as I was to know. She snuggled confidentially up to me and said :

"Guess how much he is worth—you never can!"

I pretended to consider the matter deeply, she watching my anxious and laboring countenance with a devouring and delighted interest ; and when, at last, I gave it up and begged her to appease my longing by telling me herself how much this polar Vanderbilt was worth, she put her mouth close to my ear and whispered, impressively :

"*Twenty-two fish-hooks*—not bone, but foreign— *made out of real iron !*"

Then she sprang back dramatically, to observe

the effect. I did my level best not to disappoint
her. I turned pale and murmured :

"Great Scott !"

"It's as true as you live, Mr. Twain !"

"Lasca, you are deceiving me — you cannot
mean it."

She was frightened and troubled. She exclaimed :

"Mr. Twain, every word of it is true — every
word. You believe me—you *do* believe me, now
don't you? *Say* you believe me—*do* say you believe me !"

"I—well, yes, I do—I am *trying* to. But it was
all so *sudden*. So sudden and prostrating. You
shouldn't do such a thing in that sudden way.
It—"

"Oh, I'm *so* sorry! If I had only thought—"

"Well, it's all right, and I don't blame you any
more, for you are young and thoughtless, and of
course you couldn't foresee what an effect—"

"But oh, dear, I ought certainly to have *known*
better. Why—"

"You see, Lasca, if you had said five or six
hooks, to start with, and then gradually—"

"Oh, I see, I see—then gradually added one,
and then two, and then—ah, why couldn't I have
thought of that !"

" Never mind, child, it's all right—I am better now—I shall be over it in a little while. *But*—to spring the whole twenty-two on a person unprepared and not very strong anyway—"

" Oh, it *was* a crime! But you forgive me—say you forgive me. Do!"

After harvesting a good deal of very pleasant coaxing and petting and persuading, I forgave her and she was happy again, and by-and-by she got under way with her narrative once more. I presently discovered that the family treasury contained still another feature—a jewel of some sort, apparently—and that she was trying to get around speaking squarely about it, lest I get paralyzed again. But I wanted to know about that thing, too, and urged her to tell me what it was. She was afraid. But I insisted, and said I would brace myself this time and be prepared, then the shock would not hurt me. She was full of misgivings, but the temptation to reveal that marvel to me and enjoy my astonishment and admiration was too strong for her, and she confessed that she had it on her person, and said that if I was *sure* I was prepared—and so on and so on—and with that she reached into her bosom and brought out a battered square of brass, watching my eye anxiously the while. I fell over against her in a quite well-acted faint,

14

which delighted her heart and nearly frightened it out of her, too, at the same time. When I came to and got calm, she was eager to know what I thought of her jewel.

"What do I think of it? I think it is the most exquisite thing I ever saw."

"Do you really? How nice of you to say that! But it *is* a love, now isn't it?"

"Well, I should say so! I'd rather own it than the equator."

"I thought you would admire it," she said. "I think it is *so* lovely. And there isn't another one in all these latitudes. People have come all the way from the Open Polar Sea to look at it. Did you ever see one before?"

I said no, this was the first one I had ever seen. It cost me a pang to tell that generous lie, for I had seen a million of them in my time, this humble jewel of hers being nothing but a battered old New York Central baggage-check.

"Land!" said I, "you don't go about with it on your person this way, alone and with no protection, not even a dog?"

"Ssh! not so loud," she said. "Nobody knows I carry it with me. They think it is in papa's treasury. That is where it generally is."

"Where is the treasury?"

It was a blunt question, and for a moment she looked startled and a little suspicious, but I said:

"Oh, come, don't you be afraid about me. At home we have seventy millions of people, and although I say it myself that shouldn't, there is not one person among them all but would trust me with untold fish-hooks."

This reassured her, and she told me where the hooks were hidden in the house. Then she wandered from her course to brag a little about the size of the sheets of transparent ice that formed the windows of the mansion, and asked me if I had ever seen their like at home, and I came right out frankly and confessed that I hadn't, which pleased her more than she could find words to dress her gratification in. It was so easy to please her, and such a pleasure to do it that I went on and said—

"Ah, Lasca, you *are* a fortunate girl!—this beautiful house, this dainty jewel, that rich treasure, all this elegant snow, and sumptuous icebergs and limitless sterility, and public bears and walruses, and noble freedom and largeness, and everybody's admiring eyes upon you, and everybody's homage and respect at your command without the asking; young, rich, beautiful, sought, courted, envied, not a requirement unsatisfied, not a desire ungratified, nothing to wish for that you cannot have—it is im-measurable good-fortune ! I have seen myriads of girls, but none of whom these extraordinary things could be truthfully said but you alone. And you are worthy—worthy of it all, Lasca—I believe it in my heart."

It made her infinitely proud and happy to hear me say this, and she thanked me over and over again for that closing remark, and her voice and eyes showed that she was touched. Presently she said :

" Still, it is not all sunshine — there is a cloudy side. The burden of wealth is a heavy one to bear. Sometimes I have doubted if it were not better to be poor — at least not inordinately rich. It pains me to see neighboring tribesmen stare as they pass by, and overhear them say, reverently, one to another, ' There—that is she—the million-aire's daughter !' And sometimes they say sor-rowfully, ' She is rolling in fish-hooks, and I — I have nothing.' It breaks my heart. When I was a child and we were poor, we slept with the door open, if we chose, but now—now we have to have a night-watchman. In those days my father was gentle and courteous to all ; but now he is austere and haughty, and cannot abide familiarity. Once his family were his sole thought, but now he goes about thinking of his fish-hooks all the time. And his wealth makes everybody cringing and obsequious to him. Formerly nobody laughed at his jokes, they being always stale and far-fetched and poor, and destitute of the one element that can really justify a joke — the element of humor; but now everybody laughs and cackles at those dismal things, and if any fails to do it my father is deeply displeased, and shows it. Formerly his opinion was not sought upon any matter and was not valuable when he volunteered it; it has that infirmity yet, but, nevertheless, it is sought by all and applauded by all — and he helps do the applauding himself, having no true delicacy and a plentiful want of tact. He has lowered the tone of all our tribe. Once they were a frank and manly race, now they are measly hypocrites, and sodden with servility. In my heart of hearts I hate all the ways of millionaires! Our tribe was once plain, simple folk, and content with the bone fish-hooks of their fathers; now they are eaten up with avarice and would sacrifice every sentiment of honor and honesty to possess themselves of the debasing iron fish-hooks of the foreigner. However, I must not dwell on these sad things. As I have said, it was my dream to be loved for myself alone.

"At last, this dream seemed about to be fulfilled.

A stranger came by, one day, who said his name was Kalula. I told him my name, and he said he loved me. My heart gave a great bound of gratitude and pleasure, for I had loved him at sight, and now I said so. He took me to his breast and said he would not wish to be happier than he was now. We went strolling together far over the ice-floes, telling all about each other, and planning, oh, the loveliest future! When we were tired at last we sat down and ate, for he had soap and candles and I had brought along some blubber. We were hungry, and nothing was ever so good.

" He belonged to a tribe whose haunts were far to the north, and I found that he had never heard of my father, which rejoiced me exceedingly. I mean he had heard of the millionaire, but had never heard his name—so, you see, he could not know that I was the heiress. You may be sure that I did not tell him. I was loved for myself at last, and was satisfied. I was so happy—oh, happier than you can think!

" By-and-by it was toward supper time, and I led him home. As we approached our house he was amazed, and cried out:

" 'How splendid! Is *that* your father's?'

" It gave me a pang to hear that tone and see that admiring light in his eye, but the feeling quickly passed away, for I loved him so, and he looked so handsome and noble. All my family of aunts and uncles and cousins were pleased with him, and many guests were called in, and the house was shut up tight and the rag lamps lighted, and when everything was hot and comfortable and suffocating, we began a joyous feast in celebration of my betrothal.

"When the feast was over, my father's vanity overcame him, and he could not resist the temptation to show off his riches and let Kalula see what grand good-fortune he had stumbled into — and mainly, of course, he wanted to enjoy the poor man's amazement. I could have cried — but it would have done no good to try to dissuade my father, so I said nothing, but merely sat there and suffered.

"My father went straight to the hiding-place, in full sight of everybody, and got out the fish-hooks and brought them and flung them scatteringly over my head, so that they fell in glittering confusion on the platform at my lover's knee.

"Of course, the astounding spectacle took the poor lad's breath away. He could only stare in stupid astonishment, and wonder how a single individual could possess such incredible riches.

Then presently he glanced brilliantly up and exclaimed :

"'Ah, it is *you* who are the renowned millionaire !'

"My father and all the rest burst into shouts of happy laughter, and when my father gathered the treasure carelessly up as if it might be mere rubbish and of no consequence, and carried it back to its place, poor Kalula's surprise was a study. He said :

"'Is it possible that you put such things away without counting them ?'

"My father delivered a vain-glorious horse-laugh, and said :

"'Well, truly, a body may know *you* have never been rich, since a mere matter of a fish - hook or two is such a mighty matter in your eyes.'

"Kalula was confused, and hung his head, but said :

"'Ah, indeed, sir, I was never worth the value of the barb of one of those precious things, and I have never seen any man before who was so rich in them as to render the counting of his hoard worth while, since the wealthiest man I have ever known, till now, was possessed of but three.'

"My foolish father roared again with jejune delight, and allowed the impression to remain that he was not accustomed to count his hooks and keep sharp watch over them. He was showing off, you see. Count them? Why, he counted them every day!

"I had met and got acquainted with my darling just at dawn; I had brought him home just at dark, three hours afterward — for the days were shortening toward the six-months night at that time. We kept up the festivities many hours; then, at last, the guests departed and the rest of us distributed ourselves along the walls on sleeping-benches, and soon all were steeped in dreams but me. I was too happy, too excited, to sleep. After I had lain quiet a long, long time, a dim form passed by me and was swallowed up in the gloom that pervaded the farther end of the house. I could not make out who it was, or whether it was man or woman. Presently that figure or another one passed me going the other way. I wondered what it all meant, but wondering did no good; and while I was still wondering I fell asleep.

"I do not know how long I slept, but at last I came suddenly broad awake and heard my father say in a terrible voice, 'By the great Snow God, there's a fish-hook gone!' Something told me that that meant sorrow for me, and the blood in my veins turned cold. The presentiment was con-

firmed in the same instant : my father shouted,
' Up, everybody, and seize the stranger !' Then
there was an outburst of cries and curses from all
sides, and a wild rush of dim forms through the
obscurity. I flew to my beloved's help, but what
could I do but wait and wring my hands?—he was
already fenced away from me by a living wall, he
was being bound hand and foot. Not until he was
secured would they let me get to him. I flung
myself upon his poor insulted form and cried my
grief out upon his breast while my father and all
my family scoffed at me and heaped threats and
shameful epithets upon him. He bore his ill usage
with a tranquil dignity which endeared him to me
more than ever and made me proud and happy to
suffer with him and for him. I heard my father
order that the elders of the tribe be called together
to try my Kalula for his life.

"' What ?' I said, ' before any search has been
made for the lost hook?'

"' Lost hook !' they all shouted, in derision ; and
my father added, mockingly, ' Stand back, everybody, and be properly serious — she is going to
hunt up that *lost* hook ; oh, without doubt she will
find it !'—whereat they all laughed again.

"I was not disturbed—I had no fears, no doubts.
I said :

"'It is for you to laugh now; it is your turn. But ours is coming; wait and see.'

"I got a rag-lamp. I thought I should find that miserable thing in one little moment; and I set about the matter with such confidence that those people grew grave, beginning to suspect that perhaps they had been too hasty. But, alas and alas!—oh, the bitterness of that search! *at last I gave up* There was deep silence while one might count his fingers ten or twelve times, then my heart began to sink, and around me the mockings began again, and grew steadily louder and more assured, until at last, when I gave up, they burst into volley after volley of cruel laughter.

"None will ever know what I suffered then. But my love was my support and my strength, and I took my rightful place at my Kalula's side, and put my arm about his neck, and whispered in his ear, saying:

"'You are innocent, my own—that I know; but say it to me yourself, for my comfort, then I can bear whatever is in store for us.'

"He answered:

"'As surely as I stand upon the brink of death at this moment, I am innocent. Be comforted, then, O bruised heart; be at peace, O thou breath of my nostrils, life of my life!'

"'Now, then, let the elders come!'—and as I

said the words there was a gathering sound of crunching snow outside, and then a vision of stooping forms filing in at the door—the elders.

"My father formally accused the prisoner, and detailed the happenings of the night. He said that the watchman was outside the door, and that in the house were none but the family and the stranger. 'Would the family steal their own property?' He paused. The elders sat silent many minutes; at last, one after another said to his neighbor, 'This looks bad for the stranger'—sorrowful words for me to hear. Then my father sat down. O miserable, miserable me! at that very moment I could have proved my darling innocent, but I did not know it!

"The chief of the court asked:

"'Is there any here to defend the prisoner?'

"I rose and said:

"'Why should *he* steal that hook, or any or all of them? In another day he would have been heir to the whole!'

"I stood waiting. There was a long silence, the steam from the many breaths rising about me like a fog. At last, one elder after another nodded his head slowly several times, and muttered, 'There is force in what the child has said.' Oh, the heart-lift that was in those words!—so transient, but, oh, so precious! I sat down.

" 'If any would say further, let him speak now, or after hold his peace,' said the chief of the court.

" My father rose and said :

" ' In the night a form passed by me in the gloom, going toward the treasury, and presently returned. I think, now, it was the stranger.'

" Oh, I was like to swoon! I had supposed that that was my secret ; not the grip of the great Ice God himself could have dragged it out of my heart. The chief of the court said sternly to my poor Kalula :

" ' Speak !'

" Kalula hesitated, then answered :

" ' It was I. I could not sleep for thinking of the beautiful hooks. I went there and kissed them and fondled them, to appease my spirit and drown it in a harmless joy, then I put them back. I may have dropped one, but I stole none.'

" Oh, a fatal admission to make in such a place ! There was an awful hush. I knew he had pronounced his own doom, and that all was over. On every face you could see the words hieroglyphed : ' It is a confession !—and paltry, lame, and thin.'

" I sat drawing in my breath in faint gasps— and waiting. Presently, I heard the solemn words

I knew were coming; and each word, as it came, was a knife in my heart:

"'It is the command of the court that the accused be subjected to the *trial by water*.'

"Oh, curses be upon the head of him who brought 'trial by water' to our land! It came, generations ago, from some far country that lies none knows where. Before that, our fathers used augury and other unsure methods of trial, and doubtless some poor, guilty creatures escaped with their lives sometimes; but it is not so with trial by water, which is an invention by wiser men than we poor, ignorant savages are. By it the innocent are proved innocent, without doubt or question, for they drown; and the guilty are proven guilty with the same certainty, for they do not drown. My heart was breaking in my bosom, for I said, 'He is innocent, and he will go down under the waves and I shall never see him more.'

"I never left his side after that. I mourned in his arms all the precious hours, and he poured out the deep stream of his love upon me, and oh, I was so miserable and so happy! At last, they tore him from me, and I followed sobbing after them, and saw them fling him into the sea—then I covered my face with my hands. Agony? Oh, I know the deepest deeps of that word!

"The next moment the people burst into a shout of malicious joy, and I took away my hands, startled. Oh, bitter sight — he was *swimming!* My heart turned instantly to stone, to ice. I said, 'He was guilty, and he lied to me!' I turned my back in scorn and went my way homeward.

"They took him far out to sea and set him on an iceberg that was drifting southward in the great waters. Then my family came home, and my father said to me:

"'Your thief sent his dying message to you, saying, "Tell her I am innocent, and that all the days and all the hours and all the minutes while I starve and perish I shall love her and think of her and bless the day that gave me sight of her sweet face." Quite pretty, even poetical!'

"I said, 'He is dirt—let me never hear mention of him again.' And oh, to think—he *was* innocent all the time!

"Nine months—nine dull, sad months—went by, and at last came the day of the Great Annual Sacrifice, when all the maidens of the tribe wash their faces and comb their hair. With the first sweep of my comb, out came the fatal fish-hook from where it had been all those months nestling, and I fell fainting into the arms of my remorseful father! Groaning, he said, 'We murdered him, and I shall

never smile again !' He has kept his word. Listen :
from that day to this not a month goes by that I
do not comb my hair.   But oh, where is the good
of it all now !"

So ended the poor maid's humble little tale—
whereby we learn that since a hundred million dollars in New York and twenty-two fish-hooks on the
border of the Arctic Circle represent the same
financial supremacy, a man in straitened circumstances is a fool to stay in New York when he can
buy ten cents' worth of fish-hooks and emigrate.

HOW TO TELL A STORY

THE HUMOROUS STORY AN AMERICAN DEVELOPMENT—
ITS DIFFERENCE FROM COMIC AND WITTY STORIES

I DO not claim that I can tell a story as it ought to be told. I only claim to know how a story ought to be told, for I have been almost daily in the company of the most expert story-tellers for many years.

There are several kinds of stories, but only one difficult kind—the humorous. I will talk mainly about that one. The humorous story is American, the comic story is English, the witty story is French. The humorous story depends for its effect upon the *manner* of the telling; the comic story and the witty story upon the *matter*.

The humorous story may be spun out to great length, and may wander around as much as it pleases, and arrive nowhere in particular; but the comic and witty stories must be brief and end with a point. The humorous story bubbles gently along, the others burst.

15

The humorous story is strictly a work of art—
high and delicate art—and only an artist can tell
it; but no art is necessary in telling the comic and
the witty story; anybody can do it. The art of
telling a humorous story—understand, I mean by
word of mouth, not print—was created in America,
and has remained at home.

The humorous story is told gravely; the teller
does his best to conceal the fact that he even dimly suspects that there is anything funny about it;
but the teller of the comic story tells you before-
hand that it is one of the funniest things he has
ever heard, then tells it with eager delight, and is
the first person to laugh when he gets through.
And sometimes, if he has had good success, he is
so glad and happy that he will repeat the "nub" of
it and glance around from face to face, collecting
applause, and then repeat it again. It is a pathetic
thing to see.

Very often, of course, the rambling and disjointed
humorous story finishes with a nub, point, snapper,
or whatever you like to call it. Then the listener
must be alert, for in many cases the teller will divert
attention from that nub by dropping it in a carefully casual and indifferent way, with the pretence
that he does not know it is a nub.

Artemus Ward used that trick a good deal; then,

when the belated audience presently caught the joke, he would look up with innocent surprise, as if wondering what they had found to laugh at. Dan Setchell used it before him, Nye and Riley and others use it to-day.

But the teller of the comic story does not slur the nub; he shouts it at you—every time. And when he prints it, in England, France, Germany, and Italy, he italicizes it, puts some whooping exclamation-points after it, and sometimes explains it in a parenthesis. All of which is very depressing, and makes one want to renounce joking and lead a better life.

Let me set down an instance of the comic method, using an anecdote which has been popular all over the world for twelve or fifteen hundred years. The teller tells it in this way:

THE WOUNDED SOLDIER

In the course of a certain battle a soldier whose leg had been shot off appealed to another soldier who was hurrying by to carry him to the rear, informing him at the same time of the loss which he had sustained; whereupon the generous son of Mars, shouldering the unfortunate, proceeded to carry out his desire. The bullets and cannon-balls were flying in all directions, and presently one of the latter took the wounded man's head off—without, however, his deliverer being aware of it. In no long time he was hailed by an officer, who said:

"Where are you going with that carcass?"

"To the rear, sir—he's lost his leg!"

"His leg, forsooth?" responded the astonished officer; "you mean his head, you booby."

Whereupon the soldier dispossessed himself of his burden, and stood looking down upon it in great perplexity. At length he said:

"It is true, sir, just as you have said." Then after a pause he added, "*But he* TOLD *me* IT WAS HIS LEG!!!!!"

Here the narrator bursts into explosion after explosion of thunderous horse-laughter, repeating that nub from time to time through his gaspings and shriekings and suffocatings.

It takes only a minute and a half to tell that in its comic-story form; and isn't worth the telling, after all. Put into the humorous-story form it takes ten minutes, and is about the funniest thing I have ever listened to—as James Whitcomb Riley tells it.

He tells it in the character of a dull-witted old farmer who has just heard it for the first time, thinks it is unspeakably funny, and is trying to repeat it to a neighbor. But he can't remember it; so he gets all mixed up and wanders hopelessly round and round, putting in tedious details that don't belong in the tale and only retard it; taking them out conscientiously and putting in others that are just as useless; making minor mistakes now and then and stopping to correct them and explain how he came to make them; remembering things which he forgot to put in in their proper place and going back to put them in there; stopping his narrative a good while in order to try to recall the name of the soldier that was hurt, and finally remembering that the soldier's name was not mentioned, and remarking placidly that the name is of no real importance, anyway—better, of course, if one knew it, but not essential, after all—and so on, and so on, and so on.

The teller is innocent and happy and pleased with himself, and has to stop every little while to hold himself in and keep from laughing outright; and does hold in, but his body quakes in a jelly-like way with interior chuckles; and at the end of the ten minutes the audience have laughed until they are exhausted, and the tears are running down their faces.

The simplicity and innocence and sincerity and unconsciousness of the old farmer are perfectly simulated, and the result is a performance which is thoroughly charming and delicious. This is art— and fine and beautiful, and only a master can compass it; but a machine could tell the other story.

To string incongruities and absurdities together in a wandering and sometimes purposeless way, and seem innocently unaware that they are absurdities, is the basis of the American art, if my position is correct. Another feature is the slurring of the point. A third is the dropping of a studied remark apparently without knowing it, as if one were thinking aloud. The fourth and last is the pause.

Artemus Ward dealt in numbers three and four a good deal. He would begin to tell with great animation something which he seemed to think was wonderful; then lose confidence, and after an apparently absent-minded pause add an incongruous remark in a soliloquizing way; and that was the remark intended to explode the mine—and it did.

For instance, he would say eagerly, excitedly, "I once knew a man in New Zealand who hadn't a tooth in his head"—here his animation would die out; a silent, reflective pause would follow, then he would say dreamily, and as if to himself,

" and yet that man could beat a drum better than any man I ever saw."

The pause is an exceedingly important feature in any kind of story, and a frequently recurring feature, too. It is a dainty thing, and delicate, and also uncertain and treacherous; for it must be exactly the right length—no more and no less—or it fails of its purpose and makes trouble. If the pause is too short the impressive point is passed, and the audience have had time to divine that a surprise is intended—and then you can't surprise them, of course.

On the platform I used to tell a negro ghost story that had a pause in front of the snapper on the end, and that pause was the most important thing in the whole story. If I got it the right length precisely, I could spring the finishing ejaculation with effect enough to make some impressible girl deliver a startled little yelp and jump out of her seat—and that was what I was after. This story was called " The Golden Arm," and was told in this fashion. You can practise with it yourself —and mind you look out for the pause and get it right.

THE GOLDEN ARM

Once 'pon a time dey wuz a monsus mean man, en he live 'way out in de prairie all 'lone by hisself, 'cep'n he had a wife. En bimeby she died, en he tuk en toted her way out dah in de prairie en buried her. Well, she had a golden arm—all solid gold, fum de shoulder down. He wuz pow'ful mean—pow'ful; en dat night he couldn't sleep, caze he want dat golden arm so bad.

When it come midnight he couldn't stan' it no mo'; so he git up, he did, en tuck his lantern en shoved out thoo de storm en dug her up en got de golden arm; en he bent his head down 'gin de win', en plowed en plowed en plowed thoo de snow. Den all on a sudden he stop (make a considerable pause here, and look startled, and take a listening attitude) en say: "My *lan'*, what's dat!"

En he listen—en listen—en de win' say (set your teeth together and imitate the wailing and wheezing singsong of the wind), " Bzzz-z-zzz "—en den, way back yonder whah de grave is, he hear a *voice!*—he hear a voice all mix' up in de win'—can't hardly tell 'em 'part—" Bzzz-zzz—W-h-o—g-o-t—m-y—g-o-l-d-e-n *arm?*—zzz—zzz—W-h-o g-o-t m-y g-o-l-d-e-n *arm?*" (You must begin to shiver violently now.)

En he begin to shiver en shake, en say, "Oh, my! *Oh*, my lan'!" en de win' blow de lantern out, en de snow en sleet blow in his face en mos' choke him, en he start a-plowin' knee-deep toward home mos' dead, he so sk'yerd—en pooty soon he hear de voice agin, en (pause) it 'us comin' *after* him! " Bzzz — zzz—zzz —W-h-o—g-o-t—m-y—g-o-l-d-e-n —*arm?*"

When he git to de pasture he hear it agin—closter now, en a-*comin!*—a-comin' back dah in de dark en de storm—(repeat the wind and the voice).   When he git to de house he rush up-stairs en jump in de bed en kiver up, head and years, en lay dah shiverin' en shakin'—en den way out dah he hear it *agin!* —en a-*comin'!*   En bimeby he hear (pause—awed, listening attitude)—pat—pat—pat—*hit's a-comin' up-stairs!*   Den he hear de latch, en he *know* it's in de room!

Den pooty soon he know it's a-*stannin' by de bed!* (Pause.)   Den—he know it's a-*bendin' down over him*—en he cain't skasely git his breath!   Den— den—he seem to feel someth'n *c-o-l-d*, right down 'most agin his head!   (Pause.)

Den de voice say, *right at his year,* " W-h-o—g-o-t —m-y—g-o-l-d-e-n *arm?*"   (You must wail it out very plaintively and accusingly; then you stare steadily and impressively into the face of the farthest-gone auditor—a girl, preferably—and let that awe-inspiring pause begin to build itself in the deep hush.   When it has reached exactly the right length, jump suddenly at that girl and yell, " *You've* got it!"

If you've got the *pause* right, she'll fetch a dear little yelp and spring right out of her shoes. But you *must* get the pause right; and you will find it the most troublesome and aggravating and uncertain thing you ever undertook.)

ABOUT PLAY-ACTING

I

I HAVE a project to suggest. But first I will write a chapter of introduction.

I have just been witnessing a remarkable play, here at the Burg Theatre in Vienna. I do not know of any play that much resembles it. In fact, it is such a departure from the common laws of the drama that the name "play" doesn't seem to fit it quite snugly. However, whatever else it may be, it is in any case a great and stately metaphysical poem, and deeply fascinating. "Deeply fascinating" is the right term: for the audience sat four hours and five minutes without thrice breaking into applause, except at the close of each act; sat rapt and silent—fascinated. This piece is "The Master of Palmyra." It is twenty years old; yet I doubt if you have ever heard of it. It is by Wilbrandt, and is his masterpiece and the work which is to make his name permanent in German literature. It has never been played anywhere except in Berlin and in the great Burg Theatre in Vienna. Yet whenever it is put on the stage it packs the house, and the free list is suspended. I know people who have seen it ten times; they know the most of it by heart; they do not tire of it; and they say they shall still be quite willing to go and sit under its spell whenever they get the opportunity.

There is a dash of metempsychosis in it—and it is the strength of the piece. The play gave me the sense of the passage of a dimly connected procession of dream-pictures. The scene of it is Palmyra in Roman times. It covers a wide stretch of time—I don't know how many years—and in the course of it the chief actress is reincarnated several times: four times she is a more or less young woman, and once she is a lad. In the first act she is *Zoe*—a Christian girl who has wandered across the desert from Damascus to try to Christianize the Zeus-worshipping pagans of Palmyra. In this character she is wholly spiritual, a religious enthusiast, a devotee who covets martyrdom—and gets it.

After many years she appears in the second act as *Phœbe*, a graceful and beautiful young light-o'-love from Rome, whose soul is all for the shows and luxuries and delights of this life—a dainty and capricious featherhead, a creature of shower and sunshine, a spoiled child, but a charming one. In the third act, after an interval of many years, she reappears as *Persida*, mother of a daughter in the fresh bloom of youth. She is now a sort of combination of her two earlier selves: in religious loyalty and subjection she is *Zoe;* in triviality of character and shallowness of judgment—together with a touch of vanity in dress—she is *Phœbe*.

After a lapse of years she appears in the fourth act as *Nymphas*, a beautiful boy, in whose character the previous incarnations are engagingly mixed.

And after another stretch of years all these heredities are joined in the *Zenobia* of the fifth act— a person of gravity, dignity, sweetness, with a heart filled with compassion for all who suffer, and a hand prompt to put into practical form the heart's benignant impulses.

You will easily concede that the actress who proposes to discriminate nicely these five characters, and play them to the satisfaction of a cultivated and exacting audience, has her work cut out for her. Mme. Hohenfels has made these parts her peculiar property; and she is well able to meet all the requirements. You perceive, now, where the chief part of the absorbing fascination of this piece lies; it is in watching this extraordinary artist melt these five characters into each other—grow, shade by shade, out of one and into another through a stretch of four hours and five minutes.

There are a number of curious and interesting features in this piece. For instance, its hero, *Appelles*, young, handsome, vigorous, in the first act, remains so all through the long flight of years covered by the five acts. Other men, young in the first act, are touched with gray in the second, are old and racked with infirmities in the third; in the fourth, all but one are gone to their long home, and he is a blind and helpless hulk of ninety or a hundred years. It indicates that the stretch of time covered by the piece is seventy years or more. The scenery undergoes decay, too—the decay of age, assisted and perfected by a conflagration. The fine new temples and palaces of the second act are by-and-by a wreck of crumbled walls and prostrate columns, mouldy, grass-grown, and desolate; but their former selves are still recognizable in their ruins. The aging men and the aging scenery together convey a profound illusion of that long lapse of time: they make you live it yourself! You leave the theatre with the weight of a century upon you.

Another strong effect: Death, in person, walks about the stage in every act. So far as I could make out, he was supposedly not visible to any excepting two persons—the one he came for and *Appelles*. He used various costumes: but there was always more black about them than any other tint; and so they were always sombre. Also they were always deeply impressive and, indeed, awe-inspiring. The face was not subjected to changes, but remained the same, first and last—a ghastly white. To me he was always welcome, he seemed so real —the actual Death, not a play-acting artificiality. He was of a solemn and stately carriage; and he had a deep voice, and used it with a noble dignity. Wherever there was a turmoil of merry-making or fighting or feasting or chaffing or quarrelling, or a gilded pageant, or other manifestation of our trivial and fleeting life, into it drifted that black figure with the corpse-face, and looked its fateful look and passed on; leaving its victim shuddering and smitten. And always its coming made the fussy human pack seem infinitely pitiful and shabby and hardly worth the attention of either saving or damning.

In the beginning of the first act the young girl *Zoe* appears by some great rocks in the desert, and sits down, exhausted, to rest. Presently arrive a pauper couple, stricken with age and infirmities; and they begin to mumble and pray to the Spirit of Life, who is said to inhabit that spot. The

Spirit of Life appears; also Death — uninvited. They are (supposably) invisible. Death, tall, black-robed, corpse-faced, stands motionless and waits. The aged couple pray to the Spirit of Life for a means to prop up their existence and continue it. Their prayer fails. The Spirit of Life prophesies *Zoe's* martyrdom: it will take place before night. Soon *Appelles* arrives, young and vigorous and full of enthusiasm; he has led a host against the Persians and won the battle; he is the pet of fortune, rich, honored, beloved, " Master of Palmyra." He has heard that whoever stretches himself out on one of those rocks there, and asks for a deathless life, can have his wish. He laughs at the tradition, but wants to make the trial anyway. The invisible Spirit of Life warns him: " Life without end can be regret without end." But he persists: let him keep his youth, his strength, and his mental faculties unimpaired, and he will take all the risks. He has his desire.

From this time forth, act after act, the troubles and sorrows and misfortunes and humiliations of life beat upon him without pity or respite; but he will not give up, he will not confess his mistake. Whenever he meets Death he still furiously defies him—but Death patiently waits. He, the healer of sorrows, is man's best friend: the recognition of this will come. As the years drag on, and on, and on, the friends of the *Master's* youth grow old; and one by one they totter to the grave: he goes on with his proud fight, and will not yield. At length he is wholly alone in the world; all his friends are dead; last of all, his darling of darlings, his son, the lad *Nymphas*, who dies in his arms. His pride is broken now; and he would welcome Death, if Death would come, if Death would hear his prayers and give him peace. The closing act is fine and pathetic. *Appelles* meets *Zenobia*, the helper of all who suffer, and tells her his story, which moves her pity. By common report she is endowed with more than earthly powers; and, since he cannot have the boon of death, he appeals to her to drown his memory in forgetfulness of his griefs — forgetfulness, "which is death's equivalent." She says (roughly translated), in an exaltation of compassion:

"Come to me!
  Kneel; and may the power be granted me
  To cool the fires of this poor, tortured brain,
  And bring it peace and healing."

He kneels. From her hand, which she lays upon his head, a mysterious influence steals through him; and he sinks into a dreamy tranquillity.

16

" Oh, if I could but so drift
　Through this soft twilight into the night of peace,
　Never to wake again !
　(*Raising his hand, as if in benediction.*)
　O mother earth, farewell !
　Gracious thou wert to me.　Farewell !
　Appelles goes to rest."

Death appears behind him and encloses the up-lifted hand in his.　*Appelles* shudders, wearily and slowly turns, and recognizes his life-long adver-sary.　He smiles and puts all his gratitude into one simple and touching sentence, " Ich danke dir," and dies.

Nothing, I think, could be more moving, more beautiful, than this close.　This piece is just one long, soulful, sardonic laugh at human life.　Its title might properly be " Is Life a Failure?" and leave the five acts to play with the answer.　I am not at all sure that the author meant to laugh at life.　I only notice that he has done it.　Without putting into words any ungracious or discourteous things about life, the episodes in the piece seem to be saying all the time, inarticulately : " Note what a silly, poor thing human life is ; how childish its ambitions, how ridiculous its pomps, how trivial its dignities, how cheap its heroisms, how capricious its course, how brief its flight, how stingy in hap-piness, how opulent in miseries, how few its prides, how multitudinous its humiliations, how comic its tragedies, how tragic its comedies, how wearisome and monotonous its repetition of its stupid history through the ages, with never the introduction of a new detail, how hard it has tried, from the Creation down, to play itself upon its possessor as a boon, and has never proved its case in a single instance!"

Take note of some of the details of the piece. Each of the five acts contains an independent tragedy of its own. In each act somebody's edifice of hope, or of ambition, or of happiness, goes down in ruins. Even *Appelles'* perennial youth is only a long tragedy, and his life a failure. There are two martyrdoms in the piece; and they are curiously and sarcastically contrasted. In the first act the pagans persecute *Zoe*, the Christian girl, and a pagan mob slaughters her. In the fourth act those same pagans—now very old and zealous—are become Christians, and they persecute the pagans: a mob of them slaughters the pagan youth, *Nymphas*, who is standing up for the old gods of his fathers. No remark is made about this picturesque failure of civilization; but there it stands, as an unworded suggestion that civilization, even when Christianized, was not able wholly to subdue the natural man in that old day—just as in our day the spectacle of a shipwrecked French crew clubbing women and children who tried to climb into the lifeboats suggests that civilization has not succeeded in entirely obliterating the natural man even yet. Common sailors! A year ago, in Paris, at a fire, the aristocracy of the same nation clubbed girls and women out of the way to save themselves. Civilization tested at top and bottom both, you see. And in still another panic of fright we have this same "tough" civilization saving its honor by condemning an innocent man to multiform death, and hugging and whitewashing the guilty one.

In the second act a grand Roman official is not above trying to blast *Appelles'* reputation by falsely charging him with misappropriating public moneys. *Appelles*, who is too proud to endure even the suspicion of irregularity, strips himself to naked poverty to square the unfair account; and *his* troubles begin: the blight which is to continue and spread strikes his life; for the frivolous, pretty creature whom he has brought from Rome has no taste for poverty, and agrees to elope with a more competent candidate. Her presence in the house has previously brought down the pride and broken the heart of *Appelles'* poor old mother; and *her* life is a failure. Death comes for her, but is willing to trade her for the Roman girl; so the bargain is struck with *Appelles*, and the mother is spared for the present.

No one's life escapes the blight. *Timoleus*, the gay satirist of the first two acts, who scoffed at the pious hypocrisies and money-grubbing ways of the great Roman lords, is grown old and fat and blear-eyed and racked with disease in the third, has lost his stately purities, and watered the acid of his wit. *His* life has suffered defeat. Unthinkingly he swears by Zeus—from ancient habit—and then quakes with fright; for a fellow-communicant is passing by. Reproached by a pagan friend of his youth for his apostasy, he confesses that principle, when unsupported by an assenting stomach, has to climb down. One must have bread; and "the bread is Christian now." Then the poor old wreck, once so proud of his iron rectitude, hobbles away, coughing and barking.

In that same act *Appelles* gives his sweet young Christian daughter and her fine young pagan lover his consent and blessing, and makes them utterly happy—for five minutes. Then the priest and the mob come, to tear them apart and put the girl in a nunnery; for marriage between the sects is forbidden. *Appelles'* wife could dissolve the rule; and she wants to do it; but under priestly pressure she wavers; then, fearing that in providing happiness for her child she would be committing a sin dangerous to herself, she goes over to the opposition, and throws the casting vote for the nunnery. The blight has fallen upon the young couple, and *their* life is a failure.

In the fourth act, *Longinus*, who made such a prosperous and enviable start in the first act, is left alone in the desert, sick, blind, helpless, incredibly old, to die: not a friend left in the world—another ruined life. And in that act, also, *Appelles'* worshipped boy, *Nymphas*, done to death by the mob, breathes out his last sigh in his father's arms—one more failure. In the fifth act, *Appelles* himself dies, and is glad to do it; he who so ignorantly rejoiced, only four acts before, over the splendid present of an earthly immortality—the very worst failure of the lot!

II

Now I approach my project. Here is the thea-tre-list for Saturday, May 7, 1898 — cut from the advertising columns of a New York paper:

Now I arrive at my project, and make my suggestion. From the look of this lightsome feast, I
conclude that what you need is a tonic. Send for
" The Master of Palmyra." You are trying to
make yourself believe that life is a comedy, that
its sole business is fun, that there is nothing serious
in it. You are ignoring the skeleton in your closet.
Send for " The Master of Palmyra." You are
neglecting a valuable side of your life; presently
it will be atrophied. You are eating too much
mental sugar; you will bring on Bright's disease of
the intellect. You need a tonic; you need it very
much. Send for "The Master of Palmyra." You
will not need to translate it: its story is as plain
as a procession of pictures.

I have made my suggestion. Now I wish to put
an annex to it. And that is this: It is right and
wholesome to have those light comedies and entertaining shows; and I shouldn't wish to see them
diminished. But none of us is *always* in the
comedy spirit; we have our graver moods; they
come to us all; the lightest of us cannot escape
them. These moods have their appetites—healthy
and legitimate appetites—and there ought to be
some way of satisfying them. It seems to me that
New York ought to have one theatre devoted to
tragedy. With her three millions of population,

and seventy outside millions to draw upon, she can afford it, she can support it. America devotes more time, labor, money, and attention to distributing literary and musical culture among the general public than does any other nation, perhaps; yet here you find her neglecting what is possibly the most effective of all the breeders and nurses and disseminators of high literary taste and lofty emotion—the tragic stage. To leave that powerful agency out is to haul the culture-wagon with a crippled team. Nowadays, when a mood comes which only Shakspeare can set to music, what must we do? Read Shakspeare ourselves! Isn't it pitiful? It is playing an organ solo on a jew's-harp. *We* can't read. None but the Booths can do it.

Thirty years ago Edwin Booth played "Hamlet" a hundred nights in New York. With three times the population, how often is "Hamlet" played now in a year? If Booth were back now in his prime, how often could he play it in New York? Some will say twenty-five nights. I will say three hundred, and say it with confidence. The tragedians are dead; but I think that the taste and intelligence which made their market are not.

What *has* come over us English-speaking people?

During the first half of this century tragedies and great tragedians were as common with us as farce and comedy; and it was the same in England. Now we have not a tragedian, I believe; and London, with her fifty shows and theatres, has but three, I think. It is an astonishing thing, when you come to consider it. Vienna remains upon the ancient basis: there has been no change. She sticks to the former proportions: a number of rollicking comedies, admirably played, every night; and also every night at the Burg Theatre—that wonder of the world for grace and beauty and richness and splendor and costliness—a majestic drama of depth and seriousness, or a standard old tragedy. It is only within the last dozen years that men have learned to do miracles on the stage in the way of grand and enchanting scenic effects; and it is at such a time as this that we have reduced our scenery mainly to different breeds of parlors and varying aspects of furniture and rugs. I think we must have a Burg in New York, and Burg scenery, and a great company like the Burg company. Then, with a tragedy-tonic once or twice a month, we shall enjoy the comedies all the better. Comedy keeps the heart sweet; but we all know that there is wholesome refreshment for both mind and heart in an occasional climb among the pomps of the intellectual snow-summits built by Shakspeare and those others. Do I seem to be preaching? It is out of my line: I only do it because the rest of the clergy seem to be on vacation.

CONCERNING THE JEWS

SOME months ago I published a magazine article* descriptive of a remarkable scene in the Imperial Parliament in Vienna. Since then I have received from Jews in America several letters of inquiry. They were difficult letters to answer, for they were not very definite. But at last I have received a definite one. It is from a lawyer, and he really asks the questions which the other writers probably believed they were asking. By help of this text I will do the best I can to publicly answer this correspondent, and also the others—at the same time apologizing for having failed to reply privately. The lawyer's letter reads as follows:

"I have read 'Stirring Times in Austria.' One point in particular is of vital import to not a few thousand people, including myself, being a point about which I have often wanted to address a question to some disinterested person. The show of military force in the Austrian Parliament, which precipitated the riots, was not introduced by any Jew.

---

* See HARPER'S MAGAZINE for March, 1898.

No Jew was a member of that body.   No Jewish question
was involved in the Ausgleich or in the language proposition.   No Jew was insulting anybody.   In short, no Jew
was doing any mischief toward anybody whatsoever.   In
fact, the Jews were the only ones of the nineteen different
races in Austria which did not have a party—they are absolutely non-participants.   Yet in your article you say that
in the rioting which followed, all classes of people were
unanimous only on one thing, viz., in being against the
Jews.   Now will you kindly tell me why, in your judgment,
the Jews have thus ever been, and are even now, in these
days of supposed intelligence, the butt of baseless, vicious
animosities?   I dare say that for centuries there has been
no more quiet, undisturbing, and well-behaving citizen, as
a class, than that same Jew.   It seems to me that ignorance
and fanaticism cannot alone account for these horrible and
unjust persecutions.

" Tell me, therefore, from your vantage-point of cold view,
what in your mind is the cause.   Can American Jews do
anything to correct it either in America or abroad ?   Will
it ever come to an end ?   Will a Jew be permitted to live
honestly, decently, and peaceably like the rest of mankind ?
What has become of the Golden Rule ?"

I will begin by saying that if I thought myself
prejudiced against the Jew, I should hold it fairest
to leave this subject to a person not crippled in
that way.   But I think I have no such prejudice.
A few years ago a Jew observed to me that there
was no uncourteous reference to his people in my
books, and asked how it happened.   It happened
because the disposition was lacking.   I am quite

sure that (bar one) I have no race prejudices, and I think I have no color prejudices nor caste prejudices nor creed prejudices. Indeed, I know it. I can stand any society. All that I care to know is that a man is a human being—that is enough for me; he can't be any worse. I have no special regard for Satan; but I can at least claim that I have no prejudice against him. It may even be that I lean a little his way, on account of his not having a fair show. All religions issue bibles against him, and say the most injurious things about him, but we never hear *his* side. We have none but the evidence for the prosecution, and yet we have rendered the verdict. To my mind, this is irregular. It is un-English; it is un-American; it is French. Without this precedent Dreyfus could not have been condemned. Of course Satan has some kind of a case, it goes without saying. It may be a poor one, but that is nothing; that can be said about any of us. As soon as I can get at the facts I will undertake his rehabilitation myself, if I can find an unpolitic publisher. It is a thing which we ought to be willing to do for any one who is under a cloud. We may not pay him reverence, for that would be indiscreet, but we can at least respect his talents. A person who has for untold centuries maintained the imposing position of spiritual head of four-fifths of the human race, and political head of the whole of it, must be granted the possession of executive abilities of the loftiest order. In his large presence the other popes and politicians shrink to midges for the microscope. I would like to see him. I would rather see him and shake him by the tail than any other member of the European Concert. In the present paper I shall allow myself to use the word Jew as if it stood for both religion and race. It is handy; and, besides, that is what the term means to the general world.

In the above letter one notes these points:

1. The Jew is a well-behaved citizen.

2. Can ignorance and fanaticism *alone* account for his unjust treatment?

3. Can Jews do anything to improve the situation?

4. The Jews have no party; they are non-participants.

5. Will the persecution ever come to an end?

6. What has become of the Golden Rule?

Point No. 1.—We must grant proposition No. 1 for several sufficient reasons. The Jew is not a disturber of the peace of any country. Even his enemies will concede that. He is not a loafer, he is not a sot, he is not noisy, he is not a brawler nor a rioter, he is not quarrelsome. In the statistics of crime his presence is conspicuously rare—in all countries. With murder and other crimes of violence he has but little to do: he is a stranger to the hangman. In the police court's daily long roll of "assaults" and "drunk and disorderlies" his name seldom appears. That the Jewish home is a home in the truest sense is a fact which no one will dispute. The family is knitted together by the strongest affections; its members show each other every due respect; and reverence for the elders is an inviolate law of the house. The Jew is not a burden on the charities of the state nor of the city; these could cease from their functions without affecting him. When he is well enough, he works; when he is incapacitated, his own people take care of him. And not in a poor and stingy way, but with a fine and large benevolence. His race is entitled to be called the most benevolent of all the races of men. A Jewish beggar is not impossible, perhaps; such a thing may exist, but there are few men that can say they have seen that spectacle. The Jew has been staged in many uncomplimentary forms, but, so far as I know, no dramatist has done him the injustice to stage him as a beggar. Whenever a Jew has real need to beg, his people save him from the necessity of doing it. The charitable institutions of the Jews are supported by Jewish money, and amply. The Jews make no noise about it; it is done quietly; they do not nag and pester and harass us for contributions; they give us peace, and set us an example—an example which we have not found ourselves able to follow; for by nature we are not free givers, and have to be patiently and persistently hunted down in the interest of the unfortunate.

These facts are all on the credit side of the proposition that the Jew is a good and orderly citizen. Summed up, they certify that he is quiet, peaceable, industrious, unaddicted to high crimes and brutal dispositions; that his family life is commendable; that he is not a burden upon public charities; that he is not a beggar; that in benevolence he is above the reach of competition. These are the very quint-essentials of good citizenship. If you can add that he is as honest as the average of his neighbors— But I think that question is affirmatively answered by the fact that he is a successful business man. The basis of successful business is honesty; a business cannot thrive where the parties to it cannot trust each other. In the matter of numbers the Jew counts for little in the overwhelming population of New York; but that his honesty counts for much is guaranteed by the fact that the immense wholesale business houses of

17

Broadway, from the Battery to Union Square, is substantially in his hands.

I suppose that the most picturesque example in history of a trader's trust in his fellow-trader was one where it was not Christian trusting Christian, but Christian trusting Jew. That Hessian Duke who used to sell his subjects to George III. to fight George Washington with got rich at it; and by-and-by, when the wars engendered by the French Revolution made his throne too warm for him, he was obliged to fly the country. He was in a hurry, and had to leave his earnings behind—$9,000,000. He had to risk the money with some one without security. He did not select a Christian, but a Jew —a Jew of only modest means, but of high character; a character so high that it left him lonesome— Rothschild of Frankfort. Thirty years later, when Europe had become quiet and safe again, the Duke came back from overseas, and the Jew returned the loan, with interest added.*

---

* Here is another piece of picturesque history; and it reminds us that shabbiness and dishonesty are not the monopoly of any race or creed, but are merely human :

"Congress has passed a bill to pay $379.56 to Moses Pendergrass, of Libertyville, Missouri. The story of the reason of this liberality is pathetically interesting, and shows the sort of pickle that an honest man may get into who undertakes to do an honest job of work for Uncle Sam. In 1886 Moses Pendergrass put in a bid for

The Jew has his other side. He has some discreditable ways, though he has not a monopoly of them, because he cannot get entirely rid of vexa-

the contract to carry the mail on the route from Knob Lick to Libertyville and Coffman, thirty miles a day, from July 1, 1887, for one year. He got the postmaster at Knob Lick to write the letter for him, and while Moses intended that his bid should be $400, his scribe carelessly made it $4. Moses got the contract, and did not find out about the mistake until the end of the first quarter, when he got his first pay. When he found at what rate he was working he was sorely cast down, and opened communication with the Post-Office Department. The department informed him that he must either carry out his contract or throw it up, and that if he threw it up his bondsmen would have to pay the government $1459.85 damages. So Moses carried out his contract, walked thirty miles every week-day for a year, and carried the mail, and received for his labor $4—or, to be accurate, $6.84 ; for, the route being extended after his bid was accepted, the pay was proportionately increased. Now, after ten years, a bill was finally passed to pay to Moses the difference between what he earned in that unlucky year and what he received."

The *Sun*, which tells the above story, says that bills were introduced in three or four Congresses for Moses' relief, and that committees repeatedly investigated his claim.

It took six Congresses, containing in their persons the compressed virtues of 70,000,000 of people, and cautiously and carefully giving expression to those virtues in the fear of God and the next election, eleven years to find out some way to cheat a fellow-Christian out of about $13 on his honestly executed contract, and out of nearly $300 due him on its enlarged terms. And they succeeded. During the same time they paid out $1,000,000,000 in pensions—a third of it unearned and undeserved. This indicates a splendid all-around competency in theft, for it starts with farthings, and works its industries all the way up to ship-loads. It may be possible that the Jews can beat this, but the man that bets on it is taking chances.

tious Christian competition. We have seen that he seldom transgresses the laws against crimes of violence. Indeed, his dealings with courts are almost restricted to matters connected with commerce. He has a reputation for various small forms of cheating, and for practising oppressive usury, and for burning himself out to get the insurance, and for arranging cunning contracts which leave him an exit but lock the other man in, and for smart evasions which find him safe and comfortable just within the strict letter of the law, when court and jury know very well that he has violated the spirit of it. He is a frequent and faithful and capable officer in the civil service, but he is charged with an unpatriotic disinclination to stand by the flag as a soldier—like the Christian Quaker.

Now if you offset these discreditable features by the creditable ones summarized in a preceding paragraph beginning with the words, " These facts are all on the credit side," and strike a balance, what must the verdict be ? This, I think : that, the merits and demerits being fairly weighed and measured on both sides, the Christian can claim no superiority over the Jew in the matter of good citizenship.

Yet in all countries, from the dawn of history, the Jew has been persistently and implacably hated, and with frequency persecuted.

Point No. 2.—" Can fanaticism *alone* account for this ?"

Years ago I used to think that it was responsible for nearly all of it, but latterly I have come to think that this was an error. Indeed, it is now my conviction that it is responsible for hardly any of it.

In this connection I call to mind Genesis, chapter xlvii.

We have all thoughtfully—or unthoughtfully— read the pathetic story of the years of plenty and the years of famine in Egypt, and how Joseph, with that opportunity, made a corner in broken hearts, and the crusts of the poor, and human liberty—a corner whereby he took a nation's money all away, to the last penny ; took a nation's livestock all away, to the last hoof ; took a nation's land away, to the last acre ; then took the nation itself, buying it for bread, man by man, woman by woman, child by child, till all were slaves ; a corner which took everything, left nothing ; a corner so stupendous that, by comparison with it, the most gigantic corners in subsequent history are but baby things, for it dealt in hundreds of millions of bushels, and its profits were reckonable by hundreds of millions of dollars, and it was a disaster so crushing that its effects have not wholly disappeared from

Egypt to-day, more than three thousand years after the event.

Is it presumable that the eye of Egypt was upon Joseph the foreign Jew all this time? I think it likely. Was it friendly? We must doubt it. Was Joseph establishing a character for his race which would survive long in Egypt? and in time would his name come to be familiarly used to express that character—like Shylock's? It is hardly to be doubted. Let us remember that this was *centuries before the crucifixion*.

I wish to come down eighteen hundred years later and refer to a remark made by one of the Latin historians. I read it in a translation many years ago, and it comes back to me now with force. It was alluding to a time when people were still living who could have seen the Savior in the flesh. Christianity was so new that the people of Rome had hardly heard of it, and had but confused notions of what it was. The substance of the remark was this: Some Christians were persecuted in Rome through error, they being " *mistaken for Jews.*"

The meaning seems plain. These pagans had nothing against Christians, but they were quite ready to persecute Jews. For some reason or other they hated a Jew before they even knew what a Christian was. May I not assume, then, that the persecution of Jews is a thing which *ante-dates* Christianity and was not born of Christianity? I think so. What was the origin of the feeling?

When I was a boy, in the back settlements of the Mississippi Valley, where a gracious and beautiful Sunday-school simplicity and unpracticality prevailed, the "Yankee" (citizen of the New England States) was hated with a splendid energy. But religion had nothing to do with it. In a trade, the Yankee was held to be about five times the match of the Westerner. His shrewdness, his insight, his judgment, his knowledge, his enterprise, and his formidable cleverness in applying these forces were frankly confessed, and most competently cursed.

In the cotton States, after the war, the simple and ignorant negroes made the crops for the white planter on shares. The Jew came down in force, set up shop on the plantation, supplied all the negro's wants on credit, and at the end of the season was proprietor of the negro's share of the present crop and of part of his share of the next one. Before long, the whites detested the Jew, and it is doubtful if the negro loved him.

The Jew is being legislated out of Russia. The reason is not concealed. The movement was instituted because the Christian peasant and villager stood no chance against his commercial abilities. He was always ready to lend money on a crop, and sell vodka and other necessaries of life on credit while the crop was growing. When settlement day came he owned the crop; and next year or year after he owned the farm, like Joseph.

In the dull and ignorant England of John's time everybody got into debt to the Jew. He gathered all lucrative enterprises into his hands; he was the king of commerce; he was ready to be helpful in all profitable ways; he even financed crusades for the rescue of the Sepulchre. To wipe out his account with the nation and restore business to its natural and incompetent channels he had to be banished the realm.

For the like reasons Spain had to banish him four hundred years ago, and Austria about a couple of centuries later.

In all the ages Christian Europe has been obliged to curtail his activities. If he entered upon a mechanical trade, the Christian had to retire from it. If he set up as a doctor, he was the best one, and he took the business. If he exploited agriculture, the other farmers had to get at something else. Since there was no way to successfully compete with him in any vocation, the law had to step

in and save the Christian from the poor-house.
Trade after trade was taken away from the Jew by
statute till practically none was left.   He was forbidden to engage in agriculture; he was forbidden
to practise law; he was forbidden to practise
medicine, except among Jews; he was forbidden
the handicrafts.   Even the seats of learning and
the schools of science had to be closed against this
tremendous antagonist.   Still, almost bereft of em-
ployments, he found ways to make money, even
ways to get rich.   Also ways to invest his takings
well, for usury was not denied him.   In the hard
conditions suggested, the Jew without brains could
not survive, and the Jew with brains had to keep
them in good training and well sharpened up, or
starve.   Ages of restriction to the one tool which
the law was not able to take from him—his brain
—have made that tool singularly competent; ages
of compulsory disuse of his hands have atrophied
them, and he never uses them now.   This history
has a very, very commercial look, a most sordid
and practical commercial look, the business aspect
of a Chinese cheap-labor crusade.   Religious prejudices may account for one part of it, but not for
the other nine.

Protestants have persecuted Catholics, but they
did not take their livelihoods away from them.

The Catholics have persecuted the Protestants with bloody and awful bitterness, but they never closed agriculture and the handicrafts against them. Why was that? That has the candid look of genuine religious persecution, not a trade-union boycott in a religious disguise.

The Jews are harried and obstructed in Austria and Germany, and lately in France; but England and America give them an open field and yet survive. Scotland offers them an unembarrassed field too, but there are not many takers. There are a few Jews in Glasgow, and one in Aberdeen; but that is because they can't earn enough to get away. The Scotch pay themselves that compliment, but it is authentic.

I feel convinced that the Crucifixion has not much to do with the world's attitude towards the Jew; that the reasons for it are older than that event, as suggested by Egypt's experience and by Rome's regret for having persecuted an unknown quantity called a Christian, under the mistaken impression that she was merely persecuting a Jew. *Merely* a Jew—a skinned eel who was used to it, presumably. I am persuaded that in Russia, Austria, and Germany nine-tenths of the hostility to the Jew comes from the average Christian's inability to compete successfully with the average

Jew in business—in either straight business or the questionable sort.

In Berlin, a few years ago, I read a speech which frankly urged the expulsion of the Jews from Germany; and the agitator's *reason* was as frank as his proposition. It was this: *that eighty-five per cent.* of the successful lawyers of Berlin were Jews, and that about the same percentage of the great and lucrative businesses of all sorts in Germany were in the hands of the Jewish race! Isn't it an amazing confession? It was but another way of saying that in a population of 48,000,000, of whom only 500,000 were registered as Jews, eighty-five per cent. of the brains and honesty of the whole was lodged in the Jews. I must insist upon the honesty —it is an essential of successful business, taken by and large. Of course it does not rule out rascals entirely, even among Christians, but it is a good working rule, nevertheless. The speaker's figures may have been inexact, but *the motive of persecution* stands out as clear as day.

The man claimed that in Berlin the banks, the newspapers, the theatres, the great mercantile, shipping, mining, and manufacturing interests, the big army and city contracts, the tramways, and pretty much all other properties of high value, and *also* the small businesses, were in the hands of the

Jews. He said the Jew was pushing the Christian to the wall all along the line; that it was all a Christian could do to scrape together a living; and that the Jew *must* be banished, and soon—there was no other way of saving the Christian. Here in Vienna, last autumn, an agitator said that all these disastrous details were true of Austria-Hungary also; and in fierce language he demanded the expulsion of the Jews. When politicians come out without a blush and read the baby act in this frank way, *unrebuked*, it is a very good indication that they have a market back of them, and know where to fish for votes.

You note the crucial point of the mentioned agitation; the argument is that the Christian cannot *compete* with the Jew, and that hence his very bread is in peril. To human beings this is a much more hate-inspiring thing than is any detail connected with religion. With most people, of a necessity, bread and meat take first rank, religion second. I am convinced that the persecution of the Jew is not due in any large degree to religious prejudice.

No, the Jew is a money-getter; and in getting his money he is a very serious obstruction to less capable neighbors who are on the same quest. I think that that is the trouble. In estimating worldly values the Jew is not shallow, but deep. With precocious wisdom he found out in the morning of time that some men worship rank, some worship heroes, some worship power, some worship God, and that over these ideals they dispute and cannot unite—but that they all worship money; so he made it the end and aim of his life to get it. He was at it in Egypt thirty-six centuries ago; he was at it in Rome when that Christian got persecuted by mistake for him; he has been at it ever since. The cost to him has been heavy; his success has made the whole human race his enemy—but it has paid, for it has brought him envy, and that is the only thing which men will sell both soul and body to get. He long ago observed that a millionaire commands respect, a two-millionaire homage, a multi-millionaire the deepest deeps of adoration. We all know that feeling; we have seen it express itself. We have noticed that when the average man mentions the name of a multi-millionaire he does it with that mixture in his voice of awe and reverence and lust which burns in a Frenchman's eye when it falls on another man's centime.

Point No. 4.—" The Jews have no party; they are non-participants."

Perhaps you have let the secret out and given

yourself away. It seems hardly a credit to the
race that it is able to say that; or to you, sir, that
you can say it without remorse; more that you
should offer it as a plea against maltreatment, injustice, and oppression. Who gives the Jew the
right, who gives any race the right, to sit still, in a
free country, and let somebody else look after its
safety? The oppressed Jew was entitled to all
pity in the former times under brutal autocracies,
for he was weak and friendless, and had no way
to help his case. But he has ways now, and he
has had them for a century, but I do not see that
he has tried to make serious use of them. When
the Revolution set him free in France it was an
act of grace—the grace of other people; he does
not appear in it as a helper. I do not know that
he helped when England set him free. Among
the Twelve Sane Men of France who have stepped
forward with great Zola at their head to fight
(and win, I hope and believe*) the battle for the
most infamously misused Jew of modern times,
do you find a great or rich or illustrious Jew
helping? In the United States he was created
free in the beginning—he did not need to help,
of course. In Austria and Germany and France

* The article was written in the summer of 1898.—ED.

he has a vote, but of what considerable use is
it to him? He doesn't seem to know how to
apply it to the best effect. With all his splendid capacities and all his fat wealth he is to-day not
politically important in any country. In America,
as early as 1854, the ignorant Irish hod-carrier, who
had a spirit of his own and a way of exposing it to
the weather, made it apparent to all that he must
be politically reckoned with; yet fifteen years before that we hardly knew what an Irishman looked
like. As an intelligent force and numerically, he
has always been away down, but he has governed
the country just the same. It was because he was
organized. It made his vote valuable—in fact,
essential.

You will say the Jew is everywhere numerically
feeble. That is nothing to the point—with the
Irishman's history for an object-lesson. But I am
coming to your numerical feebleness presently. In
all parliamentary countries you could no doubt
elect Jews to the legislatures—and even *one* member in such a body is sometimes a force which
counts. How deeply have you concerned yourselves about this in Austria, France, and Germany?
Or even in America, for that matter? You remark
that the Jews were not to blame for the riots in
this Reichsrath here, and you add with satisfaction

that there wasn't one in that body. That is not strictly correct; if it were, would it not be in order for you to explain it and apologize for it, not try to make a merit of it? But I think that the Jew was by no means in as large force there as he ought to have been, with his chances. Austria opens the suffrage to him on fairly liberal terms, and it must surely be his own fault that he is so much in the background politically.

As to your numerical weakness. I mentioned some figures awhile ago—500,000—as the Jewish population of Germany. I will add some more—6,000,000 in Russia, 5,000,000 in Austria, 250,000 in the United States. I take them from memory; I read them in the *Cyclopædia Britannica* ten or twelve years ago. Still, I am entirely sure of them. If those statistics are correct, my argument is not as strong as it ought to be as concerns America, but it still has strength. It is plenty strong enough as concerns Austria, for ten years ago 5,000,000 was nine per cent. of the empire's population. The Irish would govern the Kingdom of Heaven if they had a strength there like that.

I have some suspicions; I got them at second-hand, but they have remained with me these ten or twelve years. When I read in the *C. B.* that the Jewish population of the United States was 250,-

ooo, I wrote the editor, and explained to him that I was personally acquainted with more Jews than that in my country, and that his figures were without a doubt a misprint for 25,000,000. I also added that I was personally acquainted with *that* many there; but that was only to raise his confidence in me, for it was not true. His answer miscarried, and I never got it; but I went around talking about the matter, and people told me they had reason to suspect that for business reasons many Jews whose dealings were mainly with the Christians did not report themselves as Jews in the census. It looked plausible; it looks plausible yet. Look at the city of New York; and look at Boston, and Philadelphia, and New Orleans, and Chicago, and Cincinnati, and San Francisco — how your race swarms in those places!—and everywhere else in America, down to the least little village. Read the signs on the marts of commerce and on the shops; Goldstein (gold stone), Edelstein (precious stone), Blumenthal (flower-vale), Rosenthal (rose-vale), Veilchenduft (violet odor), Singvogel (song-bird), Rosenzweig (rose branch), and all the amazing list of beautiful and enviable names which Prussia and Austria glorified you with so long ago. It is another instance of Europe's coarse and cruel persecution of your race; not that it was coarse and

18

cruel to outfit it with pretty and poetical names
like those, but that it was coarse and cruel to make
it *pay* for them or else take such hideous and often
indecent names that to-day their owners never use
them; or, if they do, only on official papers. And
it was the many, not the few, who got the odious
names, they being too poor to bribe the officials to
grant them better ones.

Now why was the race renamed? I have been
told that in Prussia it was given to using fictitious
names, and often changing them, so as to beat the
tax-gatherer, escape military service, and so on;
and that finally the idea was hit upon of furnishing
all the inmates of a house with *one and the same
surname*, and then holding the house responsible
right along for those inmates, and accountable for
any disappearances that might occur; it made the
Jews keep track of *each other*, for self-interest's
sake, and saved the government the trouble.*

* In Austria the renaming was merely done because the Jews in
some newly acquired regions had no surnames, but were mostly
named Abraham and Moses, and therefore the tax-gatherer could
not tell t'other from which, and was likely to lose his reason over
the matter. The renaming was put into the hands of the War Department, and a charming mess the graceless young lieutenants
made of it. To them a Jew was of no sort of consequence, and
they labelled the race in a way to make the angels weep. As an
example, take these two: *Abraham Bellyache* and *Schmul Godbe-
damned.—Culled from "Namens-Studien," by Karl Emil Franzos.*

If that explanation of how the Jews of Prussia came to be renamed is correct, if it is true that they fictitiously registered themselves to gain certain advantages, it may possibly be true that in America they refrain from registering themselves as Jews to fend off the damaging prejudices of the Christian customer. I have no way of knowing whether this notion is well founded or not. There may be other and better ways of explaining why only that poor little 250,000 of our Jews got into the *Cyclopædia*. I may, of course, be mistaken, but I am strongly of the opinion that we have an immense Jewish population in America.

Point No. 3.—"Can Jews do anything to improve the situation?"

I think so. If I may make a suggestion without seeming to be trying to teach my grandmother how to suck eggs, I will offer it. In our days we have learned the value of combination. We apply it everywhere—in railway systems, in trusts, in trade unions, in Salvation Armies, in minor politics, in major politics, in European Concerts. Whatever our strength may be, big or little, we *organize* it. We have found out that that is the only way to get the most out of it that is in it. We know the weakness of individual sticks, and the strength of the concentrated fagot. Suppose you try a scheme

like this, for instance.   In England and America
put every Jew on the census-book *as* a Jew (in case
you have not been doing that).   Get up volunteer
regiments composed of Jews solely, and, when the
drum beats, fall in and go to the front, so as to re-
move the reproach that you have few Massénas
among you, and that you feed on a country but
don't like to fight for it.   Next, in politics, organize you strength, band together, and deliver the
casting vote where you can, and, where you can't,
compel as good terms as possible.   You huddle to
yourselves already in all countries, but you huddle
to no sufficient purpose, politically speaking.   You
do not seem to be organized, except for your charities.   There you are omnipotent ; there you compel your due of recognition—you do not have to
beg for it.   It shows what you can do when you
band together for a definite purpose.

And then from America and England you can
encourage your race in Austria, France, and Germany, and materially help it.   It was a pathetic
tale that was told by a poor Jew in Galicia a fortnight ago during the riots, after he had been raided
by the Christian peasantry and despoiled of everything he had.   He said his vote was of no value
to him, and he wished he could be excused from
casting it, for, indeed, casting it was a sure *damage*

to him, since no matter which party he voted for, the other party would come straight and take its revenge out of him. Nine per cent. of the population of the empire, these Jews, and apparently they cannot put a plank into any candidate's platform! If you will send our Irish lads over here I think they will organize your race and change the aspect of the Reichsrath.

You seem to think that the Jews take no hand in politics here, that they are "absolutely non-participants." I am assured by men competent to speak that this is a very large error, that the Jews are exceedingly active in politics all over the empire, but that they scatter their work and their votes among the numerous parties, and thus lose the advantages to be had by concentration. I think that in America they scatter too, but you know more about that than I do.

Speaking of concentration, Dr. Herzl has a clear insight into the value of that. Have you heard of his plan? He wishes to gather the Jews of the world together in Palestine, with a government of their own—under the suzerainty of the Sultan, I suppose. At the Convention of Berne, last year, there were delegates from everywhere, and the proposal was received with decided favor. I am not the Sultan, and I am not objecting; but if that concentration of the cunningest brains in the world were going to be made in a free country (bar Scotland), I think it would be politic to stop it. It will not be well to let the race find out its strength. If the horses knew theirs, we should not ride any more.

Point No. 5.—"Will the persecution of the Jews ever come to an end?"

On the score of religion, I think it has already come to an end. On the score of race prejudice and trade, I have the idea that it will continue. That is, here and there in spots about the world, where a barbarous ignorance and a sort of mere animal civilization prevail; but I do not think that elsewhere the Jew need now stand in any fear of being robbed and raided. Among the high civilizations he seems to be very comfortably situated indeed, and to have more than his proportionate share of the prosperities going. It has that look in Vienna. I suppose the race prejudice cannot be removed; but he can stand that; it is no particular matter. By his make and ways he is substantially a foreigner wherever he may be, and even the angels dislike a foreigner. I am using this word foreigner in the German sense—*stranger*. Nearly all of us have an antipathy to a stranger, even of our own nationality. We pile gripsacks in a vacant

seat to keep him from getting it ; and a dog goes
further, and does as a savage would—challenges
him on the spot. The German dictionary seems
to make no distinction between a stranger and a
foreigner ; in its view a stranger *is* a foreigner—a
sound position, I think. You will always be by
ways and habits and predilections substantially
strangers—foreigners—wherever you are, and that
will probably keep the race prejudice against you
alive.

But you were the favorites of Heaven originally,
and your manifold and unfair prosperities convince
me that you have crowded back into that snug
place again. Here is an incident that is significant.
Last week in Vienna a hailstorm struck the pro-
digious Central Cemetery and made wasteful destruction there. In the Christian part of it, according to the official figures, 621 window-panes were
broken ; more than 900 singing-birds were killed ;
five great trees and many small ones were torn to
shreds and the shreds scattered far and wide by
the wind ; the ornamental plants and other decora-
tions of the graves were ruined, and more than a
hundred tomb-lanterns shattered ; and it took the
cemetery's whole force of 300 laborers more than
three days to clear away the storm's wreckage. In
the report occurs this remark—and in its italics

you can hear it grit its Christian teeth: "... le-diglich die *israelitische* Abtheilung des Friedhofes vom Hagelwetter *gänzlich verschont* worden war." Not a hailstone hit the Jewish reservation! Such nepotism makes me tired.

Point No. 6.—"What has become of the Golden Rule?"

It exists, it continues to sparkle, and is well taken care of. It is Exhibit A in the Church's assets, and we pull it out every Sunday and give it an airing. But you are not permitted to try to smuggle it into this discussion, where it is irrelevant and would not feel at home. It is strictly religious furniture, like an acolyte, or a contribution-plate, or any of those things. It has never been intruded into business; and Jewish persecution is not a religious passion, it is a business passion.

To conclude.—If the statistics are right, the Jews constitute but *one per cent.* of the human race. It suggests a nebulous dim puff of star-dust lost in the blaze of the Milky Way. Properly the Jew ought hardly to be heard of; but he is heard of, has always been heard of. He is as prominent on the planet as any other people, and his commercial importance is extravagantly out of proportion to the smallness of his bulk. His contributions to the world's list of great names in literature, science, art, music, finance, medicine, and abstruse learning are also away out of proportion to the weakness of his numbers. He has made a marvellous fight in this world, in all the ages; and has done it with his hands tied behind him. He could be vain of himself, and be excused for it. The Egyptian, the Babylonian, and the Persian rose, filled the planet with sound and splendor, then faded to dream-stuff and passed away; the Greek and the Roman followed, and made a vast noise, and they are gone; other peoples have sprung up and held their torch high for a time, but it burned out, and they sit in twilight now, or have vanished. The Jew saw them all, beat them all, and is now what he always was, exhibiting no decadence, no infirmities of age, no weakening of his parts, no slowing of his energies, no dulling of his alert and aggressive mind. All things are mortal but the Jew; all other forces pass, but he remains. What is the secret of his immortality?

Postscript—THE JEW AS SOLDIER

When I published the above article in HARPER'S MONTHLY, I was ignorant — like the rest of the Christian world — of the fact that the Jew had a record as a soldier. I have since seen the official statistics, and I find that he furnished soldiers and high officers to the Revolution, the War of 1812, and the Mexican War. In the Civil War he was represented in the armies and navies of both the North and the South by 10 per cent. of his numerical strength—the same percentage that was furnished by the Christian populations of the two sections. This large fact means more than it seems to mean ; for it means that the Jew's patriotism was not merely level with the Christian's, but overpassed it. When the Christian volunteer arrived in camp he got a welcome and applause, but as a rule the Jew got a snub. His company was not desired, and he was made to feel it. That he nevertheless conquered his wounded pride and sacrificed both that and his blood for his flag raises the average and quality of his patriotism above the Christian's. His record for capacity, for fidelity, and for gallant soldiership in the field is as good as any one's. This is true of the Jewish private soldiers and the Jewish generals alike. Major-General O. O. Howard speaks of one of his Jewish staff-officers as being " of the bravest and best "; of another—killed at Chancellorsville—as being "a true friend and a brave officer"; he highly praises two of his Jewish brigadier-generals ; finally, he uses these strong words : " Intrinsically there are no more patriotic men to be found in the country than those who claim to be of Hebrew descent, and who served with me in parallel commands or more directly under my instructions."

Fourteen Jewish Confederate and Union families contributed, between them, fifty-one soldiers to the war. Among these, a father and three sons; and another, a father and four sons.

In the above article I was not able to endorse the common reproach that the Jew is willing to feed upon a country but not to fight for it, because I did not know whether it was true or false. I supposed it to be true, but it is not allowable to endorse wandering maxims upon supposition—except when one is trying to make out a case. That slur upon the Jew cannot hold up its head in presence of the figures of the War Department. It has done its work, and done it long and faithfully, and with high approval: it ought to be pensioned off now, and retired from active service.

STIRRING TIMES IN AUSTRIA

I.—THE GOVERNMENT IN THE FRYING-PAN

HERE in Vienna in these closing days of 1897 one's blood gets no chance to stagnate. The atmosphere is brimful of political electricity. All conversation is political; every man is a battery, with brushes overworn, and gives out blue sparks when you set him going on the common topic. Everybody has an opinion, and lets you have it frank and hot, and out of this multitude of counsel you get merely confusion and despair. For no one really understands this political situation, or can tell you what is going to be the outcome of it.

Things have happened here recently which would set any country but Austria on fire from end to end, and upset the government to a certainty; but no one feels confident that such results will follow here. Here, apparently, one must wait and see what will happen, then he will know, and not before; guessing is idle; guessing cannot help the matter. This is what the wise tell you; they all say it; they say it every day, and it is the sole detail upon which they all agree.

There is some approach to agreement upon another point: that there will be no revolution. Men say: "Look at our history—revolutions have not been in our line; and look at our political map—its construction is unfavorable to an organized uprising, and without unity what could a revolt accomplish? It is *dis*union which has held our empire together for centuries, and what it has done in the past it may continue to do now and in the future."

The most intelligible sketch I have encountered of this unintelligible arrangement of things was contributed to the *Traveler's Record* by Mr. Forrest Morgan, of Hartford, three years ago. He says:

"The Austro-Hungarian Monarchy is the patchwork quilt, the Midway Plaisance, the national chain-gang of Europe; a state that is not a nation, but a collection of nations, some with national memories and aspirations and others without, some occupying distinct provinces almost purely their own, and others mixed with alien races, but each with a different language and each mostly holding the others foreigners as much as if the link of a common government did not exist. Only one of its races even now comprises so much as *one-fourth* of the whole, and not another so much as *one-sixth;* and each has remained for ages as unchanged in isolation, however mingled together in locality, as globules of oil in water. There is nothing else in the modern world that is nearly like it, though there have been plenty in past ages; it seems unreal and impossible even though we know it is true; it violates all our feeling as to what a country should be in order to have a right to exist; and it seems as though it was too ramshackle to go on holding together any length of time. Yet it has survived, much in its present shape, two centuries of storms that have swept perfectly unified countries from existence and others that have brought it to the verge of ruin, has survived formidable European coalitions to dismember it, and has steadily gained force after each; forever changing in its exact make-up, losing in the West but gaining in the East, the changes leave the structure as firm as ever, like the dropping off and adding on of logs in a raft, its mechanical union of pieces showing all the vitality of genuine national life."

That seems to confirm and justify the prevalent Austrian faith that in this confusion of unrelated and irreconcilable elements, this condition of incurable disunion, there is strength — for the government. Nearly every day some one explains to me that a revolution would not succeed here. " It couldn't, you know. Broadly speaking, all the nations in the empire hate the government — but they all hate each other too, and with devoted and enthusiastic bitterness; no two of them can combine; the nation that rises must rise alone; then the others would joyfully join the government against her, and she would have just a fly's chance against a combination of spiders. This government is entirely independent. It can go its own road, and do as it pleases; it has nothing to fear. In countries like England and America, where there is one tongue and the public interests are common, the government must take account of public opinion; but in Austria-Hungary there are nineteen public opinions—one for each state. No —two or three for each state, since there are two or three nationalities in each. A government cannot satisfy all these public opinions; it can only go through the motions of trying. This government does that. It goes through the motions, and they do not succeed; but that does not worry the government much."

The next man will give you some further information. "The government has a policy—a wise one—and sticks steadily to it. This policy is— *tranquillity:* keep this hive of excitable nations as quiet as possible; encourage them to amuse themselves with things less inflammatory than politics. To this end it furnishes them an abundance of Catholic priests to teach them to be docile and obedient, and to be diligent in acquiring ignorance about things here below, and knowledge about the kingdom of heaven, to whose historic delights they are going to add the charm of their society by-and-by; and further—to this same end—it cools off the newspapers every morning at five o'clock, whenever warm events are happening." There is a censor of the press, and apparently he is always on duty and hard at work. A copy of each morning paper is brought to him at five o'clock. His official wagons wait at the doors of the newspaper offices and scud to him with the first copies that come from the press. His company of assistants read every line

FAC-SIMILE OF A CENSORED NEWSPAPER

in these papers, and mark everything which seems to have a dangerous look; then he passes final judgment upon these markings. Two things conspire to give to the results a capricious and unbalanced look: his assistants have diversified notions as to what is dangerous and what isn't; he can't get time to examine their criticisms in much detail;

and so sometimes the very same matter which is suppressed in one paper fails to be damned in another one, and gets published in full feather and unmodified. Then the paper in which it was suppressed blandly copies the forbidden matter into its evening edition—provokingly giving credit and detailing all the circumstances in courteous and inoffensive language—and of course the censor cannot say a word.

Sometimes the censor sucks all the blood out of a newspaper and leaves it colorless and inane; sometimes he leaves it undisturbed, and lets it talk out its opinions with a frankness and vigor hardly to be surpassed, I think, in the journals of any country. Apparently the censor sometimes revises his verdicts upon second thought, for several times lately he has suppressed journals after their issue and partial distribution. The distributed copies are then sent for by the censor and destroyed. I have two of these, but at the time they were sent for I could not remember what I had done with them.

If the censor did his work before the morning edition was printed, he would be less of an inconvenience than he is; but, of course, the papers cannot wait many minutes after five o'clock to get his verdict; they might as well go out of business as do that; so they print and take the chances. Then,

19

if they get caught by a suppression, they must strike out the condemned matter and print the edition over again. That delays the issue several hours, and is expensive besides. The government gets the suppressed edition for nothing. If it bought it, that would be joyful, and would give great satisfaction. Also, the edition would be larger. Some of the papers do not replace the condemned paragraphs with other matter; they merely snatch them out and leave blanks behind — mourning blanks, marked " *Confiscated*."

The government discourages the dissemination of newspaper information in other ways. For instance, it does not allow newspapers to be sold on the streets; therefore the newsboy is unknown in Vienna. And there is a stamp duty of nearly a cent upon each copy of a newspaper's issue. Every American paper that reaches me has a stamp upon it, which has been pasted there in the post-office or downstairs in the hotel office; but no matter who put it there, I have to pay for it, and that is the main thing. Sometimes friends send me so many papers that it takes all I can earn that week to keep this government going.

I must take passing notice of another point in the government's measures for maintaining tranquillity. Everybody says it does not like to see any individual attain to commanding influence in the country, since such a man can become a disturber and an inconvenience. "We have as much talent as the other nations," says the citizen, resignedly, and without bitterness, "but for the sake of the general good of the country we are discouraged from making it over-conspicuous; and not only discouraged, but tactfully and skilfully prevented from doing it, if we show too much persistence. Consequently we have no renowned men; in centuries we have seldom produced one—that is, seldom allowed one to produce himself. We can say to-day what no other nation of first importance in the family of Christian civilization can say— that there exists no Austrian who has made an enduring name for himself which is familiar all around the globe."

Another helper toward tranquillity is the army. It is as pervasive as the atmosphere. It is everywhere. All the mentioned creators, promoters, and preservers of the public tranquillity do their several shares in the quieting work. They make a restful and comfortable serenity and reposefulness. This is disturbed sometimes for a little while: a mob assembles to protest against something; it gets noisy—noisier—still noisier—finally *too* noisy; then the persuasive soldiery come charging down upon it, and in a few minutes all is quiet again, and there is no mob.

There is a Constitution and there is a Parliament. The House draws its membership of 425 deputies from the nineteen or twenty states heretofore mentioned. These men represent peoples who speak eleven languages. That means eleven distinct varieties of jealousies, hostilities, and warring interests. This could be expected to furnish forth a parliament of a pretty inharmonious sort, and make legislation difficult at times—and it does that. The parliament is split up into many parties—the Clericals, the Progressists, the German Nationalists, the Young Czechs, the Social Democrats, the Christian Socialists, and some others—and it is difficult to get up working combinations among them. They prefer to fight apart sometimes.

The recent troubles have grown out of Count Badeni's necessities. He could not carry on his government without a majority vote in the House at his back, and in order to secure it he had to make a trade of some sort. He made it with the Czechs—the Bohemians. The terms were not easy for him: he must pass a bill making the Czech tongue the official language in Bohemia in place of the German. This created a storm. All the Germans in Austria were incensed. In numbers they form but a fourth part of the empire's population, but they urge that the country's public business should be conducted in one common tongue, and that tongue a world language—which German is.

However, Badeni secured his majority. The German element in parliament was apparently become helpless. The Czech deputies were exultant.

Then the music began. Bedani's voyage, instead of being smooth, was disappointingly rough from the start. The government must get the *Ausgleich* through. It must not fail. Bedani's majority was ready to carry it through; but the minority was determined to obstruct it and delay it until the obnoxious Czech-language measure should be shelved.

The *Ausgleich* is an Adjustment, Arrangement, Settlement, which holds Austria and Hungary together. It dates from 1867, and has to be renewed every ten years. It establishes the share which Hungary must pay toward the expenses of the imperial government. Hungary is a kingdom (the Emperor of Austria is its King), and has its own parliament and governmental machinery. But it has no foreign office, and it has no army—at least its army is a part of the imperial army, is paid out of the imperial treasury, and is under the control of the imperial war office.

The ten-year rearrangement was due a year ago, but failed to connect. At least completely. A year's compromise was arranged. A new arrangement must be effected before the last day of this year. Otherwise the two countries become separate entities. The Emperor would still be King of Hungary—that is, King of an independent foreign country. There would be Hungarian custom-houses on the Austrian frontier, and there would be a Hungarian army and a Hungarian foreign office. Both countries would be weakened by this, both would suffer damage.

The Opposition in the House, although in the minority, had a good weapon to fight with in the pending *Ausgleich*. If it could delay the *Ausgleich* a few weeks, the government would doubtless have to withdraw the hated language bill or lose Hungary.

The Opposition began its fight. Its arms were the Rules of the House. It was soon manifest that by applying these Rules ingeniously it could make the majority helpless, and keep it so as long as it pleased. It could shut off business every now and then with a motion to adjourn. It could require the ayes and noes on the motion, and use up thirty minutes on that detail. It could call for the reading and verification of the minutes of the pre-

ceding meeting, and use up half a day in that way. It could require that several of its members be entered upon the list of permitted speakers previously to the opening of a sitting; and as there is no time limit, further delays could thus be accomplished.

These were all lawful weapons, and the men of the Opposition (technically called the Left) were within their rights in using them. They used them to such dire purpose that all parliamentary business was paralyzed. The Right (the government side) could accomplish nothing. Then it had a saving idea. This idea was a curious one. It was to have the Presidents and Vice-Presidents of the parliament trample the Rules under foot upon occasion!

This, for a profoundly embittered minority constructed out of fire and gun-cotton! It was time for idle strangers to go and ask leave to look down out of a gallery and see what would be the result of it.

II.—A Memorable Sitting

And now took place that memorable sitting of the House which broke two records. It lasted the best part of two days and a night, surpassing by half an hour the longest sitting known to the

world's previous parliamentary history, and breaking the long-speech record with Dr. Lecher's
twelve-hour effort, the longest flow of unbroken
talk that ever came out of one mouth since the
world began.

At 8.45, on the evening of the 28th of October,
when the House had been sitting a few minutes
short of ten hours, Dr. Lecher was granted the
floor. It was a good place for theatrical effects. I
think that no other Senate House is so shapely as
this one, or so richly and showily decorated. Its
plan is that of an opera-house. Up toward the
straight side of it—the stage side—rise a couple of
terraces of desks for the ministry, and the official
clerks or secretaries—terraces thirty feet long, and
each supporting about half a dozen desks with
spaces between them. Above these is the President's terrace, against the wall. Along it are distributed the proper accommodations for the presiding officer and his assistants. The wall is of
richly colored marble highly polished, its panelled
sweep relieved by fluted columns and pilasters of
distinguished grace and dignity, which glow softly
and frostily in the electric light. Around the
spacious half-circle of the floor bends the great
two-storied curve of the boxes, its frontage elabo-
rately ornamented and sumptuously gilded. On the

floor of the House the 425 desks radiate fanwise from the President's tribune.

The galleries are crowded on this particular evening, for word has gone about that the *Ausgleich* is before the House; that the President, Ritter von Abrahamowicz, has been throttling the Rules; that the Opposition are in an inflammable state in consequence, and that the night session is likely to be of an exciting sort.

The gallery guests are fashionably dressed, and the finery of the women makes a bright and pretty show under the strong electric light. But down on the floor there is no costumery.

The deputies are dressed in day clothes; some of the clothes neat and trim, others not; there may be three members in evening dress, but not more. There are several Catholic priests in their long black gowns, and with crucifixes hanging from their necks. No member wears his hat. One may see by these details that the aspects are not those of an evening sitting of an English House of Commons, but rather those of a sitting of our House of Representatives.

In his high place sits the President, Abrahamowicz, object of the Opposition's limitless hatred. He is sunk back in the depths of his arm-chair, and has his chin down. He brings the ends of his spread fingers together in front of his breast, and reflectively taps them together, with the air of one who would like to begin business but must wait, and be as patient as he can. It makes you think of Richelieu. Now and then he swings his head up to the left or to the right and answers something which some one has bent down to say to him. Then he taps his fingers again. He looks tired, and maybe a trifle harassed. He is a gray - haired, long, slender man, with a colorless long face, which, in repose, suggests a death-mask; but when not in repose is tossed and rippled by a turbulent smile which washes this way and that, and is not easy to keep up with—a pious smile, a holy smile, a saintly smile, a deprecating smile, a beseeching and suppli-cating smile; and when it is at work the large mouth opens, and the flexible lips crumple, and unfold, and crumple again, and move around in a genial and persuasive and angelic way, and expose large glimpses of the teeth; and that interrupts the sacredness of the smile and gives it momentarily a mixed worldly and political and satanic cast. It is a most interesting face to watch. And then the long hands and the body — they furnish great and frequent help to the face in the business of adding to the force of the statesman's words.

To change the tense. At the time of which I

have just been speaking the crowds in the galleries were gazing at the stage and the pit with rapt interest and expectancy. One half of the great fan of desks was in effect empty, vacant; in the other half several hundred members were bunched and jammed together as solidly as the bristles in a brush; and they also were waiting and expecting. Presently the Chair delivered this utterance :

"Dr. Lecher has the floor."

Then burst out such another wild and frantic and deafening clamor as has not been heard on this planet since the last time the Comanches surprised a white settlement at midnight. Yells from the Left, counter-yells from the Right, explosions of yells from all sides at once, and all the air sawed and pawed and clawed and cloven by a writhing confusion of gesturing arms and hands. Out of the midst of this thunder and turmoil and tempest rose Dr. Lecher, serene and collected, and the providential length of him enabled his head to show out above it. He began his twelve-hour speech. At any rate, his lips could be seen to move, and that was evidence. On high sat the President, imploring order, with his long hands put together as in prayer, and his lips visibly but not hearably speaking. At intervals he grasped his bell and swung it up and down with vigor, adding its keen clamor to the storm weltering there below.

Dr. Lecher went on with his pantomime speech, contented, untroubled. Here and there and now and then powerful voices burst above the din, and delivered an ejaculation that was heard. Then the din ceased for a moment or two, and gave opportunity to hear what the Chair might answer; then the noise broke out again. Apparently the President was being charged with all sorts of illegal exercises of power in the interest of the Right (the government side): among these, with arbitrarily closing an Order of Business before it was finished; with an unfair distribution of the right to the floor; with refusal of the floor, upon quibble and protest, to members entitled to it; with stopping a speaker's speech upon quibble and protest; and with other transgressions of the Rules of the House. One of the interrupters who made himself heard was a young fellow of slight build and neat dress, who stood a little apart from the solid crowd and leaned negligently, with folded arms and feet crossed, against a desk. Trim and handsome; strong face and thin features; black hair roughed up; parsimonious mustache; resonant great voice, of good tone and pitch. It is Wolf, capable and hospitable with sword and pistol; fighter of the

DR. ORTON LECHER

recent duel with Count Badeni, the head of the government. He shot Badeni through the arm, and then walked over in the politest way and inspected his game, shook hands, expressed regret, and all that. Out of him came early this thundering peal, audible above the storm :

"I demand the floor. I wish to offer a motion."

In the sudden lull which followed, the President answered, "Dr. Lecher has the floor."

Wolf. "I move the close of the sitting !"

P. "Representative Lecher has the floor." [Stormy outburst from the Left—that is, the Opposition.]

Wolf. "I demand the floor for the introduction of a formal motion. [Pause.] Mr. President, are you going to grant it, or not? [Crash of approval from the Left.] I will keep on demanding the floor till I get it."

P. "I call Representative Wolf to order. Dr. Lecher has the floor."

Wolf. "Mr. President, are you going to observe the Rules of this House?" [Tempest of applause and confused ejaculations from the Left—a boom and roar which long endured, and stopped all business for the time being.]

Dr. von Pessler. "By the Rules motions are in order, and the Chair *must* put them to vote."

For answer the President (who is a Pole—I make this remark in passing) began to jangle his bell with energy at the moment that that wild pandemonium of voices burst out again.

Wolf (hearable above the storm). " Mr. President, I demand the floor. We intend to find out, here and now, which is the hardest, *a Pole's skull or a German's !*"

This brought out a perfect cyclone of satisfaction from the Left. In the midst of it some one again moved an adjournment. The President blandly answered that Dr. Lecher had the floor. Which was true ; and he was speaking, too, calmly, earnestly, and argumentatively; and the official stenographers had left their places and were at his elbows taking down his words, he leaning and orating into their ears—a most curious and interesting scene.

Dr. von Pessler (to the Chair). " Do not drive us to extremities !"

The tempest burst out again : yells of approval from the Left, catcalls and ironical laughter from the Right. At this point a new and most effective noise-maker was pressed into service. Each desk has an extension, consisting of a removable board eighteen inches long, six wide, and a half-inch thick. A member pulled one of these out and began to belabor the top of his desk with it. Instantly other members followed suit, and perhaps you can imagine the result. Of all conceivable rackets it is the most ear-splitting, intolerable, and altogether fiendish.

The persecuted President leaned back in his chair, closed his eyes, clasped his hands in his lap, and a look of pathetic resignation crept over his long face. It is the way a country schoolmaster used to look in days long past when he had refused his school a holiday and it had risen against him in ill-mannered riot and violence and insurrection. Twice a motion to adjourn had been offered—a motion always in order in other Houses, and doubtless so in this one also. The President had refused to put these motions. By consequence, he was not in a pleasant place now, and was having a right hard time. Votes upon motions, whether carried or defeated, could make endless delay, and postpone the *Ausgleich* to next century.

In the midst of these sorrowful circumstances and this hurricane of yells and screams and satanic clatter of desk-boards, Representative Dr. Kronawetter unfeelingly reminds the Chair that a motion has been offered, and adds: " Say yes, or no ! What do you sit there for, and give no answer?"

P. " After I have given a speaker the floor, I cannot give it to another. After Dr. Lecher is though, I will put your motion." [Storm of indignation from the Left.]

Wolf (to the Chair). "Thunder and lightning! look at the Rule governing the case!"

Kronawetter. "I move the close of the sitting! And I demand the ayes and noes!"

Dr. Lecher. "Mr. President, have I the floor?"

P. "You have the floor."

Wolf (to the Chair, in a stentorian voice which cleaves its way through the storm). "It is by such brutalities as these that you drive us to extremities! Are you waiting till some one shall throw into your face the word that shall describe what you are bringing about?* [Tempest of insulted fury from the Right.] *Is that what you are waiting for, old Grayhead?*" [Long-continued clatter of desk-boards from the Left, with shouts of "The vote! the vote!" An ironical shout from the Right, "Wolf is boss!"]

Wolf keeps on demanding the floor for his motion. At length—

P. "I call Representative Wolf to order! Your conduct is unheard of, sir! You forget that you are in a parliament; you must remember where you are, sir." [Applause from the Right. Dr. Lecher

* That is, *revolution.*

is still peacefully speaking, the stenographers listening at his lips.]

Wolf (banging on his desk with his desk-board).
"I demand the floor for my motion! I won't
stand this trampling of the Rules under foot—no,
not if I die for it! I will never yield! You have
got to stop me by force. Have I the floor?"

P. "Representative Wolf, what kind of behavior
is this? I call you to order again. You should
have some regard for your dignity."

Dr. Lecher speaks on. Wolf turns upon him
with an offensive innuendo.

Dr. Lecher. "Mr. Wolf, I beg you to refrain
from that sort of suggestions." [Storm of hand-
clapping from the Right.]

This was applause from the enemy, for Lecher
himself, like Wolf, was an Obstructionist.

Wolf growls to Lecher, "You can scribble that
applause in your album!"

P. "Once more I call Representative Wolf to
order! Do not forget that you are a Representative, sir."

Wolf (slam-banging with his desk-board). "I will
force this matter! Are you going to grant me the
floor, or not?"

And still the sergeant-at-arms did not appear. It
was because there wasn't any. It is a curious thing,

20

but the Chair has no effectual means of compelling order.

After some more interruptions:

Wolf (banging with his board). " I demand the floor. I will not yield!"

P. " I have no recourse against Representative Wolf. In the presence of behavior like this it is to be regretted that such is the case." [A shout from the Right, " Throw him out !"]

It is true, he had no effective recourse. He had an official called an " Ordner," whose help he could invoke in desperate cases, but apparently the Ordner is only a persuader, not a compeller. Apparently he is a sergeant-at-arms who is not loaded ; a good enough gun to look at, but not valuable for business.

For another twenty or thirty minutes Wolf went on banging with his board and demanding his rights; then at last the weary President threatened to summon the dread order-maker. But both his manner and his words were reluctant. Evidently it grieved him to have to resort to this dire extremity. He said to Wolf, " If this goes on, I shall feel obliged to summon the Ordner, and beg him to restore order in the House."

Wolf. " I'd like to see you do it ! Suppose you fetch in a few policemen too ! [Great tumult.]

Are you going to put my motion to adjourn, or not?"

Dr. Lecher continues his speech. Wolf accompanies him with his board-clatter.

The President despatches the Ordner, Dr. Lang (himself a deputy), on his order-restoring mission. Wolf, with his board uplifted for defence, confronts the Ordner with a remark which Boss Tweed might have translated into " Now let's see what you are going to do about it !" [Noise and tumult all over the House.]

Wolf stands upon his rights, and says he will maintain them till he is killed in his tracks. Then he resumes his banging, the President jangles his bell and begs for order, and the rest of the House augment the racket the best it can.

Wolf. " I require an adjournment, because I find myself personally threatened. [Laughter from the Right.] Not that I fear for myself; I am only anxious about what will happen to the man who touches me."

The Ordner. " I am not going to fight with you."

Nothing came of the efforts of the angel of peace, and he presently melted out of the scene and disappeared. Wolf went on with his noise and with his demands that he be granted the floor, resting his board at intervals to discharge criticisms and epithets at the Chair. Once he reminded the Chairman of his violated promise to grant him (Wolf) the floor, and said, "Whence I came, we call promise-breakers rascals!" And he advised the Chairman to take his conscience to bed with him and use it as a pillow. Another time he said that the Chair was making itself ridiculous before all Europe. In fact, some of Wolf's language was almost unparliamentary. By-and-by he struck the idea of beating out a *tune* with his board. Later he decided to stop asking for the floor, and to confer it upon himself. And so he and Dr. Lecher now spoke at the same time, and mingled their speeches with the other noises, and nobody heard either of them. Wolf rested himself now and then from speech-making by reading, in his clarion voice, from a pamphlet.

I will explain that Dr. Lecher was not making a twelve-hour speech for pastime, but for an important purpose. It was the government's intention to push the *Ausgleich* through its preliminary stages in this one sitting (for which it was the Order of the Day), and then by vote refer it to a select committee. It was the Majority's scheme—as charged by the Opposition—to drown debate upon the bill by pure noise—drown it out and stop it. The debate being thus ended, the vote upon the reference

SCENE IN THE AUSTRIAN PARLIAMENT-HOUSE DURING DR. LECHER'S TWELVE HOURS' SPEECH

would follow—with victory for the government. But into the government's calculations had not entered the possibility of a single-barrelled speech which would occupy the entire time-limit of the sitting, and also get itself delivered in spite of all the noise. Goliath was not expecting David. But David was there; and during twelve hours he tranquilly pulled statistical, historical, and argumentative pebbles out of his scrip and slung them at the giant; and when he was done he was victor, and the day was saved.

In the English House an obstructionist has held the floor with Bible-readings and other outside matters; but Dr. Lecher could not have that restful and recuperative privilege—he must confine himself strictly to the subject before the House. More than once when the President could not hear him because of the general tumult, he sent persons to listen and report as to whether the orator was speaking to the subject or not.

The subject was a peculiarly difficult one, and it would have troubled any other deputy to stick to it three hours without exhausting his ammunition, because it required a vast and intimate knowledge —detailed and particularized knowledge—of the commercial, railroading, financial, and international banking relations existing between two great sov-

ereignties, Hungary and the Empire. But Dr.
Lecher is President of the Board of Trade of his
city of Brünn, and was master of the situation.
His speech was not formally prepared. He had a
few notes jotted down for his guidance; he had his
facts in his head; his heart was in his work; and
for twelve hours he stood there, undisturbed by
the clamor around him, and with grace and ease
and confidence poured out the riches of his mind,
in closely reasoned arguments, clothed in eloquent
and faultless phrasing.

He is a young man of thirty-seven. He is tall
and well-proportioned, and has cultivated and for-
tified his muscle by mountain-climbing. If he were
a little handsomer he would sufficiently reproduce
for me the Chauncey Depew of the great New England dinner nights of some years ago; he has Depew's charm of manner and graces of language and
delivery.

There was but one way for Dr. Lecher to hold
the floor—he must stay on his legs. If he should
sit down to rest a moment, the floor would be taken
from him by the enemy in the Chair. When he
had been talking three or four hours he himself
proposed an adjournment, in order that he might
get some rest from his wearing labors; but he limited his motion with the condition that if it was

lost he should be allowed to continue his speech,
and if it carried he should have the floor at the next
sitting. Wolf was now appeased, and withdrew his
own thousand-times-offered motion, and Dr. Lecher's was voted upon—and lost. So he went on
speaking.

By one o'clock in the morning, excitement and
noise-making had tired out nearly everybody but
the orator. Gradually the seats of the Right un-
derwent depopulation; the occupants had slipped
out to the refreshment-rooms to eat and drink, or
to the corridors to chat. Some one remarked that
there was no longer a quorum present, and moved
a call of the House. The Chair (Vice-President
Dr. Kramarz) refused to put it to vote. There was
a small dispute over the legality of this ruling, but
the Chair held its ground.

The Left remained on the battle-field to support
their champion. He went steadily on with his
speech; and always it was strong, virile, felicitous,
and to the point. He was earning applause, and
this enabled his party to turn that fact to account.
Now and then they applauded him a couple of
minutes on a stretch, and during that time he could
stop speaking and rest his voice without having the
floor taken from him.

At a quarter to two a member of the Left demanded that Dr. Lecher be allowed a recess for rest, and said that the Chairman was "heartless." Dr. Lecher himself asked for ten minutes. The Chair allowed him five. Before the time had run out Dr. Lecher was on his feet again.

Wolf burst out again with a motion to adjourn. Refused by the Chair. Wolf said the whole parliament wasn't worth a pinch of powder. The Chair retorted that that was true in a case where a single member was able to make all parliamentary business impossible. Dr. Lecher continued his speech.

The members of the Majority went out by detachments from time to time and took naps upon sofas in the reception-rooms; and also refreshed themselves with food and drink — in quantities nearly unbelievable—but the Minority stayed loyally by their champion. Some distinguished deputies of the Majority stayed by him too, compelled thereto by admiration of his great performance. When a man has been speaking eight hours, is it conceivable that he can still be interesting, still fascinating? When Dr. Lecher had been speaking eight hours he was still compactly surrounded by friends who would not leave him and by foes (of all parties) who *could* not; and all hung enchanted and wondering upon his words, and all testified their admiration with constant and cordial outbursts of applause.   Surely this was a triumph without precedent in history.

During the twelve-hour effort friends brought to the orator three glasses of wine, four cups of coffee, and one glass of beer—a most stingy re-enforcement of his wasting tissues, but the hostile Chair would permit no addition to it.   But, no matter, the Chair could not beat that man.   He was a garrison holding a fort, and was not to be starved out.

When he had been speaking eight hours his pulse was 72; when he had spoken twelve, it was 100.

He finished his long speech in these terms, as nearly as a permissibly free translation can convey them :

"I will now hasten to close my examination of the subject.   I conceive that we of the Left have made it clear to the honorable gentlemen of the other side of the House that we are stirred by no intemperate enthusiasm for this measure in its present shape. . . .

"What we require, and shall fight for with all lawful weapons, is a formal, comprehensive, and definitive solution and settlement of these vexed matters.   We desire the restoration of the earlier condition of things; the cancellation of all this incapable government's pernicious trades with Hungary; and then—release from the sorry burden of the Badeni ministry!

"I voice the hope—I know not if it will be ful-filled—I voice the deep and sincere and patriotic hope that the committee into whose hands this bill will eventually be committed will take its stand upon high ground, and will return the *Ausgleich-Provisorium* to this House in a form which shall make it the protector and promoter alike of the great interests involved and of the honor of our fatherland." After a pause, turning toward the government benches: "But in any case, gentlemen of the Majority, make sure of this: henceforth, as before, you will find us at our post. The Germans of Austria will neither surrender nor die!"

Then burst a storm of applause which rose and fell, rose and fell, burst out again and again and again, explosion after explosion, hurricane after hurricane, with no apparent promise of ever com-ing to an end; and meantime the whole Left was surging and weltering about the champion, all bent upon wringing his hand and congratulating him and glorifying him.

Finally he got away, and went home and ate five loaves and twelve baskets of fishes, read the morn-ing papers, slept three hours, took a short drive, then returned to the House and sat out the rest of the thirty-three-hour session.

To merely *stand up* in one spot twelve hours on a stretch is a feat which very few men could achieve; to add to the task the utterance of a hundred thousand words would be beyond the possibilities of the most of those few; to superimpose the requirement that the words should be put into the form of a compact, coherent, and symmetrical oration would probably rule out the rest of the few, bar Dr. Lecher.

III.—Curious Parliamentary Etiquette

In consequence of Dr. Lecher's twelve-hour speech and the other obstructions furnished by the Minority, the famous thirty-three-hour sitting of the House accomplished nothing. The government side had made a supreme effort, assisting itself with all the helps at hand, both lawful and unlawful, yet had failed to get the *Ausgleich* into the hands of a committee. This was a severe defeat. The Right was mortified, the Left jubilant.

Parliament was adjourned for a week—to let the members cool off, perhaps—a sacrifice of precious time, for but two months remained in which to carry the all-important *Ausgleich* to a consummation.

If I have reported the behavior of the House in-
telligibly, the reader has been surprised at it, and
has wondered whence these law-makers come and
what they are made of ; and he has probably supposed that the conduct exhibited at the Long Sitting was far out of the common, and due to special
excitement and irritation. As to the make-up of
the House, it is this: the deputies come from all
the walks of life and from all the grades of society.
There are princes, counts, barons, priests, peasants,
mechanics, laborers, lawyers, judges, physicians,
professors, merchants, bankers, shopkeepers. They
are religious men, they are earnest, sincere, devoted,
and they hate the Jews. The title of Doctor is so
common in the House that one may almost say
that the deputy who does not bear it is by that
reason conspicuous. I am assured that it is not a
self-granted title, and not an honorary one, but an
earned one ; that in Austria it is very seldom conferred as a mere compliment; that in Austria the
degrees of Doctor of Music, Doctor of Philosophy,
and so on, are not conferred by the seats of learning; and so, when an Austrian is called Doctor
it means that he is either a lawyer or a physician,
and that he is not a self-educated man, but is college-bred, and has been diplomaed for merit.

That answers the question of the constitution of

the House.   Now as to the House's curious manners.   The manners exhibited by this convention
of Doctors were not at that time being tried as a
wholly new experiment.   I will go back to a previous sitting in order to show that the deputies had
already had some practice.

There had been an incident.   The dignity of the
House had been wounded by improprieties indulged
in in its presence by a couple of its members.
This matter was placed in the hands of a committee
to determine where the guilt lay, and the degree
of it, and also to suggest the punishment.   The
chairman of the committee brought in his report.
By this it appeared that, in the course of a speech,
Deputy Schrammel said that religion had no
proper place in the public schools—it was a private
matter.   Whereupon Deputy Gregorig shouted,
" How about free love !"

To this, Deputy Iro flung out this retort : " Soda-
water at the Wimberger !"

This appeared to deeply offend Deputy Gregorig, who shouted back at Iro, " You cowardly blatherskite, say that again !"

The committee had sat three hours.   Gregorig
had apologized ; Iro had explained.   Iro explained
that he didn't say anything about soda-water at
the Wimberger.   He explained in writing, and was

very explicit: "I declare *upon my word of honor* that I did not say the words attributed to me."

Unhappily for his word of honor, it was proved by the official stenographers and by the testimony of several deputies that he *did* say them.

The committee did not officially know why the apparently inconsequential reference to soda-water at the Wimberger should move Deputy Gregorig to call the utterer of it a cowardly blatherskite; still, after proper deliberation, it was of the opinion that the House ought to formally censure the whole business. This verdict seems to have been regarded as sharply severe. I think so because Deputy Dr. Lueger, Bürgermeister of Vienna, felt it a duty to soften the blow to his friend Gregorig by showing that the soda-water remark was not so innocuous as it might look; that, indeed, Gregorig's tough retort was justifiable—and he proceeded to explain why. He read a number of scandalous post-cards which he intimated had proceeded from Iro, as indicated by the handwriting, though they were anonymous. Some of them were posted to Gregorig at his place of business, and could have been read by all his subordinates; the others were posted *to Gregorig's wife*. Lueger did not say—but everybody knew—that the cards referred to a matter of town gossip which made Mr. Gregorig a chief actor in a tavern scene where siphon-squirting played a prominent and humorous part, and wherin women had a share.

There were several of the cards; more than several, in fact; no fewer than five were sent in one day. Dr. Lueger read some of them, and described others. Some of them had pictures on them; one a picture of a hog with a monstrous snout, and beside it a squirting soda-siphon; below it some sarcastic doggerel.

Gregorig deals in shirts, cravats, etc. One of the cards bore these words: "Much-respected Deputy and collar-sewer—or *stealer*."

Another: "Hurrah for the Christian-Social work among the women-assemblages! Hurrah for the soda-squirter!" Comment by Dr. Lueger; "I cannot venture to read the rest of that one, nor the signature, either."

Another: "Would you mind telling me if . . ." Comment by Dr. Lueger: "The rest of it is not properly readable."

To Deputy Gregorig's wife: "Much-respected Madam Gregorig,—The undersigned desires an invitation to the next soda-squirt." Comment by Dr. Lueger: "Neither the rest of the card nor the signature can I venture to read to the House, so vulgar are they."

The purpose of this card—to expose Gregorig to his family—was repeated in others of these anonymous missives.

The House, by vote, censured the two improper deputies.

This may have had a modifying effect upon the phraseology of the membership for a while, and upon its general exuberance also, but it was not for long. As has been seen, it had become lively once more on the night of the Long Sitting. At the next sitting after the long one there was certainly no lack of liveliness. The President was persistently ignoring the Rules of the House in the interest of the government side, and the Minority were in an unappeasable fury about it. The ceaseless din and uproar, the shouting and stamping and desk-banging, were deafening, but through it all burst voices now and then that made themselves heard. Some of the remarks were of a very candid sort, and I believe that if they had been uttered in our House of Representatives they would have attracted attention. I will insert some samples here. Not in their order, but selected on their merits:

Dr. Mayreder (to the President). "You have lied! You conceded the floor to me; make it good, or you have lied!"

Mr. Glöckner (to the President). " Leave ! Get out !"

Wolf (indicating the President). " There sits a man to whom a certain title belongs !"

Unto Wolf, who is continuously reading, in a powerful voice, from a newspaper, arrive these personal remarks from the Majority : " Oh, shut your mouth !" " Put him out !" " Out with him !" Wolf stops reading a moment to shout at Dr. Lueger, who has the floor but cannot get a hearing, " Please, Betrayer of the People, begin !"

Dr. Lueger. " Meine Herren—" [" Oho !" and groans.]

Wolf. " *That's* the holy light of the Christian Socialists !"

Mr. Kletzenbauer (Christian Socialist). " Dam—nation ! are you ever going to quiet down ?"

Wolf discharges a galling remark at Mr. Wohlmeyer.

Wohlmeyer (responding). " You Jew, you !"

There is a moment's lull, and Dr. Lueger begins his speech. Graceful, handsome man, with winning manners and attractive bearing, a bright and easy speaker, and is said to know how to trim his political sails to catch any favoring wind that blows. He manages to say a few words, then the tempest overwhelms him again.

21

Wolf stops reading his paper a moment to say a drastic thing about Lueger and his Christian-Social pieties, which sets the C. S.'s in a sort of frenzy.

Mr. Vielohlawek. "You leave the Christian Socialists alone, you word-of-honor-breaker! Obstruct all you want to, but you leave *them* alone! You've no business in this House; you belong in a gin-mill!"

Mr. Prochazka. "In a lunatic-asylum you mean!"

Vielohlawek. "It's a pity that such a man should be leader of the Germans; he disgraces the German name!"

Dr. Scheicher. "It's a shame that the like of him should insult us."

Strohbach (to Wolf). "Contemptible cub—we will bounce thee out of this!" [It is inferable that the "thee" is not intended to indicate affection this time, but to re-enforce and emphasize Mr. Strohbach's scorn.]

Dr. Scheicher. "His insults are of no consequence. He wants his ears boxed."

Dr. Lueger (to Wolf). "You'd better worry a trifle over your Iro's word of honor. You are behaving like a street arab."

Dr. Scheicher. "It is infamous!"

Dr. Lueger. "And *these* shameless creatures are the leaders of the German People's Party!"

Meantime Wolf goes whooping along with his newspaper readings in great contentment.

Dr. Pattai. "Shut up! Shut up! Shut *up!* You haven't the floor!"

Strohbach. "The miserable cub!"

Dr. Lueger (to Wolf, raising his voice strenuously above the storm). "You are a wholly honorless street brat!" [A voice, "Fire the rapscallion out!" But Wolf's soul goes marching noisily on just the same.]

Schönerer (vast and muscular, and endowed with the most powerful voice in the Reichsrath ; comes ploughing down through the standing crowds, red, and choking with anger; halts before Deputy Wohlmeyer, grabs a rule and smashes it with a blow upon a desk, threatens Wohlmeyer's face with his fist, and bellows out some personalities, and a promise). "Only you wait—we'll teach you." [A whirlwind of offensive retorts assails him from the band of meek and humble Christian Socialists compacted around their leader, that distinguished religious expert, Dr. Lueger, Bürgermeister of Vienna. Our breath comes in excited gasps now, and we are full of hope. We imagine that we are back fifty years ago in the Arkansas Legislature, and we think we know what is going to happen, and are glad we came, and glad we are up in the gallery, out of the way, where we can see the whole thing and yet not have to supply any of the material for the inquest. However, as it turns out, our confidence is abused, our hopes are misplaced.]

Dr. Pattai (wildly excited). "You quiet down, or we shall turn ourselves loose! There will be cuffing of ears!"

Prochazka (in a fury). "No—*not* ear-boxing, but genuine *blows!*"

Vielohlawek. "I would rather take my hat off to a Jew than to Wolf!"

Strohbach (to Wolf). "Jew flunky! Here we have been fighting the Jews for ten years, and now you are helping them to power again. How much do you get for it?"

Holansky. "What he wants is a strait-jacket!"

Wolf continues his readings. It is a market report now.

Remark flung across the House to Schönerer: "*Die Grossmutter auf dem Misthaufen erzeugt worden!*"

It will be judicious not to translate that. Its flavor is pretty high, in any case, but it becomes particularly gamy when you remember that the first gallery was well stocked with ladies.

Apparently it was a great hit. It fetched thunders of joyous enthusiam out of the Christian Socialists, and in their rapture they flung biting epithets with wasteful liberality at specially detested members of the Opposition; among others, this one at Schönerer: *"Bordell in der Krugerstrasse!"* Then they added these words, which they whooped, howled, and also even sang, in a deep-voiced chorus: *"Schmul Leeb Kohn! Schmul Leeb Kohn! Schmul Leeb Kohn!* and made it splendidly audible above the banging of deskboards and the rest of the roaring cyclone of fiend-ish noises. [A gallery witticism comes flitting by from mouth to mouth around the great curve: "The swan-song of Austrian representative government!" You can note its progress by the applausive smiles and nods it gets as it skims along.]

Kletzenbauer. "Holofernes, where is Judith?" [Storm of laughter.]

Gregorig (the shirt-merchant). "This Wolf-Theatre is costing 6000 florins!"

Wolf (with sweetness). "Notice him, gentlemen; it is Mr. Gregorig." [Laughter.]

Vielohlawek (to Wolf). "You Judas!"

Schneider. "Brothel-knight!"

Chorus of Voices. "East-German offal tub!"

And so the war of epithets crashes along, with never-diminishing energy for a couple of hours.

The ladies in the gallery were learning. That was well; for by-and-by ladies will form a part of the membership of all the legislatures in the world; as soon as they can prove competency they will be admitted. At present men only are competent to legislate; therefore they look down upon women, and would feel degraded if they had to have them for colleagues in their high calling.

Wolf is yelling another market report now.

Gessman. "Shut up, infamous louse-brat!"

During a momentary lull Dr. Lueger gets a hearing for three sentences of his speech. They demand and require that the President shall suppress the four noisiest members of the Opposition.

Wolf (with a that-settles-it toss of the head). "The shifty trickster of Vienna has spoken!"

Iro belonged to Schönerer's party. The word-of-honor incident has given it a new name. Gregorig is a Christian Socialist, and hero of the post-cards and the Wimberger soda-squirting incident. He stands vast and conspicuous, and conceited and self-satisfied, and roosterish and inconsequential, at Lueger's elbow, and is proud and cocky to be in such great company. He looks very well indeed; really majestic, and aware of it. He crows out his little empty remark now and then, and looks as pleased as if he had been delivered of the *Ausgleich*. Indeed, he does look notably fine. He wears almost the only dress vest on the floor; it exposes a continental spread of white shirt-front; his hands are posed at ease in the lips of his trousers pockets; his head is tilted back complacently; he is attitudinizing; he is playing to the gallery. However, they are all doing that. It is curious to see. Men who only vote, and can't make speeches, and don't know how to invent witty ejaculations, wander about the vacated parts of the floor, and stop in a good place and strike attitudes—attitudes suggestive of weighty thought, mostly—and glance furtively up at the galleries to see how it works; or a couple will come together and shake hands in an artificial way, and laugh a gay manufactured laugh, and do some constrained and self-conscious attitudinizing; and *they* steal glances at the galleries to see if they are getting notice. It is like a scene on the stage—by-play by minor actors at the back while the stars do the great work at the front. Even Count Badeni attitudinizes for a moment; strikes a reflective Napoleonic attitude of fine picturesqueness—but soon thinks better of it and desists. There are two who do not attitudinize— poor harried and insulted President Abrahamowicz, who seems wholly miserable, and can find no way to put in the dreary time but by swinging his bell and by discharging occasional remarks which nobody can hear; and a resigned and patient priest, who sits lonely in a great vacancy on Majority territory and munches an apple.

Schönerer uplifts his fog-horn of a voice and shakes the roof with an insult discharged at the Majority.

Dr. Leuger. " The Honorless Party would better keep still here !"

Gregorig (the echo, swelling out his shirt-front). " Yes, keep quiet, pimp !"

Schönerer (to Lueger). " Political mountebank !"

Prochazka (to Schönerer). " Drunken clown !"

During the final hour of the sitting many happy phrases were distributed through the proceedings. Among them were these—and they are strikingly good ones :

" Blatherskite !"

" Blackguard !"

" Scoundrel !"

" Brothel-daddy !"

This last was the contribution of Dr. Gessman, and gave great satisfaction. And deservedly. It seems to me that it was one of the most sparkling things that was said during the whole evening.

At half past two in the morning the House adjourned. The victory was with the Opposition. No; not quite that. The effective part of it was snatched away from them by an unlawful exercise of Presidential force — another contribution toward driving the mistreated Minority out of their minds.

At other sittings of the parliament, gentlemen of the Opposition, shaking their fists toward the President, addressed him as " Polish Dog." At one sitting an angry deputy turned upon a colleague and shouted,

"———— ———— ———— ———— ————!"

You must try to imagine what it was. If I should offer it even in the original it would probably not get by the Magazine editor's blue pencil; to offer a translation would be to waste my ink, of course. This remark was frankly printed in its entirety by one of the Vienna dailies, but the others disguised the toughest half of it with stars.

If the reader will go back over this chapter and gather its array of extraordinary epithets into a bunch and examine them, he will marvel at two things: how this convention of gentlemen could consent to use such gross terms; and why the users were allowed to get out of the place alive. There is no way to understand this strange situa-

tion. If every man in the House were a professional blackguard, and had his home in a sailor
boarding-house, one could still not understand it;
for although that sort do use such terms, they
never *take* them. These men are not professional
blackguards; they are mainly gentlemen, and educated; yet they use the terms, and take them too.
They really seem to attach no consequence to
them. One cannot say that they act like schoolboys; for that is only almost true, not entirely.
Schoolboys blackguard each other fiercely, and by
the hour, and one would think that nothing would
ever come of it but noise; but that would be a
mistake. Up to a certain limit the result would be
noise only, but, that limit overstepped, trouble
would follow right away. There are certain phrases
—phrases of a peculiar character—phrases of the
nature of that reference to Schönerer's grandmother, for instance—which not even the most
spiritless schoolboy in the English-speaking world
would allow to pass unavenged. One difference
between schoolboys and the law-makers of the
Reichsrath seems to be that the law-makers have
no limit, no danger-line. Apparently they may
call each other what they please, and go home un-
mutilated.

Now, in fact, they did have a scuffle on two occasions, but it was not on account of names called. There has been no scuffle where *that* was the cause.

It is not to be inferred that the House lacks a sense of honor because it lacks delicacy. That would be an error. Iro was caught in a lie, and it profoundly disgraced him. The House cut him, turned its back upon him. He resigned his seat; otherwise he would have been expelled. But it was lenient with Gregorig, who had called Iro a cowardly blatherskite in debate. It merely went through the form of mildly censuring him. That did not trouble Gregorig.

The Viennese say of themselves that they are an easy-going, pleasure-loving community, making the best of life, and not taking it very seriously. Nevertheless, they are grieved about the ways of their parliament, and say quite frankly that they are ashamed. They claim that the low condition of the parliament's manners is new, not old. A gentleman who was at the head of the government twenty years ago confirms this, and says that in his time the parliament was orderly and well-behaved. An English gentleman of long residence here endorses this, and says that a low order of politicians originated the present forms of questionable speech on the stump some years ago, and imported them into the parliament.* However, some day there will be a Minister of Etiquette and a sergeant-at-arms, and then things will go better. I mean if parliament and the Constitution survive the present storm.

IV.—The Historic Climax

During the whole of November things went from bad to worse. The all-important *Ausgleich* remained hard aground, and could not be sparred off. Badeni's government could not withdraw the Language Ordinance and keep its majority, and the Opposition could not be placated on easier terms. One night, while the customary pandemonium was crashing and thundering along at its best, a fire broke out. It was a surging, struggling, shoulder-to-shoulder scramble. A great many blows were struck. Twice Schönerer lifted one of the heavy ministerial fauteuils—some say with one hand—and threatened members of the Majority with it, but it was wrenched away from him; a member hammered Wolf over the head

---

* "In that gracious bygone time when a mild and good-tempered spirit was the atmosphere of our House, when the manner of our speakers was studiously formal and academic, and the storms and explosions of to-day were wholly unknown," etc.—*Translation of the opening remark of an editorial in this morning's Neue Freie Presse, December 11.*

with the President's bell, and another member choked him; a professor was flung down and belabored with fists and choked; he held up an open penknife as a defence against the blows; it was snatched from him and flung to a distance; it hit a peaceful Christian Socialist who wasn't doing anything, and brought blood from his hand. This was the only blood drawn. The men who got hammered and choked looked sound and well next day. The fists and the bell were not properly handled, or better results would have been apparent. I am quite sure that the fighters were not in earnest.

On Thanksgiving Day the sitting was a history-making one. On that day the harried, bedeviled, and despairing government went insane. In order to free itself from the thraldom of the Opposition it committed this curiously juvenile crime : it moved an important change of the Rules of the House, forbade debate upon the motion, put it to a stand-up vote instead of ayes and noes, and then gravely claimed that it had been adopted ; whereas, to even the dullest witness—if I without immodesty may pretend to that place—it was plain that nothing legitimately to be called a vote had been taken at all.

I think that Saltpeter never uttered a truer thing than when he said, "Whom the gods would destroy they first make mad." Evidently the government's mind was tottering when this bald insult to the House was the best way it could contrive for getting out of the frying-pan.

The episode would have been funny if the matter at stake had been a trifle; but in the circumstances it was pathetic. The usual storm was raging in the House. As usual, many of the Majority and the most of the Minority were standing up— to have a better chance to exchange epithets and make other noises. Into this storm Count Falkenhayn entered, with his paper in his hand; and at once there was a rush to get near him and hear him read his motion. In a moment he was walled in by listeners. The several clauses of his motion were loudly applauded by these allies, and as loudly disapplauded—if I may invent a word—by such of the Opposition as could hear his voice. When he took his seat the President promptly put the motion—persons desiring to vote in the affirmative, *stand up!* The House was already standing up; had been standing for an hour; and before a third of it had found out what the President had been saying, he had proclaimed the adoption of the motion! And only a few heard *that*. In fact, when that House is legislating you can't tell it from artillery practice.

You will realize what a happy idea it was to side-track the lawful ayes and noes and substitute a stand-up vote by this fact: that a little later, when a deputation of deputies waited upon the President and asked him if he was actually willing to claim that that measure had been passed, he answered, "Yes—and *unanimously*." It shows that in effect the whole House was on its feet when that trick was sprung.

The "Lex Falkenhayn," thus strangely born, gave the President power to suspend for three days any deputy who should continue to be disorderly after being called to order twice, and it also placed at his disposal such force as might be necessary to make the suspension effective. So the House had a sergeant-at-arms at last, and a more formidable one, as to power, than any other legislature in Christendom had ever possessed. The Lex Falkenhayn also gave the House itself authority to suspend members for *thirty* days.

On these terms the *Ausgleich* could be put through in an hour—apparently. The Opposition would have to sit meek and quiet, and stop obstructing, or be turned into the street, deputy after deputy, leaving the Majority an unvexed field for its work.

Certainly the thing looked well. The government was out of the frying-pan at last. It congratulated itself, and was almost girlishly happy. Its stock rose suddenly from less than nothing to a premium. It confessed to itself, with pride, that its Lex Falkenhayn was a master-stroke—a work of genius.

However, there were doubters—men who were troubled, and believed that a grave mistake had been made. It might be that the Opposition was crushed, and profitably for the country, too; but the *manner* of it—the *manner* of it! That was the serious part. It could have far-reaching results; results whose gravity might transcend all guessing. It might be the initial step toward a return to government by force, a restoration of the irresponsible methods of obsolete times.

There were no vacant seats in the galleries next day. In fact, standing-room outside the building was at a premium. There were crowds there, and a glittering array of helmeted and brass-buttoned police, on foot and on horseback, to keep them from getting too much excited. No one could guess what was going to happen, but every one felt that *something* was going to happen, and hoped he might have a chance to see it, or at least get the news of it while it was fresh.

At noon the House was empty—for I do not

count myself. Half an hour later the two galleries were solidly packed, the floor still empty. Another half-hour later Wolf entered and passed to his place; then other deputies began to stream in, among them many forms and faces grown familiar of late. By one o'clock the membership was present in full force. A band of Socialists stood grouped against the ministerial desks, in the shadow of the Presidential tribune. It was observable that these official strongholds were now protected against rushes by bolted gates, and that these were in ward of servants wearing the House's livery. Also the removable desk-boards had been taken away, and nothing left for disorderly members to slat with.

There was a pervading, anxious hush—at least what stood very well for a hush in that House. It was believed by many that the Opposition was cowed, and that there would be no more obstruction, no more noise. That was an error.

Presently the President entered by the distant door to the right, followed by Vice-President Fuchs, and the two took their way down past the Polish benches toward the tribune. Instantly the customary storm of noises burst out, and rose higher and higher, and wilder and wilder, and really seemed to surpass anything that had gone before it in that place. The President took his seat, and begged

22

for order, but no one could hear him. His lips moved—one could see that; he bowed his body forward appealingly, and spread his great hand eloquently over his breast—one could see that; but as concerned his uttered words, he probably could not hear them himself. Below him was that crowd of two dozen Socialists glaring up at him, shaking their fists at him, roaring imprecations and insulting epithets at him. This went on for some time. Suddenly the Socialists burst through the gates and stormed up through the ministerial benches, and a man in a red cravat reached up and snatched the documents that lay on the President's desk and flung them abroad. The next moment he and his allies were struggling and fighting with the half-dozen uniformed servants who were there to protect the new gates. Meantime a detail of Socialists had swarmed up the side steps and overflowed the President and the Vice, and were crowding and shouldering and shoving them out of the place. They crowded them out, and down the steps and across the House, past the Polish benches; and all about them swarmed hostile Poles and Czechs, who resisted them. One could see fists go up and come down, with other signs and shows of a heady fight; then the President and the Vice disappeared through the door of entrance, and the victorious Socialists turned and marched back, mounted the tribune, flung the President's bell and his remaining papers abroad, and then stood there in a compact little crowd, eleven strong, and held the place as if it were a fortress. Their friends on the floor were in a frenzy of triumph, and manifested it in their deafening way. The whole House was on its feet, amazed and wondering.

It was an astonishing situation, and imposingly dramatic. Nobody had looked for this. The unexpected had happened. What next? But there *can* be no next; the play is over; the grand climax is reached; the possibilities are exhausted; ring down the curtain.

Not yet. That distant door opens again. And now we see what history will be talking of five centuries hence: a uniformed and helmeted battalion of bronzed and stalwart men marching in double file down the floor of the House—a free parliament profaned by an invasion of brute force!

It was an odious spectacle—odious and awful. For one moment it was an unbelievable thing—a thing beyond all credibility; it must be a delusion, a dream, a nightmare. But no, it was real—pitifully real, shamefully real, hideously real. These sixty policemen had been soldiers, and they went at their work with the cold unsentimentality of their trade. They ascended the steps of the tribune, laid their hands upon the inviolable persons of the representatives of a nation, and dragged and tugged and hauled them down the steps and out at the door; then ranged themselves in stately military array in front of the ministerial estrade, and so stood.

It was a tremendous episode. The memory of it will outlast all the thrones that exist to-day. In the whole history of free parliaments the like of it had been seen but three times before. It takes its imposing place among the world's unforgettable things. I think that in my lifetime I have not twice seen abiding history made before my eyes, but I know that I have seen it once.

Some of the results of this wild freak followed instantly. The Badeni government came down with a crash; there was a popular outbreak or two in Vienna; there were three or four days of furious rioting in Prague, followed by the establishing there of martial law; the Jews and Germans were harried and plundered, and their houses destroyed; in other Bohemian towns there was rioting—in some cases the Germans being the rioters, in others the Czechs—and in all cases the Jew had to roast, no matter which side he was on. We are well along in December now ;* the next new Minister-President has not been able to patch up a peace among the warring factions of the parliament, therefore there is no use in calling it together again for the present ; public opinion believes that parliamentary government and the Constitution are actually threatened with extinction, and that the permanency of the monarchy itself is a not absolutely certain thing !

Yes, the Lex Falkenhayn was a great invention, and did what was claimed for it—it got the government out of the frying-pan.

* It is the 9th.—M. T.

THE AUSTRIAN EDISON KEEPING
SCHOOL AGAIN

BY a paragraph in the *Freie Presse* it appears
that Jan Szczepanik, the youthful inventor
of the "telelectroscope" (for seeing at great
distances) and some other scientific marvels, has
been having an odd adventure, by help of the state.
Vienna is hospitably ready to smile whenever
there is an opportunity, and this seems to be a fair
one. Three or four years ago, when Szczepanik
was nineteen or twenty years old, he was a schoolmaster in a Moravian village, on a salary of—I
forget the amount, but no matter; there was not
enough of it to remember. His head was full of
inventions, and in his odd hours he began to plan
them out. He soon perfected an ingenious invention for applying photography to pattern-designing
as used in the textile industries, whereby he proposed to reduce the customary outlay of time,
labor, and money expended on that department of
loom-work to next to nothing. He wanted to

carry his project to Vienna and market it, and, as he could not get leave of absence, he made his trip without leave. This lost him his place, but did not gain him his market. When his money ran out he went back home, and was presently reinstated. By-and-by he deserted once more, and went to Vienna, and this time he made some friends who assisted him, and his invention was sold to England and Germany for a great sum. During the past three years he has been experimenting and investigating in velvety comfort. His most picturesque achievement is his telelectroscope, a device which a number of able men—including Mr. Edison, I think—had already tried their hands at, with prospects of eventual success. A Frenchman came near to solving the difficult and intricate problem fifteen years ago, but an essential detail was lacking which he could not master, and he suffered defeat. Szczepanik's experiments with his pattern-designing project revealed to him the secret of the lacking detail. He perfected his invention, and a French syndicate has bought it, and saved it for exhibition and fortune-making at the Paris world's fair.

As a schoolmaster Szczepanik was exempt from military duty. When he ceased from teaching, being an educated man he could have had himself enrolled as a one-year volunteer; but he forgot to do it, and this exposed him to the privilege, and also the necessity, of serving *three* years in the army. In the course of duty, the other day, an official discovered the inventor's indebtedness to the state, and took the proper measures to collect. At first there seemed to be no way for the inventor (and the state) out of the difficulty. The authorities were loath to take the young man out of his great laboratory, where he was helping to shove the whole human race along on its road to new prosperities and scientific conquests, and suspend operations in his mental Klondike three years, while he punched the empty air with a bayonet in a time of peace; but there was the law, and how was it to be helped? It was a difficult puzzle, but the authorities labored at it until they found a forgotten law some wherewhich furnished a loop-hole— a large one, and a long one, too, as it looks to me. By this piece of good-luck Szczepanik is saved from soldiering, but he becomes a schoolmaster again; and it is a sufficiently picturesque billet, when you examine it. He must go back to his village every two months, and teach his school half a day—from early in the morning until noon; and, to the best of my understanding of the published terms, he must keep this up the rest of his life! I hope so, just for the romantic poeticalness of it. He is twenty-four, strongly and compactly built, and comes of an ancestry accustomed to waiting to see its great-grandchildren married. It is almost certain that he will live to be ninety. I hope so. This promises him sixty-six years of useful school service. Dissected, it gives him a chance to teach school 396 half-days, make 396 railway trips going, and 396 back, pay bed and board 396 times in the village, and lose possibly 1200 days from his laboratory work—that is to say, three years and three months or so. And he already owes three years to this same account. This has been overlooked; I shall call the attention of the authorities to it. It may be possible for him to get a compromise on this compromise by doing his three years in the army, and saving one; but I think it can't happen. This government "holds the age" on him; it has what is technically called a "good thing" in financial circles, and knows a good thing when it sees it. I know the inventor very well, and he has my sympathy. This is friendship. But I am throwing my influence with the government. This is politics.

Szczepanik left for his village in Moravia day before yesterday to "do time" for the first time under his sentence. Early yesterday morning he

started for the school in a fine carriage, which was
stocked with fruits, cakes, toys, and all sorts of
knick-knacks, rarities, and surprises for the children,
and was met on the road by the school and a body
of schoolmasters from the neighboring districts,
marching in column, with the village authorities at
the head, and was received with the enthusiastic
welcome proper to the man who had made their
village's name celebrated, and conducted in state
to the humble doors which had been shut against
him as a deserter three years before. It is out of
materials like these that romances are woven ; and
when the romancer has done his best, he has not
improved upon the unpainted facts. Szczepanik
put the sapless school-books aside, and led the
children a holiday dance through the enchanted
lands of science and invention, explaining to them
some of the curious things which he had contrived,
and the laws which governed their construction
and performance, and illustrating these matters
with pictures and models and other helps to a clear
understanding of their fascinating mysteries. After
this there was play and a distribution of the fruits
and toys and things ; and after this, again, some
more science, including the story of the invention
of the telephone, and an explanation of its character and laws, for the convict had brought a tele-

phone along. The children saw that wonder for the first time, and they also personally tested its powers and verified them.

Then school "let out"; the teacher got his certificate, all signed, stamped, taxed, and so on, said good-bye, and drove off in his carriage under a storm of " *Do widzenia !*" (" *Au revoir !*") from the children, who will resume their customary sobrieties until he comes in August and uncorks his flask of scientific fire-water again.

TRAVELLING WITH A REFORMER

L AST spring I went out to Chicago to see the Fair, and although I did not see it my trip was not wholly lost—there were compensations. In New York I was introduced to a major in the regular army who said he was going to the Fair, and we agreed to go together. I had to go to Boston first, but that did not interfere; he said he would go along and put in the time. He was a handsome man, and built like a gladiator. But his ways were gentle, and his speech was soft and persuasive. He was companionable, but exceedingly reposeful. Yes, and wholly destitute of the sense of humor. He was full of interest in everything that went on around him, but his serenity was indestructible; nothing disturbed him, nothing excited him.

But before the day was done I found that deep down in him somewhere he had a passion, quiet as he was—a passion for reforming petty public abuses. He stood for citizenship — it was his

hobby. His idea was that every citizen of the re-
public ought to consider himself an unofficial
policeman, and keep unsalaried watch and ward
over the laws and their execution. He thought
that the only effective way of preserving and protecting public rights was for each citizen to do
his share in preventing or punishing such in-
fringements of them as came under his personal
notice.

It was a good scheme, but I thought it would
keep a body in trouble all the time; it seemed to
me that one would be always trying to get offend-
ing little officials discharged, and perhaps getting
laughed at for all reward. But he said no, I had
the wrong idea; that there was no occasion to get
anybody discharged; that in fact you *mustn't* get
anybody discharged; that that would itself be a
failure; no, one must reform the man—reform him
and make him useful where he was.

" Must one report the offender and then beg his
superior not to discharge him, but reprimand him
and keep him ?"

" No, that is not the idea; you don't report him
at all, for then you risk his bread and butter. You
can act as if you are *going* to report him—when
nothing else will answer. But that's an extreme
case. That is a sort of *force*, and force is bad.

Diplomacy is the effective thing.   Now if a man
has tact—if a man will exercise diplomacy—"

For two minutes we had been standing at a telegraph wicket, and during all this time the Major
had been trying to get the attention of one of the
young operators, but they were all busy skylarking.
The Major spoke now, and asked one of them to
take his telegram.   He got for reply:

" I reckon you can wait a minute, can't you?"
and the skylarking went on.

The Major said yes, he was not in a hurry.
Then he wrote another telegram:

"*President Western Union Tel. Co.:*

" Come and dine with me this evening. I can tell you
how business is conducted in one of your branches."

Presently the young fellow who had spoken so
pertly a little before reached out and took the telegram, and when he read it he lost color and began
to apologize and explain. He said he would lose
his place if this deadly telegram was sent, and he
might never get another. If he could be let off
this time he would give no cause of complaint
again.   The compromise was accepted.

As we walked away, the Major said:

" Now, you see, that was diplomacy—and you
see how it worked.   It wouldn't do any good to

bluster, the way people are always doing—that boy can always give you as good as you send, and you'll come out defeated and ashamed of yourself pretty nearly always. But you see he stands no chance against diplomacy. Gentle words and diplomacy—those are the tools to work with."

"Yes, I see; but everybody wouldn't have had your opportunity. It isn't everybody that is on those familiar terms with the president of the Western Union."

"Oh, you misunderstand. I don't know the president—I only use him diplomatically. It is for his good and for the public good. There's no harm in it."

I said, with hesitation and diffidence:

"But is it ever right or noble to tell a lie?"

He took no note of the delicate self-righteousness of the question, but answered, with undisturbed gravity and simplicity:

"Yes, sometimes. Lies told to injure a person and lies told to profit yourself are not justifiable, but lies told to help another person, and lies told in the public interest—oh, well, that is quite another matter. Anybody knows that. But never mind about the methods: you see the result. That youth is going to be useful now, and well-behaved. He had a good face. He was worth saving. Why, he was worth saving on his mother's account if not his own. Of course, he has a mother—sisters, too. Damn these people who are always forgetting that! Do you know, I've never fought a duel in my life—never once—and yet have been challenged, like other people. I could always see the other man's unoffending women folks or his little children standing between him and me. *They* hadn't done anything—I couldn't break *their* hearts you know."

He corrected a good many little abuses in the course of the day, and always without friction—always with a fine and dainty " diplomacy " which left no sting behind; and he got such happiness and such contentment out of these performances that I was obliged to envy him his trade—and perhaps would have adopted it if I could have managed the necessary deflections from fact as confidently with my mouth as I believe I could with a pen, behind the shelter of print, after a little practice.

Away late that night we were coming up-town in a horse-car when three boisterous roughs got aboard, and began to fling hilarious obscenities and profanities right and left among the timid passengers, some of whom were women and children. Nobody resisted or retorted; the conductor tried soothing words and moral suasion, but the roughs only called him names and laughed at him. Very soon I saw that the Major realized that this was a matter which was in his line; evidently he was turning over his stock of diplomacy in his mind and getting ready. I felt that the first diplomatic remark he made in this place would bring down a landslide of ridicule upon him, and maybe something worse; but before I could whisper to him and check him he had begun, and it was too late. He said, in a level and dispassionate tone:

"Conductor, you must put these swine out. I will help you."

I was not looking for that. In a flash the three roughs plunged at him. But none of them arrived. He delivered three such blows as one could not expect to encounter outside the prize-ring, and neither of the men had life enough left in him to get up from where he fell. The Major dragged them out and threw them off the car, and we got under way again.

I was astonished; astonished to see a lamb act so; astonished at the strength displayed, and the clean and comprehensive result; astonished at the brisk and business-like style of the whole thing. The situation had a humorous side to it, considering how much I had been hearing about mild persuasion and gentle diplomacy all day from this

23

pile-driver, and I would have liked to call his attention to that feature and do some sarcasms about
it; but when I looked at him I saw that it would
be of no use—his placid and contented face had no
ray of humor in it; he would not have understood.
When we left the car, I said :

"That was a good stroke of diplomacy — three
good strokes of diplomacy, in fact."

"*That ?* That wasn't diplomacy. You are quite
in the wrong. Diplomacy is a wholly different
thing. One cannot apply it to that sort, they
would not understand it. No, that was not diplomacy; it was force."

"Now that you mention it, I—yes, I think perhaps you are right."

"Right? Of course I am right. It was just
force."

"I think, myself, it had the outside aspect of it.
Do you often have to reform people in that way?"

"Far from it. It hardly ever happens. Not
oftener than once in half a year, at the outside."

"Those men will get well?"

"Get well? Why certainly they will. They
are not in any danger. I know how to hit and
where to hit. You noticed that I did not hit them
under the jaw. That would have killed them."

I believed that. I remarked—rather wittily, as I

thought—that he had been a lamb all day, but now had all of a sudden developed into a ram—battering-ram ; but with dulcet frankness and simplicity he said no, a battering-ram was quite a different thing and not in use now. This was maddening, and I came near bursting out and saying he had no more appreciation of wit than a jackass—in fact, I had it right on my tongue, but did not say it, knowing there was no hurry and I could say it just as well some other time over the telephone.

We started to Boston the next afternoon. The smoking - compartment in the parlor - car was full, and we went into the regular smoker. Across the aisle in the front seat sat a meek, farmer-looking old man with a sickly pallor in his face, and he was holding the door open with his foot to get the air. Presently a big brakeman came rushing through, and when he got to the door he stopped, gave the farmer an ugly scowl, then wrenched the door to with such energy as to almost snatch the old man's boot off. Then on he plunged about his business. Several passengers laughed, and the old gentleman looked pathetically pained and grieved.

After a little the conductor passed along, and the Major stopped him and asked him a question in his habitually courteous way:

" Conductor, where does one report the misconduct of a brakeman? Does one report to you?"

"You can report him at New Haven if you want to. What has he been doing?"

The Major told the story. The conductor seemed amused. He said, with just a touch of sarcasm in his bland tones:

"As I understand you, the brakeman didn't *say* anything."

"No, he didn't say anything."

"But he scowled, you say."

"Yes."

"And snatched the door loose in a rough way."

"Yes."

"That's the whole business, is it?"

"Yes, that is the whole of it."

The conductor smiled pleasantly, and said:

"Well, if you want to report him, all right, but I don't quite make out what it's going to amount to. You'll say—as I understand you—that the brakeman insulted this old gentleman. They'll ask you what he *said*. You'll say he didn't say anything at all. I reckon they'll say, how are you going to make out an insult when you acknowledge yourself that he didn't say a word."

There was a murmur of applause at the conductor's compact reasoning, and it gave him pleasure—

you could see it in his face. But the Major was not disturbed. He said:

"There — now you have touched upon a crying defect in the complaint-system. The railway officials—as the public think and as you also seem to think—are not aware that there are any kind of insults except *spoken* ones. So nobody goes to headquarters and reports insults of manner, insults of gesture, look, and so forth ; and yet these are sometimes harder to bear than any words. They are bitter hard to bear because there is nothing tangible to take hold of; and the insulter can always say, if called before the railway officials, that he never dreamed of intending any offence. It seems to me that the officials ought to specially and urgently request the public to report *unworded* affronts and incivilities."

The conductor laughed, and said:

"Well, that *would* be trimming it pretty fine, sure !"

"But not too fine, I think. I will report this matter at New Haven, and I have an idea that I'll be thanked for it."

The conductor's face lost something of its complacency ; in fact, it settled to a quite sober cast as the owner of it moved away. I said :

"You are not really going to bother with that trifle, are you?"

"It isn't a trifle. Such things ought always to be reported. It is a public duty, and no citizen has a right to shirk it. But I sha'n't have to report this case."

"Why?"

"It won't be necessary. Diplomacy will do the business. You'll see."

Presently the conductor came on his rounds again, and when he reached the Major he leaned over and said:

"That's all right. You needn't report him. He's responsible to me, and if he does it again I'll give him a talking to."

The Major's response was cordial:

"Now that is what I like! You mustn't think that I was moved by any vengeful spirit, for that wasn't the case. It was duty—just a sense of duty, that was all. My brother-in-law is one of the directors of the road, and when he learns that you are going to reason with your brakeman the very next time he brutally insults an unoffending old man it will please him, you may be sure of that."

The conductor did not look as joyous as one might have thought he would, but on the contrary looked sickly and uncomfortable. He stood around a little ; then said :

"*I* think something ought to be done to him *now*. I'll discharge him."

" Discharge him ? What good would that do ? Don't you think it would be better wisdom to teach him better ways and keep him ?"

" Well, there's something in that. What would you suggest ?"

" He insulted the old gentleman in presence of all these people. How would it do to have him come and apologize in their presence ?"

" I'll have him here right off. And I want to say this : If people would do as you've done, and report such things to me instead of keeping mum and going off and blackguarding the road, you'd see a different state of things pretty soon. I'm much obliged to you."

The brakeman came and apologized. After he was gone the Major said :

" Now, you see how simple and easy that was. The ordinary citizen would have accomplished nothing—the brother-in-law of a director can accomplish anything he wants to."

" But are you really the brother-in-law of a director ?"

" Always. Always when the public interests require it. I have a brother-in-law on all the boards — everywhere. It saves me a world of trouble."

"It is a good wide relationship."

"Yes. I have over three hundred of them."

"Is the relationship never doubted by a conductor?"

"I have never met with a case. It is the honest truth—I never have."

"Why didn't you let him go ahead and discharge the brakeman, in spite of your favorite policy? You know he deserved it."

The Major answered with something which really had a sort of distant resemblance to impatience :

"If you would stop and think a moment you wouldn't ask such a question as that. Is a brakeman a dog, that nothing but a dog's methods will do for him? He is a man, and has a man's fight for life. And he always has a sister, or a mother, or wife and children to support. Always—there are no exceptions. When you take his living away from him you take theirs away too—and what have they done to you? Nothing. And where is the profit in discharging an uncourteous brakeman and hiring another just like him? It's unwisdom. Don't you see that the rational thing to do is to *reform* the brakeman and keep him? Of course it is."

Then he quoted with admiration the conduct of a certain division superintendent of the Consolidated road, in a case where a switchman of two years' experience was negligent once and threw a train off the track and killed several people. Citizens came in a passion to urge the man's dismissal, but the superintendent said:

" No, you are wrong. He has learned his lesson, he will throw no more trains off the track. He is twice as valuable as he was before. I shall keep him."

We had only one more adventure on the trip. Between Hartford and Springfield the train-boy came shouting in with an armful of literature and dropped a sample into a slumbering gentleman's lap, and the man woke up with a start. He was very angry, and he and a couple of friends discussed the outrage with much heat. They sent for the parlor-car conductor and described the matter, and were determined to have the boy expelled from his situation. The three complainants were wealthy Holyoke merchants, and it was evident that the conductor stood in some awe of them. He tried to pacify them, and explained that the boy was not under his authority, but under that of one of the news companies; but he accomplished nothing.

Then the Major volunteered some testimony for the defence. He said:

"I saw it all. You gentlemen have not meant to exaggerate the circumstances, but still that is what you have done. The boy has done nothing more than all train-boys do. If you want to get his ways softened down and his manners reformed, I am with you and ready to help, but it isn't fair to get him discharged without giving him a chance."

But they were angry, and would hear of no compromise. They were well acquainted with the president of the Boston & Albany, they said, and would put everything aside next day and go up to Boston and fix that boy.

The Major said he would be on hand too, and would do what he could to save the boy. One of the gentlemen looked him over, and said:

"Apparently it is going to be a matter of who can wield the most influence with the president. Do you know Mr. Bliss personally?"

The Major said, with composure:

"Yes; he is my uncle."

The effect was satisfactory. There was an awkward silence for a minute or more; then the hedging and the half-confessions of over-haste and exaggerated resentment began, and soon everything was smooth and friendly and sociable, and it was resolved to drop the matter and leave the boy's bread and butter unmolested.

It turned out as I had expected: the president of the road was not the Major's uncle at all—except by adoption, and for this day and train only.

We got into no episodes on the return journey. Probably it was because we took a night train and slept all the way.

We left New York Saturday night by the Pennsylvania road. After breakfast the next morning we went into the parlor-car, but found it a dull place and dreary. There were but few people in it and nothing going on. Then we went into the little smoking-compartment of the same car and found three gentlemen in there. Two of them were grumbling over one of the rules of the road —a rule which forbade card-playing on the trains on Sunday. They had started an innocent game of high-low-jack and been stopped. The Major was interested. He said to the third gentleman:

"Did you object to the game?"

"Not at all. I am a Yale professor and a religious man, but my prejudices are not extensive."

Then the Major said to the others:

"You are at perfect liberty to resume your game, gentlemen; no one here objects."

One of them declined the risk, but the other one said he would like to begin again if the Major would join him. So they spread an overcoat over their knees and the game proceeded. Pretty soon the parlor-car conductor arrived, and said, brusquely:

"There, there, gentlemen, that won't do. Put up the cards—it's not allowed."

The Major was shuffling. He continued to shuffle, and said:

"By whose order is it forbidden?"

"It's my order. I forbid it."

The dealing began. The Major asked:

"Did you invent the idea?"

"What idea?"

"The idea of forbidding card-playing on Sunday."

"No—of course not."

"Who did?"

"The company."

"Then it isn't your order, after all, but the company's. Is that it?"

"Yes. But you don't stop playing; I have to require you to stop playing immediately."

"Nothing is gained by hurry, and often much is lost. Who authorized the company to issue such an order?"

" My dear sir, that is a matter of no consequence to me, and—"

" But you forget that you are the only person concerned. It may be a matter of consequence to me. It is, indeed, a matter of very great importance to me. I cannot violate a legal requirement of my country without dishonoring myself; I cannot allow any man or corporation to hamper my liberties with illegal rules—a thing which railway companies are always trying to do—without dishonoring my citizenship. So I come back to that question: By whose authority has the company issued this order?"

" I don't *know*. That's *their* affair."

" Mine, too. I doubt if the company has any right to issue such a rule. This road runs through several States. Do you know what State we are in now, and what its laws are in matters of this kind?"

" Its laws do not concern me, but the company's orders do. It is my duty to stop this game, gentlemen, and it *must* be stopped."

" Possibly; but still there is no hurry. In hotels they post certain rules in the rooms, but they always quote passages from the State law as authority for these requirements. I see nothing posted here of this sort. Please produce your

authority and let us arrive at a decision, for you
see yourself that you are marring the game."

"I have nothing of the kind, but I have my
orders, and that is sufficient. They must be
obeyed."

"Let us not jump to conclusions. It will be
better all around to examine into the matter without heat or haste, and see just where we stand before either of us makes a mistake—for the curtail-
ing of the liberties of a citizen of the United
States is a much more serious matter than you
and the railroads seem to think, and it cannot be
done in my person until the curtailer proves his
right to do so. Now—"

"My dear sir, *will* you put down those cards?"

"All in good time, perhaps. It depends. You
say this order must be obeyed. *Must.* It is a
strong word. You see yourself how strong it is.
A wise company would not arm you with so drastic
an order as this, of *course*, without appointing a
penalty for its infringement. Otherwise it runs
the risk of being a dead letter and a thing to laugh
at. What is the appointed penalty for an infringement of this law?"

"Penalty? I never heard of any."

"Unquestionably you must be mistaken. Your
company orders you to come here and rudely break

up an innocent amusement, and furnishes you no way to enforce the order? Don't you see that that is nonsense? What do you *do* when people refuse to obey this order? Do you take the cards away from them?"

"No."

"Do you put the offender off at the next station?"

"Well, no—of course we couldn't if he had a ticket."

"Do you have him up before a court?"

The conductor was silent and apparently troubled. The Major started a new deal, and said:

"You see that you are helpless, and that the company has placed you in a foolish position. You are furnished with an arrogant order, and you deliver it in a blustering way, and when you come to look into the matter you find you haven't any way of enforcing obedience."

The conductor said, with chill dignity:

"Gentlemen, you have heard the order, and my duty is ended. As to obeying it or not, you will do as you think fit." And he turned to leave.

"But wait. The matter is not yet finished. I think you are mistaken about your duty being ended; but if it really is, I myself have a duty to perform yet."

"How do you mean?

"Are you going to report my disobedience at headquarters in Pittsburg?"

"No. What good would that do?"

"You must report me, or I will report you."

"Report me for what?"

"For disobeying the company's orders in not stopping this game. As a citizen it is my duty to help the railway companies keep their servants to their work."

"Are you in earnest?"

"Yes, I am in earnest. I have nothing against you as a man, but I have this against you as an officer—that you have not carried out that order, and if you don't report me I must report you. And I will."

The conductor looked puzzled, and was thoughtful a moment; then he burst out with:

"I seem to be getting *myself* into a scrape! It's all a muddle; I can't make head or tail of it; it's never happened before; they always knocked under and never said a word, and so *I* never saw how ridiculous that stupid order with no penalty is. *I* don't want to report anybody, and I don't want to *be* reported—why, it might do me no end of harm. Now *do* go on with the game—play the whole day if you want to—and don't let's have any more trouble about it!"

"No, I only sat down here to establish this gentleman's rights—he can have his place now. But before you go won't you tell me what you think the company made this rule for? Can you imagine an excuse for it? I mean a rational one—an excuse that is not on its face silly, and the invention of an idiot?"

"Well, surely I can. The reason it was made is plain enough. It is to save the feelings of the other passengers—the religious ones among them, I mean. They would not like it, to have the Sabbath desecrated by card-playing on the train."

"I just thought as much. They are willing to desecrate it themselves by travelling on Sunday, but they are not willing that other people—"

"By gracious, you've hit it! I never thought of that before. The fact is, it *is* a silly rule when you come to look into it."

At this point the train-conductor arrived, and was going to shut down the game in a very high-handed fashion, but the parlor-car conductor stopped him, and took him aside to explain. Nothing more was heard of the matter.

I was ill in bed eleven days in Chicago, and got no glimpse of the Fair, for I was obliged to return East as soon as I was able to travel. The Major secured and paid for a state-room in a sleeper the

24

day before we left, so that I could have plenty of room and be comfortable; but when we arrived at the station a mistake had been made and our car had not been put on. The conductor had reserved a section for us—it was the best he could do, he said. But the Major said we were not in a hurry, and would wait for the car to be put on. The conductor responded, with pleasant irony:

"It may be that *you* are not in a hurry, just as you say, but we *are*. Come, get aboard, gentlemen, get aboard—don't keep us waiting."

But the Major would not get aboard himself nor allow me to do it. He wanted his car, and said he must have it. This made the hurried and perspiring conductor impatient, and he said:

"It's the best we can *do*—we can't do impossibilities. You will take the section or go without. A mistake has been made and can't be rectified at this late hour. It's a thing that happens now and then, and there is nothing for it but to put up with it and make the best of it. Other people do."

Ah, that is just it, you see. If they had stuck to their rights and enforced them you wouldn't be trying to trample mine underfoot in this bland way now. I haven't any disposition to give you unnecessary trouble, but it is my duty to protect the next man from this kind of imposition. So I must have my car. Otherwise I will wait in Chicago and sue the company for violating its contract."

" Sue the company?—for a thing like that!"

" Certainly."

" Do you really mean that?

"Indeed I do."

The conductor looked the Major over wonderingly, and then said:

" It beats me—it's bran-new—I've never struck the mate to it before. But I swear I think you'd do it. Look here, I'll send for the station-master."

When the station-master came he was a good deal annoyed—at the Major, not at the person who had made the mistake. He was rather brusque, and took the same position which the conductor had taken in the beginning; but he failed to move the soft-spoken artilleryman, who still insisted that he must have his car. However, it was plain that there was only one strong side in this case, and that that side was the Major's. The station-master banished his annoyed manner, and became pleasant and even half-apologetic. This made a good opening for a compromise, and the Major made a concession. He said he would give up the engaged state-room, but he must have *a* state-room. After a deal of ransacking, one was found whose owner was persuad-able; he exchanged it for our section, and we got away at last. The conductor called on us in the evening, and was kind and courteous and obliging, and we had a long talk and got to be good friends. He said he wished the public would make trouble oftener—it would have a good effect. He said that the railroads could not be expected to do their whole duty by the traveller unless the traveller would take some interest in the matter himself.

I hoped that we were done reforming for the trip now, but it was not so. In the hotel-car, in the morning, the Major called for broiled chicken. The waiter said :

It's not in the bill of fare, sir ; we do not serve anything but what is in the bill.''

" That gentleman yonder is eating a broiled chicken."

" Yes, but that is different. He is one of the superintendents of the road."

" Then all the more must I have broiled chicken. I do not like these discriminations. Please hurry —bring me a broiled chicken."

The waiter brought the steward, who explained in a low and polite voice that the thing was impos-sible—it was against the rule, and the rule was rigid.

" Very well, then, you must either apply it impartially or break it impartially. You must take that gentleman's chicken away from him or bring me one."

The steward was puzzled, and did not quite know what to do. He began an incrherent argument, but the conductor came along just then, and asked what the difficulty was. The steward explained that here was a gentleman who was insisting on having a chicken when it was dead against the rule and not in the bill. The conductor said:

" Stick by your rules—you haven't any option. Wait a moment—is this the gentleman?" Then he laughed and said: " Never mind your rules—it's my advice, and sound; give him anything he wants —don't get him started on his rights. Give him whatever he asks for; and if you haven't got it, stop the train and get it."

The Major ate the chicken, but said he did it from a sense of duty and to establish a principle, for he did not like chicken.

I missed the Fair it is true, but I picked up some diplomatic tricks which I and the reader may find handy and useful as we go along.

PRIVATE HISTORY OF THE "JUMP-ING FROG" STORY

FIVE or six years ago a lady from Finland asked me to tell her a story in our negro dialect, so that she could get an idea of what that variety of speech was like. I told her one of Hopkinson Smith's negro stories, and gave her a copy of *Harper's Monthly* containing it. She translated it for a Swedish newspaper, but by an oversight named me as the author of it instead of Smith. I was very sorry for that, because I got a good lashing in the Swedish press, which would have fallen to his share but for that mistake; for it was shown that Boccaccio had told that very story, in his curt and meagre fashion, five hundred years before Smith took hold of it and made a good and tellable thing out of it.

I have always been sorry for Smith. But my own turn has come now. A few weeks ago Professor Van Dyke, of Princeton, asked this question:

"Do you know how old your 'Jumping Frog' story is?"

And I answered:

"Yes—forty-five years. The thing happened in Calaveras County, in the spring of 1849."

"No; it happened earlier—a couple of thousand years earlier; it is a Greek story."

I was astonished—and hurt. I said:

"I am willing to be a literary thief if it has been so ordained; I am even willing to be caught robbing the ancient dead alongside of Hopkinson Smith, for he is my friend and a good fellow, and I think would be as honest as any one if he could do it without occasioning remark; but I am not willing to antedate his crimes by fifteen hundred years. I must ask you to knock off part of that."

But the professor was not chaffing; he was in earnest, and could not abate a century. He named the Greek author, and offered to get the book and send it to me and the college text-book containing the English translation also. I thought I would like the translation best, because Greek makes me tired. January 30th he sent me the English version, and I will presently insert it in this article. It is my "Jumping Frog" tale in every essential. It is not strung out as I have strung it out, but it is all there.

To me this is very curious and interesting. Curious for several reasons. For instance :

I heard the story told by a man who was not telling it to his hearers as a thing new to them, but as a thing which *they had witnessed and would remember*. He was a dull person, and ignorant; he had no gift as a story-teller, and no invention; in his mouth this episode was merely history—history and statistics; and the gravest sort of history, too; he was entirely serious, for he was dealing with what to him were austere facts, and they interested him solely because they *were* facts; he was drawing on his memory, not his mind; he saw no humor in his tale, neither did his listeners; neither he nor they ever smiled or laughed; in my time I have not attended a more solemn conference. To him and to his fellow gold-miners there were just two things in the story that were worth considering. One was the smartness of its hero, Jim Smiley, in taking the stranger in with a loaded frog; and the other was Smiley's deep knowledge of a frog's nature—for he knew (as the narrator asserted and the listeners conceded) that a frog *likes shot* and is always ready to eat it. Those men discussed those two points, and those only. They were hearty in their admiration of them, and none of the party was aware that a first-rate story had been told in a first-rate way, and that it was brimful of a quality whose presence they never suspected—humor.

Now, then, the interesting question is, *did* the frog episode happen in Angel's Camp in the spring of '49, as told in my hearing that day in the fall of 1865? I am perfectly sure that it did. I am also sure that its duplicate happened in Bœotia a couple of thousand years ago. I think it must be a case of history actually repeating itself, and not a case of a good story floating down the ages and surviving because too good to be allowed to perish.

I would now like to have the reader examine the Greek story and the story told by the dull and solemn Californian, and observe how exactly alike they are in essentials.

[*Translation.*]

THE ATHENIAN AND THE FROG.*

An Athenian once fell in with a Bœotian who was sitting by the roadside looking at a frog. Seeing the other approach, the Bœotian said his was a remarkable frog, and asked if he would agree to start a contest of frogs, on condition that he whose frog jumped farthest should receive a large sum of money. The Athenian replied that he would if the other would fetch him a frog, for the lake was near. To this he agreed, and when he was gone the

---

* Sidgwick, *Greek Prose Composition*, page 116.

Athenian took the frog, and, opening its mouth, poured some stones into its stomach, so that it did not indeed seem larger than before, but could not jump. The Bœotian soon returned with the other frog, and the contest began. The second frog first was pinched, and jumped moderately; then they pinched the Bœotian frog. And he gathered himself for a leap, and used the utmost effort, but he could not move his body the least. So the Athenian departed with the money. When he was gone the Bœotian, wondering what was the matter with the frog, lifted him up and examined him. And being turned upsidedown, he opened his mouth and vomited out the stones.

And here is the way it happened in California:

FROM "THE CELEBRATED JUMPING FROG OF CALAVERAS COUNTY"

Well, thish-yer Smiley had rat-terriers and chicken cocks, and tom-cats, and all of them kind of things, till you couldn't rest, and you couldn't fetch nothing for him to bet on but he'd match you. He ketched a frog one day, and took him home, and said he cal'lated to educate him; and so he never done nothing for three months but set in his back yard and learn that frog to jump. And you bet you he *did* learn him, too. He'd give him a little punch behind, and the next minute you'd see that frog whirling in the air like a doughnut—see him turn one summerset, or maybe a couple if he got a good start, and come down flat-flooted and all right, like a cat. He got him up so in the matter of ketching flies, and kep' him in practice so constant, that he'd nail a fly every time as fur as he could see him. Smiley said all a frog wanted was education, and he could do 'most anything—and I believe him. Why, I've seen him set Dan'l Webster down here on this floor—Dan'l

Webster was the name of the frog—and sing out, "Flies, Dan'l, flies!" and quicker'n you could wink he'd spring straight up and snake a fly off'n the counter there, and flop down on the floor ag'in as solid as a gob of mud, and fall to scratching the side of his head with his hind foot as indifferent as if he hadn't no idea he'd been doin' any more'n any frog might do. You never see a frog so modest and straightfor'ard as he was, for all he was so gifted. And when it come to fair and square jumping on a dead level, he could get over more ground at one straddle than any animal of his breed you ever see. Jumping on a dead level was his strong suit, you understand; and when it came to that, Smiley would ante up money on him as long as he had a red. Smiley was monstrous proud of his frog, and well he might be, for fellers that had travelled and been everywheres all said he laid over any frog that ever *they* see.

Well, Smiley kep' the beast in a little lattice box, and he used to fetch him down-town sometimes and lay for a bet. One day a feller—a stranger in the camp, he was—come acrost him with his box, and says:

"What might it be that you've got in the box?"

And Smiley says, sorter indifferent-like, "It might be a parrot, or it might be a canary, maybe, but it ain't—it's only just a frog."

And the feller took it, and looked at it careful, and turned it round this way and that, and says, "H'm—so 'tis. Well, what's *he* good for?"

"Well," Smiley says, easy and careless, "he's good enough for *one* thing, I should judge—he can outjump any frog in Calaveras County."

The feller took the box again and took another long, particular look, and give it back to Smiley, and says, very deliberate: "Well," he says, "I don't see no p'ints about that frog that's any better'n any other frog."

"Maybe you don't," Smiley says. "Maybe you understand frogs and maybe you don't understand 'em; maybe you've had experience, and maybe you ain't only a amature, as it were. Anyways, I've got *my* opinion, and I'll resk forty dollars that he can outjump any frog in Calaveras County."

And the feller studies a minute, and then says, kinder sad like, "Well, I'm only a stranger here, and I ain't got no frog, but if I had a frog I'd bet you."

And then Smiley says: "That's all right—that's all right; if you'll hold my box a minute, I'll go and get you a frog." And so the feller took the box and put up his forty dollars along with Smiley's and set down to wait.

So he set there a good while thinking and thinking to hisself, and then he got the frog out and prized his mouth open and took a teaspoon and filled him full of quail shot—filled him pretty near up to his chin—and set him on the floor. Smiley he went to the swamp and slopped around in the mud for a long time, and finally he ketched a frog and fetched him in and give him to this feller, and says:

"Now, if you're ready, set him alongside of Dan'l, with his fore-paws just even with Dan'l's, and I'll give the word." Then he says, "One—two—three—*git!*" and him and the feller touched up the frogs from behind, and the new frog hopped off lively; but Dan'l give a heave, and hysted up his shoulders—so—like a Frenchman, but it warn't no use—he couldn't budge; he was planted as solid as a church, and he couldn't no more stir than if he was anchored out. Smiley was a good deal surprised, and he was disgusted, too, but he didn't have no idea what the matter was, of course.

The feller took the money and started away; and when he was going out at the door he sorter jerked his thumb over his shoulder—so—at Dan'l, and says again, very deliberate: "Well," he says, "*I* don't see no p'ints about that frog that's any better'n any other frog."

Smiley he stood scratching his head and looking down at Dan'l a long time, and at last he says, "I do wonder what in the nation that frog throwed off for—I wonder if there ain't something the matter with him—he 'pears to look mighty baggy, somehow." And he ketched Dan'l by the nape of the neck, and hefted him, and says, "Why, blame my cats if he don't weigh five pound!" and turned him upsidedown, and he belched out a double handful of shot. And then he see how it was, and he was the maddest man —he set the frog down and took out after that feller, but he never ketched him.

The resemblances are deliciously exact. There you have the wily Bœotian and the wily Jim Smiley waiting — two thousand years apart — and waiting, each equipped with his frog and "laying" for the stranger. A contest is proposed — for money. The Athenian would take a chance "if the other would fetch him a frog"; the Yankee says: "I'm only a stranger here, and I ain't got no frog; but if I had a frog I'd bet you." The wily Bœotian and the wily Californian, with that vast gulf of two thousand years between, retire eagerly and go frogging in the marsh; the Athenian and the Yankee remain behind and work a base advantage, the one with pebbles, the other with shot. Presently the contest began. In the one case "they pinched the Bœotian frog"; in the other,

"him and the feller touched up the frogs from behind." The Bœotian frog "gathered himself for a
leap" (you can just *see* him !), but "could not move
his body in the least"; the Californian frog "give
a heave, but it warn't no use—he couldn't budge."
In both the ancient and the modern cases the
strangers departed with the money. The Bœotian
and the Californian wonder what is the matter with
their frogs; they lift them and examine ; they turn
them upsidedown and out spills the informing
ballast.

Yes, the resemblances are curiously exact. I
used to tell the story of the "Jumping Frog" in
San Francisco, and presently Artemus Ward came
along and wanted it to help fill out a little book
which he was about to publish; so I wrote it out
and sent it to his publisher, Carleton ; but Carleton
thought the book had enough matter in it, so he
gave the story to Henry Clapp as a present, and
Clapp put it in his *Saturday Press*, and it killed
that paper with a suddenness that was beyond
praise. At least the paper died with that issue,
and none but envious people have ever tried to
rob me of the honor and credit of killing it. The
"Jumping Frog" was the first piece of writing of
mine that spread itself through the newspapers
and brought me into public notice. Consequently,

the *Saturday Press* was a cocoon and I the worm in it; also, I was the gay-colored literary moth which its death set free. This simile has been used before.

Early in '66 the " Jumping Frog " was issued in book form, with other sketches of mine. A year or two later Madame Blanc translated it into French and published it in the *Revue des Deux Mondes*, but the result was not what should have been expected, for the *Revue* struggled along and pulled through, and is alive yet. I think the fault must have been in the translation. I ought to have translated it myself. I think so because I examined into the matter and finally retranslated the sketch from the French back into English, to see what the trouble was; that is, to see just what sort of a focus the French people got upon it. Then the mystery was explained. In French the story is too confused and chaotic and unreposeful and ungrammatical and insane; consequently it could only cause grief and sickness—it could not kill. A glance at my retranslation will show the reader that this must be true.

[*My Retranslation.*]

THE FROG JUMPING OF THE COUNTY OF CALAVERAS.

Eh bien! this Smiley nourished some terriers à rats, and some cocks of combat, and some cats, and all sorts of things;

and with his rage of betting one no had more of repose. He trapped one day a frog and him imported with him (*et l'emporto chez lui*) saying that he pretended to make his education. You me believe if you will, but during three months he not has nothing done but to him apprehend to jump (*apprendre à sauter*) in a court retired of her mansion (*de sa maison*). And I you respond that he have succeeded. He him gives a small blow by behind, and the instant after you shall see the frog turn in the air like a grease-biscuit, make one summersault, sometimes two, when she was well started, and refall upon his feet like a cat. He him had accomplished in the art of to gobble the flies (*gober des mouches*), and him there exercised continually — so well that a fly at the most far that she appeared was a fly lost. Smiley had custom to say that all which lacked to a frog it was the education, but with the education she could do nearly all—and I him believe. *Tenez*, I him have seen pose Daniel Webster there upon this plank—Daniel Webster was the name of the frog—and to him sing, " Some flies, Daniel, some flies !"—in a flash of the eye Daniel had bounded and seized a fly here upon the counter, then jumped anew at the earth, where he rested truly to himself scratch the head with his behind-foot, as if he no had not the least idea of his superiority. Never you not have seen frog as modest, as natural, sweet as she was. And when he himself agitated to jump purely and simply upon plain earth, she does more ground in one jump than any beast of his species than you can know.

To jump plain—this was his strong. When he himself agitated for that Smiley multiplied the bets upon her as long as there to him remained a red. It must to know, Smiley was monstrously proud of his frog, and he of it was right, for some men who were travelled, who had all seen, said that they to him would be injurious to him compare to another frog. Smiley guarded Daniel in a little box lat-ticed which he carried bytimes to the village for some bet.

One day an individual stranger at the camp him arrested with his box and him said:

"What is this that you have then shut up there within?"

Smiley said, with an air indifferent:

"That could be a paroquet, or a syringe (*ou un serin*), but this no is nothing of such, it not is but a frog."

The individual it took, it regarded with care, it turned from one side and from the other, then he said:

Tiens! in effect!—At what is she good?"

"My God!" responded Smiley, always with an air disen-gaged, "she is good for one thing to my notice (*à mon avis*), she can batter in jumping (*elle peut batter en sautant*) all frogs of the county of Calaveras."

The individual retook the box, it examined of new longly, and it rendered to Smiley in saying with an air deliberate:

"*Eh bien!* I no saw not that that frog had nothing of better than each frog." (*Je ne vois pas que cette grenouille ait rien de mieux qu'aucune grenouille*). [If that isn't gram-mar gone to seed, then I count myself no judge.—M. T.]

"Possible that you not it saw not," said Smiley; "possible that you—you comprehend frogs; possible that you not you there comprehend nothing; possible that you had of the experience, and possible that you not be but an amateur. Of all manner (*de toute manière*) I bet forty dollars that she batter in jumping no matter which frog of the county of Calaveras."

The individual reflected a second, and said like sad:

"I not am but a stranger here, I no have not a frog; but if I of it had one, I would embrace the bet."

"Strong, well!" respond Smiley; "nothing of more fa-cility. If you will hold my box a minute, I go you to search a frog (*j'irai vous chercher*)."

25

Behold, then, the individual who guards the box, who puts his forty dollars upon those of Smiley, and who attends (*et qui attendre*). He attended enough longtimes, reflecting all solely. And figure you that he takes Daniel, him opens the mouth by force and with a teaspoon him fills with shot of the hunt, even him fills just to the chin, then he him puts by the earth. Smiley during these times was at slopping in a swamp. Finally he trapped (*attrapé*) a frog, him carried to that individual and said :

" Now if you be ready, put him all against Daniel, with their before-feet upon the same line, and I give the signal " —then he added : " One, two, three—advance !"

Him and the individual touched their frogs by behind, and the frog new put to jump smartly, but Daniel himself lifted ponderously, exhalted the shoulders thus, like a Frenchman—to what good? He could not budge. He is planted solid like a church, he not advance no more than if one him had put at the anchor.

Smiley was surprised and disgusted, but he not himself doubted not of the turn being intended (*mais il ne se doutait pas du tour bien entendre*). The individual empocketed the silver, himself with it went, and of it himself in going is that he no gives not a jerk of thumb over the shoulder— like that—at the poor Daniel, in saying with his air deliberate—(*L'individu empoche l'argent s'en va et en s'en allant est ce qu'il ne donne pas un coup de pouce par-dessus l'épaule, comme ça, au pauvre Daniel, en aisant de son air délibéré*).

" *Eh bien! I no see not that that frog has nothing of better than another.*"

Smiley himself scratched longtimes the head, the eyes fixed upon Daniel, until that which at last he said :

" I me demand how the devil it makes itself that this beast has refused. Is it that she had something? One would believe that she is stuffed,"

He grasped Daniel by the skin of the neck, him lifted and said:

"The wolf me bite if he no weigh not five pounds."

He him reversed and the unhappy belched two handfuls of shot (*et le malheureux*, etc.). When Smiley recognized how it was, he was like mad. He deposited his frog by the earth and ran after that individual, but he not him caught never.

It may be that there are people who can translate better than I can, but I am not acquainted with them.

So ends the private and public history of the Jumping Frog of Calaveras County, an incident which has this unique feature about it—that it is both old and new, a "chestnut" and not a "chestnut"; for it was original when it happened two thousand years ago, and was again original when it happened in California in our own time.

MY BOYHOOD DREAMS

THE dreams of my boyhood? No, they have not been realized. For all who are old, there is something infinitely pathetic about the subject which you have chosen, for in no gray-head's case can it suggest any but one thing—disappointment. Disappointment is its own reason for its pain: the quality or dignity of the hope that failed is a matter aside. The dreamer's valuation of the thing lost—not another man's—is the only standard to measure it by, and his grief for it makes it large and great and fine, and is worthy of our reverence in all cases. We should carefully remember that. There are sixteen hundred million people in the world. Of these there is but a trifling number — in fact, only thirty-eight millions — who can understand why a person should have an ambition to belong to the French army; and why, belonging to it, he should be proud of that; and why, having got down that far, he should want to go on down, down, down till he struck bottom and got on the General Staff; and why, being stripped of his livery, or set free and reinvested with his self-respect by any other quick and thorough process, let it be what it might, he should wish to return to his strange serfage. But no matter: the estimate put upon these things by the fifteen hundred and sixty millions is no proper measure of their value: the proper measure, the just measure, is that which is put upon them by Dreyfus, and is cipherable merely upon the littleness or the vastness of the *disappointment* which their loss cost him.

There you have it: the measure of the magnitude of a dream-failure is the measure of the disappointment the failure cost the dreamer; the value, in others' eyes, of the thing lost, has nothing to do with the matter. With this straightening-out and classification of the dreamer's position to help us, perhaps we can put ourselves in his place and respect his dream—Dreyfus's, and the dreams our friends have cherished and reveal to us. Some that I call to mind, some that have been revealed to me, are curious enough; but we may not smile at them, for they were precious to the dreamers, and their failure has left scars which give them dignity and pathos. With this theme in my mind, dear heads that were brown when they and mine were young together rise old and white before me now, beseeching me to speak for them, and most lovingly will I do it.

Howells, Hay, Aldrich, Matthews, Stockton, Cable, Remus—how their young hopes and ambitions come flooding back to my memory now, out of the vague far past, the beautiful past, the lamented past! I remember it so well—that night we met together—it was in Boston, and Mr. Fields was there, and Mr. Osgood, and Ralph Keeler, and Boyle O'Reilly, lost to us now these many years—and under the seal of confidence revealed to each other what our boyhood dreams had been : dreams which had not as yet been blighted, but over which was stealing the gray of the night that was to come—a night which we prophetically *felt*, and this feeling oppressed us and made us sad. I remember that Howells's voice broke twice, and it was only with great difficulty that he was able to go on ; in the end he wept. For he had hoped to be an auctioneer. He told of his early struggles to climb to his goal, and how at last he attained to within a single step of the coveted summit. But there misfortune after misfortune assailed him, and he went down, and down, and down, until now at last, weary and disheartened, he had for the present given up the struggle and become editor of the

Atlantic Monthly. This was in 1830. Seventy years are gone since, and where now is his dream? It will never be fulfilled. And it is best so; he is no longer fitted for the position; no one would take him now; even if he got it, he would not be able to do himself credit in it, on account of his deliberateness of speech and lack of trained professional vivacity; he would be put on real estate, and would have the pain of seeing younger and abler men intrusted with the furniture and other such goods—goods which draw a mixed and intellectually low order of customers, who must be beguiled of their bids by a vulgar and specialized humor and sparkle, accompanied with antics.

But it is not the thing lost that counts, but only the *disappointment* the loss brings to the dreamer that had coveted that thing and had set his heart of hearts upon it, and when we remember this, a great wave of sorrow for Howells rises in our breasts, and we wish for his sake that his fate could have been different.

At that time Hay's boyhood dream was not yet past hope of realization, but it was fading, dimming, wasting away, and the wind of a growing apprehension was blowing cold over the perishing summer of his life. In the pride of his young ambition he had aspired to be a steamboat mate; and

in fancy saw himself dominating a forecastle some
day on the Mississippi and dictating terms to
roustabouts in high and wounding tones. I look
back now, from this far distance of seventy years,
and note with sorrow the stages of that dream's
destruction. Hay's history is but Howells's, with
differences of detail. Hay climbed high toward
his ideal; when success seemed almost sure, his
foot upon the very gang-plank, his eye upon the
capstan, misfortune came and his fall began. Down
—down—down—ever down: Private Secretary to
the President; Colonel in the field; Chargé d'Affaires in Paris; Chargé d'Affaires in Vienna; Poet;
Editor of the *Tribune;* Biographer of Lincoln;
Ambassador to England; and now at last there he
lies—Secretary of State, Head of Foreign Affairs.
And he has fallen like Lucifer, never to rise again.
And his dream—where now is his dream? Gone
down in blood and tears with the dream of the
auctioneer.

And the young dream of Aldrich — where is
that? I remember yet how he sat there that night
fondling it, petting it; seeing it recede and ever
recede; trying to be reconciled and give it up, but
not able yet to bear the thought; for it had been
his hope to be a horse-doctor. He also climbed
high, but, like the others, fell; then fell again,

and yet again, and again and again. And now at last he can fall no further. He is old now, he has ceased to struggle, and is only a poet. No one would risk a horse with him now. His dream is over.

Has *any* boyhood dream ever been fulfilled? I must doubt it. Look at Brander Matthews. He wanted to be a cowboy. What is he to-day? Nothing but a professor in a university. Will he ever be a cowboy? It is hardly conceivable.

Look at Stockton. What was Stockton's young dream? He hoped to be a barkeeper. See where *he* has landed.

Is it better with Cable? What was Cable's young dream? To be ring-master in the circus, and swell around and crack the whip. What is he to-day? Nothing but a theologian and novelist.

And Uncle Remus—what was his young dream? To be a buccaneer. Look at him now.

Ah, the dreams of our youth, how beautiful they are, and how perishable! The ruins of these might-have-beens, how pathetic! The heart-secrets that were revealed that night now so long vanished, how they touch me as I give them voice! Those sweet privacies, how they endeared us to each other! We were under oath never to tell any of these things, and I have always kept that oath inviolate when speaking with persons whom I thought not worthy to hear them.

Oh, our lost Youth—God keep its memory green in our hearts! for Age is upon us, with the indignity of its infirmities, and Death beckons!

TO THE ABOVE OLD PEOPLE

Sleep! for the Sun that scores another Day
Against the Tale allotted You to stay,
   Reminding You, is Risen, and now
Serves Notice—ah, ignore it while You may!

The chill Wind blew, and those who stood before
The Tavern murmured, "Having drunk his Score,
   Why tarries He with empty Cup? Behold,
The Wine of Youth once poured, is poured no more.

"Come, leave the Cup, and on the Winter's Snow
Your Summer Garment of Enjoyment throw:
   Your Tide of Life is ebbing fast, and it,
Exhausted once, for You no more shall flow."

While yet the Phantom of false Youth was mine,
I heard a Voice from out the Darkness whine,
   "O Youth, O whither gone? Return,
And bathe my Age in thy reviving Wine."

In this subduing Draught of tender green
And kindly Absinth, with its wimpling Sheen
   Of dusky half-lights, let me drown
The haunting Pathos of the Might-Have-Been.

For every nickeled Joy, marred and brief,
We pay some day its Weight in golden Grief
   Mined from our Hearts. Ah, murmur not—
From this one-sided Bargain dream of no Relief!

The Joy of Life, that streaming through their Veins
Tumultuous swept, falls slack—and wanes
   The Glory in the Eye—and one by one
Life's Pleasures perish and make place for Pains.

Whether one hide in some secluded Nook—
Whether at Liverpool or Sandy Hook—
   'Tis one. Old Age will search him out—and He—
He—He—when ready will know where to look.

From Cradle unto Grave I keep a House
Of Entertainment where may drowse
   Bacilli and kindred Germs—or feed—or breed
Their festering Species in a deep Carouse.

Think—in this battered Caravanserai,
Whose Portals open stand all Night and Day,
   How Microbe after Microbe with his Pomp
Arrives unasked, and comes to stay.

Our ivory Teeth, confessing to the Lust
Of masticating, once, now own Disgust
   Of Clay-plug'd Cavities—full soon our Snags
Are emptied, and our Mouths are filled with Dust.

Our Gums forsake the Teeth and tender grow,
And fat, like over-ripened Figs—we know
   The Sign—the Riggs Disease is ours, and we
Must list this Sorrow, add another Woe:

Our Lungs begin to fail and soon we Cough,
And chilly Streaks play up our Backs, and off
　　Our fever'd Foreheads drips an icy Sweat—
We scoffed before, but now we may not scoff.

Some for the Bunions that afflict us prate
Of Plasters unsurpassable, and hate
　　To cut a Corn—ah cut, and let the Plaster go,
Nor murmur if the Solace come too late.

Some for the Honors of Old Age, and some
Long for its Respite from the Hum
　　And Clash of sordid Strife—O Fools,
The Past should teach them what's to Come :

Lo, for the Honors, cold Neglect instead !
For Respite, disputations Heirs a Bed
　　Of Thorns for them will furnish.　Go,
Seek not Here for Peace—but Yonder—with the Dead.

For whether Zal and Rustam heed this Sign,
And even smitten thus, will not repine,
　　Let Zal and Rustam shuffle as they may,
The Fine once levied they must Cash the Fine.

O Voices of the Long Ago that were so dear !
Fall'n Silent, now, for many a Mould'ring Year,
　　O whither are ye flown ?　Come back,
And break my Heart, but bless my grieving ear.

Some happy Day my Voice will Silent fall,
And answer not when some that love it call :
　　Be glad for Me when this you note—and think
I've found the Voices lost, beyond the Pall.

So let me grateful drain the Magic Bowl
That medicines hurt Minds and on the Soul
The Healing of its Peace doth lay—if then
Death claim me—Welcome be his Dole !

SANNA, SWEDEN, *September* 15*th.*

Private.—If you don't know what Riggs's Disease of the Teeth
is, the dentist will tell you. I've had it — and it is more than
interesting.   S. L. C.

EDITORIAL NOTE

Fearing that there might be some mistake, we submitted
a proof of this article to the (American) gentlemen named
in it, and asked them to correct any errors of detail that
might have crept in among the facts.   They reply with
some asperity that errors cannot creep in among facts where
there are no facts for them to creep in among; and that
none are discoverable in this article, but only baseless aber-
rations of a disordered mind.   They have no recollection
of any such night in Boston, nor elsewhere; and in their
opinion there was never any such night.   They have *met*
Mr. Twain, but have had the prudence not to intrust any
privacies to him—particularly under oath ; and they think
they now see that this prudence was justified, since he has
been untrustworthy enough to even betray privacies which
had no existence.   Further, they think it a strange thing
that Mr. Twain, who was never invited to meddle with
anybody's boyhood dreams but his own, has been so gratui-
tously anxious to see that other peoples are placed before
the world that he has quite lost his head in his zeal and
forgotten to make any mention of his own at all.   Provided
we insert this explanation, they are willing to let his article

pass; otherwise they must require its suppression in the interest of truth.

P. S.—These replies having left us in some perplexity, and also in some fear lest they might distress Mr. Twain if published without his privity, we judged it but fair to submit them to him and give him an opportunity to defend himself But he does not seem to be troubled, or even aware that he is in a delicate situation. He merely says:

" Do not worry about those former young people They can write good literature, but when it comes to speaking the truth, they have not had my training.—MARK TWAIN."

The last sentence seems obscure, and liable to an unfortunate construction. It plainly needs refashioning, but we cannot take the responsibility of doing it.—EDITOR.

THE END